D0149055

Intercultural Communication

Roots and Routes

Carolyn Calloway-Thomas
Indiana University

Pamela J. Cooper
Northwestern University

Cecil Blake
Indiana University Northwest

Allyn and Bacon
Boston • London • Toronto • Sydney • Tokyo • Singapore

Series Editor: Karon Bowers
Editorial Assistant: Leila Scott
Editorial-Production Administrator: Joe Sweeney
Editorial-Production Service: Walsh & Associates, Inc.
Composition Buyer: Linda Cox
Manufacturing Buyer: Dave Repetto
Cover Administrator: Jennifer Hart

Copyright © 1999 by Allyn & Bacon
A Pearson Education Company
160 Gould Street
Needham Heights, MA 02494

www.abacon.com

Library of Congress Cataloging-in-Publication Data

Calloway-Thomas, Carolyn
    Intercultural communication : roots and routes / Carolyn Calloway-Thomas, Pamela J. Cooper, Cecil Blake.
        p.   cm.
    Includes bibliographical references and index.
    ISBN 0-205-29263-1
    1. Intercultural communication.   I. Cooper, Pamela J. II. Blake, Cecil A.   III. Title.
    P94.6.C35   1998
    203.2—dc21   98-34367
                                                                          CIP

Printed in the United States of America

10   9   8   7   6   5   4   3   2   02

#39391240

CONTENTS

PREFACE

On September 30, 1997, the *New York Times*, under a heading titled, "Clash of Cultures Tears Texas City," described a riveting debate between two Hispanic women and their supervisor in the town of Amarillo (Verhovek, 1997). The supervisor and owner of a small insurance company had hired the two women because they spoke both English and Spanish. Although the women's chief responsibility was to assist the clients who spoke Spanish as their primary language, the women soon began to chat with each other in Spanish. Observing the practice, the owner asked the two Hispanic women to sign a pledge making the insurance company "an English speaking office except when we have customers who can't speak our language" (p. A10). The two Hispanic women refused to sign the pledge and ethnic tension followed.

This intercultural incident is not unusual. As one reads newspapers, books, and magazines or watches television, one can hardly ignore stories about struggles, disputes, tensions, clashes, and conflicts that occur as people try to "make sense" of their lives in an uncertain world. Increasingly, globalization is changing the way individuals define themselves on the basis of economics, religion, culture, customs, language, ethnic identity, and ancestry. Given the fact that such factors profoundly influence human interaction, it seemed desirable for us to write a textbook that offers a fascinating possibility of cultural understanding, with keen attention to both theory and performance.

This text represents a unique treatment of intercultural communication culled from the global experiences of its authors. In addition to a comprehensive approach to the subject, the text provides complete chapters on religion, the media, ethics, culture and pedagogy, and the socioeconomic dimensions of intercultural communication. In this regard, the book represents a novel approach to intercultural communication against the background of a rapidly transforming world culturally and linguistically. As people travel more and more worldwide, intercultural communication competence becomes a powerful imperative that goes beyond our traditional approaches to the topic.

The book is conceived as a text for college students and for anyone interested in and committed to improving intercultural communication. Academics, diplomats, businesspersons, teachers, foreign service officers, administrators, Peace Corps volunteers, politicians, and others who wish to add more light than shadows to the world should find this book useful.

Chapter 1 sets out a conceptual framework that distinguishes this text from many others. We use the metaphors of process and movement—"roots and routes"—to capture the ongoing dynamism of intercultural communication. The chapter shows how sociocultural and historical roots shape people's movement (routes) from one geographical space to another. It casts a fresh eye on how intercultural passages through time and space leave marks or influence the outcome of human interactions. Although the chapter is anchored theoretically, our goal is not to present theory exclusively throughout the text, but rather to demonstrate how theory animates intercultural performance. That said, we are mindful that the dynamic and complex qualities of intercultural communication cannot be captured fully through descriptive and explanatory language.

Chapter 2 addresses the critical function of context in intercultural communication. We provide a discussion of how context shapes significant sociopsychological variables such as perception and values. We argue that the critical locus of contexts contributes significantly toward managing intercultural communication with reduced potential for communication breakdown and misunderstanding.

Chapter 3 focuses on understanding cultural foundations. We discuss the concept of cultural warrants, which are grounded within societies and serve as means of justifying people's judgments and decisions. We suggest that when individuals pay attention to how warrants work, they increase their chances of becoming more competent in intercultural encounters.

Chapter 4 was prompted by the enormous role that race, ethnicity, and gender play in contemporary society. The chapter proposes that by examining the pulse points of race, ethnicity, and gender, humans are moved to stretch their imaginations and reassess the way these concepts organize their thoughts and actions.

Chapter 5, on prejudice and stereotypes, begins with the perception process and social cognition as they relate to ethnocentrism and cultural relativism. These concepts are then used to demonstrate how stereotypes and prejudices are formed. In this chapter we examine how stereotypes and prejudices can be used to shape what people say as well as their reactions to what others say.

By including information on the ethical sense, Chapter 6, we acknowledge that moral sentiments influence how humans express their most serious thoughts and feelings. In this way, we also add another dimension of communication that is missing from most intercultural texts.

Chapter 7, on religion, examines religion as a galvanizing factor in binding people together regardless of race, ethnicity, and nationality. We also look at how people abuse religion in intercultural relations and create potential contexts for discord. This chapter makes a distinct contribution by introducing a discussion about pacifism and enhanced intercultural interactions.

Chapter 8 covers language from both structural and semantic concerns and verbal styles as they relate to intercultural communication. This chapter is intended to show that language is tightly woven into intercultural experiences.

Chapter 9 begins with a general overview of nonverbal communication and its relationship to verbal communication and then moves to nonverbal behaviors across cultures. We demonstrate that although humans share much in common, they are culturally rooted in different types and categories of nonverbal actions.

Chapter 10 examines the intersection between culture, economics, and the new world order. Here we offer a picture of "roots and routes" by a different mechanism. We consider how changes in the global economic community influence intercultural dynamics. We also examine how cultural values and norms are set in the fabric of economics.

Education is the focus of Chapter 11. It takes intercultural concepts and relates them directly to the educational context, using learning styles and other factors as vehicles for understanding how people grasp ideas.

A separate chapter addresses the location of the media in propagating cultural norms and shaping humans' perceptions of themselves and others. Through an examination of situation comedies and advances in the music industry, we look at the important position media occupy in facilitating or obstructing effective intercultural relations. Chapter 12 also provides insights into the international dimensions of media and culture.

In Chapter 13, on intercultural competence, we offer our readers an even more practical, but theoretically grounded, view of intercultural communication "out there" that they can grasp and attain. Using concepts such as the family and local and global dimensions of communication, we offer general and specific routes that readers can take as they attempt to improve their intercultural communication skills.

The book concludes with a discussion of some of the major trends in diversity and intercultural communication that are shaping the future as we approach a new century. Chapter 14 also offers challenges and possibilities that could be lying ahead in an exhilarating and fascinating world.

Writing is often impossible without the help of others. We must single out the many, sometimes anonymous, individuals whom we met in our travels through Africa, Asia, Europe, and North and South America. We learned a great deal about the inhabitants of such places, and their voices echo throughout the book with stories and ideas that enriched our perspectives.

We are also indebted to the reviewers of this book—John Kares Smith, State University of New York–Oswego; Steve Duck, University of Iowa; Thomas E. Harris, University of Alabama; Dudley Cahn, State University of New York–New Paltz; Richard Armstrong, Wichita State University; Risa Dickson, California State University–San Bernadino; Barry Brummet, University of Wisconsin–Milwaukee—for very carefully scrutinizing our chapters, steering us away from some pitfalls and mines in our efforts to share our years of intellectual and intercultural exploration.

Finally, we are grateful to our spouses, Jack Edward, Rick, and Hortensia respectively, for patiently listening and offering valuable criticisms of our work.

REFERENCE

Verhovek, S. H. (1997, September 30). Clash of cultures tears Texas city. *The New York Times*, p. A10.

1

ROOTS AND ROUTES

Objectives

After reading this chapter and completing the activities, you should be able to:

1. Explain the differences between roots and routes.
2. Explain how the concept of cultural flow shapes intercultural interactions.
3. Show how roots and routes influence our interactions with others.
4. Describe some incident in your experience to which you responded incorrectly because of your own roots.
5. Give in writing why communicating interculturally is complex.
6. Distinguish between locally focused individuals and globally focused individuals.

In his absorbing work, *In My Father's House*, Kwame Anthony Appiah (1992) recounts the following incident:

> *In the midseventies I was driving with a (white) English friend in the Ghanaian city of Takoradi. My friend was at the wheel. We stopped at a road junction behind a large timber truck, and the driver, who failed to see us in his rearview mirror, backed toward us. My English friend sounded our horn, but the driver went on backing—until he hit and broke our windscreen. It was plain enough whose fault—in the sense of the legal system—the accident was. Yet none of the witnesses was willing to support our version of the story. (p. 8)*

By way of background, Appiah notes that "In other settings, one might have assumed that this was a reflection of racial solidarity" (p. 8). Instead, however, the Ghanaians refused to corroborate his and the Englishman's story because the Africans considered the issue to be between a person with money (the Englishman) and those without money (the Ghanaians). This legal and cultural system conspired against Appiah and his friend.

Appiah's point is that to reduce this sociological, legal, and economic encounter to the simplistic issue of race is self-defeating, for it omits the complexity and elegance of human behavior. Appiah is troubled by the ease with which individuals make inappropriate cultural assumptions about others, with little regard for human complexity. Rereading Appiah's story, we were struck by how pertinent it is to the present state of intercultural communication.

Today, individuals often fail to understand that communicating interculturally involves encountering surface and depth. This human shortcoming, we believe, accounts for much of the cultural mischief that exists today in communicating across race, class, ethnicity, and gender. Stories of individuals taking fragments of others' lives are abundant. At a prestigious school in California, a visiting professor was sued because a male student in her classroom felt harassed by the instructor's visual presentation of the female anatomy. And some talk radio show hosts, for example, use simplistic and unrestrained language to foster hostility and divisions among North Americans and others.

Part of this general tension, we argue, stems from the fact that, as Robert M. Pirsig (1974) observes, "We take a handful of sand from the endless landscape of awareness around us and call the handful of sand the world" (p. 81). History is replete with examples of misunderstandings that occur because of differences in color and creed or in simply ways of thinking. It is hoped that all of us are increasingly interested in how to perceive and understand human diversity. This book is an intercultural journey toward this end.

CULTURAL ROOTS

Imagine that you are about to take a trip to Borneo, a far away, enchanting land that you have never visited before. Unless you are different from most people, you will take along with you many of the habits and customs that shaped your life long before we offered you the opportunity to travel to Borneo. Here are only a few examples of the many cultural habits you will likely carry with you: a preference for eating with knives and forks, a tradition of saying "hello" when you greet others, an orientation toward using the thumb and forefingers while making a ring to express the familiar "okay" sign, and a ritual performance of eating ice cream and hamburgers. Our point is that when we travel or interact with people who are different from ourselves, we bring our culture with us, with all the possibilities for enjoyment and understanding that this baggage implies.

Further, although we actually (physically) leave our home or country for another place, or interact with individuals who are culturally different, we never entirely leave behind our roots—a major shaping mechanism that gives structure and order to our lives. Without becoming too technical, one might say that the data of our past experience constitute our roots, and the data of our past experiences meshed with roots, constitute our routes. We will discuss routes in more detail later. Indeed, communicating interculturally involves complex movement beyond our roots (both physical and attitudinal) in the process of encountering people from other cultures. The main principle governing our approach to intercultural communication is that although we cannot hope to represent the world in its entirety, we can use our culture, stories, histories, memories, and experiences to demonstrate that people are complex. In this way, we believe that people who speak with both simple and complex voices can be better understood as well as acknowledged.

The terms *cultural roots* and *cultural routes* will serve as vehicles for understanding how we conceptualize intercultural communication. But, that said, we want to resist the reduction of this book to a single theme. For human culture is a complex and multifaceted enterprise and in addressing the issue of culture we would not want to bury its many aspects in a single book. The concepts of roots and routes, however, are powerful tools for understanding how and why the "there" and "then" influence the "here" and "now," and how such interactions ultimately shape the outcome of intercultural communication.

The idea of roots and routes comes from distinctions developed by Manuel Castells (1989), Iain Chambers (1990), and Paul Gilroy (1993). Gilroy (1993) views roots as "the space constituted through and between places," and routes as the "space marked out by flows" (p. 193). We will explain routes in more detail later. Roots, however, involve specific spaces, for example, land that individuals occupy—such as home and country—that are fundamental in helping to form their attachment to ideas, concepts, and things. These "knowable places" become the focal point for one's values and symbolic of one's feelings.

These rooted spaces also include institutions of learning, such as elementary and high schools, churches, clubs, and civic and social organizations. The particular places are not as important as the attachments that people form regarding them and that subsequently shape their communication with others. For example, it is customary for one of the authors who grew up in a pastoral setting, to feel a grand sense of rootedness whenever she sees pastoral settings. The pastoral settings are powerfully evocative for her because they have locked inside them a kind of cultural DNA, or pattern of characteristics. These responses, in turn, create within her what Yi-fu Tuan (1977) calls "enchanted images of the past" (p. 150).

More than anything, roots provide a way for individuals to render their experiences meaningful. A woman traveling through the Vietnam countryside may be moved by a tour guide's references to the severe environmental degradation of Vietnam. The gracious children in Borneo may remind a man of the rich and beautiful people in his hometown of Bernice, Louisiana, or the English phrase, "It's raining cats and dogs" may evoke an exchange student's fond memories of heavy rainstorms in Puerto Rico. These are all examples of how we express our roots. These comments further illustrate the fact that stories, activities, memories, experiences, and history—along with our five senses of sight, sound, hearing, taste, and smell—also shape the way we feel about our roots. In one sense, we can say that an attachment to something and a longing for something are practical ways of determining what has meaning for us. In fact, whenever we long for something or whenever some event or person "moves us," in the sense of tapping into our most precious values and folkways, we can say that our roots are evoked.

Thus, we also conceive of roots as the specific ties that people have to particular places—wherever they believe them to be—including their home, their nation, and the site of their "guarding spirits and gods," as Tuan (1977) phrases it. These ties serve as a center for people's world views, and by extension, a shaping mechanism for their communication with others (p. 150). Connections to the past, such as a person's impulse to remember a song sung in church, or a verse recited in high school, or maybe a longing to see the mountains, springs, and ponds that framed that person's beginnings, help him or her to maintain a profound attachment to homeland or country. What is crucial about these attachments in terms of intercultural communication is that at any point this *packaging of meaning* can influence our responses to persons who are culturally different. Some of our *roots* are so firmly anchored that they make us highly resistant to other people's ideas and behavior.

One reason for this resistance arises from the fact that roots have so much to do with feelings. Roots are all the things that yoke us to the soil as a special, defining place for activities and communication events. For example, shortly after you arrive in Borneo, should you begin to miss your home, the specific content of that missing feeling constitutes part of your roots. The content might be the warmth of a roaring fire in a fireplace with your family members gathered around in lively conversation, or the content might be that you miss seeing a favorite television program that has given your life meaning. The content of roots will vary depending upon where, when, and how an individual was raised, and the nature of the interactions that occur in the "spaces through and between places," as Gilroy put it. As we noted earlier, "spaces through and between places" include physical as well as attitudinal movement. Think of these rooted spaces as receptacles in which you store your meaningful experiences as you move from one person, activity, idea, or event to another.

In his famous novel, *The Razor's Edge*, W. Somerset Maugham (1944) provides a compelling, concrete explanation of what we mean by roots.

Men and women are not only themselves. They are also the region in which they were born, the city dwelling, the farm, in which they learned to walk. They are the games they played as children and the old wives' tales they overheard. They are the food they eat and the schools they attend. They are the Gods they believe in.

In general, because people are taught so well in childhood what to value or devalue, appreciate or denigrate, love or hate, such attachments carry with them profound sentiments about how individuals should feel about where they live. Within these spaces (home, church picnics, school, football games, restaurants), people participate in cultural and social activities that anchor them to particular spots. These activities can include the songs we sing, the stories we hear, the food we eat, the Gods we worship, and the human bonds we form. Thus, roots are more than land and space; they are how and what one thinks and feels about a particular place.

These attachments vary depending upon one's culture. In his book, *From Beirut to Jerusalem*, for example, Thomas Friedman (1989) provides valuable insight on the extreme acts that individuals can commit in defense of their roots. He notes that the deep-rooted primordial identities of some Middle Easterners were instrumental in fostering tension between Jews and Arabs so powerfully that it was hard for them to find "a way to balance the intimacy and cohesion of their tribe-like groups with the demands of a nation-state that could be run by certain neutral rules and values to which everyone agreed" (pp. 91–92). There is no guarantee that individuals' attachments to place will always be positive, although usually they are, because rarely is one indifferent to one's home or nation. This attachment is key to understanding why communication between different intercultural groups can be challenging.

Because communicating interculturally invites a confrontation with diversity in ideas, concepts, beliefs, attitudes, and practices, it can involve a radical jolt to one's roots, especially since communicators are culturally and socially programmed to legitimate their own values and practices (Shweder, 1991). For example, individuals who worship their dead ancestors, or mat their hair with cow dung, or pierce their ear lobes, or eat pork weekly, can normally give others a pretty reasonable argument about why their practices are good and desirable.

Our point is that communicating interculturally is dependent upon the social milieu in which one's roots are developed; that ideas about food, rituals, churchgoing, and so forth, are highly dependent upon the specifics that one gets from one's roots.

For this reason, to communicate interculturally is to risk the possibility of giving up some of one's rooted and usual ways of communicating. Of course, this does not mean that you will become rootless. We do expect, however, that you will develop notions of "elsewhere"—the idea that communicating cross-culturally involves adjusting your ideas, thought patterns, and actions to those of others.

CULTURAL ROUTES

Your journey of discovery with people in Borneo and elsewhere will involve distance beyond your *own* cultural boundaries as you encounter new cultural meanings and ways of interacting with others. Expect all sorts of ideas, customs, and traditions to "criss-cross the patterns" of your life (Chambers, 1990, p. 47). For example, in Borneo, expect a different sense of time, "quiet and well-scrubbed" houses, Chinese restaurants, Western-style dress, quiet-spoken people, and wild pigs to hunt (Sesser, 1993). Expect as well to travel a new cultural route as you increase your fascination with a different side of life: Living in Borneo. What do we mean by cultural routes?

Routes involve physical, cultural, and social *passages* or *movement* between, as well as beyond, one's roots. They are characterized by fluidity and dynamism. Whereas an individual's roots might remain relatively stable, if the individual is to become a competent intercultural communicator, he or she relies on the flow of routes for energy. For example, a Thai rice farmer's movement between the rural areas and the city of Bangkok would constitute a flow along a route. Thus, flow carries with it a back-and-forth crossing between one's and others' actions, feelings, and thinking as a result of contact with different cultures.

Think of routes as *passages* along the intercultural road that are marked by *interconnections*, intersections, stations, and junctions. At any point along the road the intercultural communicator is confronted by new ideas and modes of thinking and doing, all of which have the potential to change or rearrange his or her roots. For example, while traveling through Borneo you might encounter the ethnic Penans, who have a different sense of time than you. Knowing this, you would not ask a Penan, "What were you doing last December 25?" because he or she would simply not understand your method of recording time past. To remember to meet you in 30 days, a Penan would put 30 knots in "a piece of rattan and untie one every sunrise" (Sesser, 1993, p. 243).

While traveling through England during the 1890s, black reformer and journalist Ida B. Wells described her experiences as "being born again in a new condition" (quoted in Gilroy, p. 18). Mrs. Wells felt that she entered England rooted in one set of assumptions and was then changed into something else as a result of her experiences, passages, and interconnections. Similarly, your travels to Borneo and elsewhere are bound to influence you in significant ways.

At any point along the road, however, you may view new things and experiences as not only challenges and opportunities, but also as threats, crises, disturbances, or limitations. As we indicated previously, encountering new and different experiences does not mean that you must toss out, give up, or surrender your own rootedness in order to communicate interculturally. But it does mean that the flow of information, ideas, concepts, beliefs, and knowledge constantly change and influence the nature of what you do and how at any given moment. Another profitable way of looking at routes is to think of them as cultural interconnections, back-and-forth passages, or exchanges linking your past to present and future interactions with others. Recall our former example concerning a woman's reaction to environmental devastation in Vietnam. As she moved from one city in Vietnam to another, the woman reacted the way she did primarily because seeing devastation and waste there evoked in her thoughts such as, "I believe we should manage well our precious resources," and "My rooted values incline me to have reverence for the good earth worldwide."

Because movement away from the soil of our ancestors can bring with it a special kind of anguish, intercultural interactions foster in some people considerable tension between their cultural roots and routes. The experience can be similar to the feeling that Romeo and Juliet had as they struggled to express their love for each other—a love that clashed with the roots of their families' quarrel. The forbidden romantic route that Romeo and Juliet took shook the rooted foundation of their world. This form of tension also can be marked by flow away from one's roots and toward another culture's ways of thinking, feeling, and doing. It is crucial to understand that at any moment the individual can retreat or advance toward new ways of perceiving the world. At most points, though, individuals will undoubtedly disturb the milieu in which they find themselves, since most humans respond meaningfully to their environment.

An American from a strongly community-based social network who enters a new place that has no pot-luck suppers, spontaneous gatherings, horseshoe pitching, and conversations over backyard fences will have to make new accommodations to replace these life-sustaining rituals. As new and different ideas and activities develop, a new communication dynamic is required. In other words, individuals who interact interculturally must see communicating "not as something that has already been achieved," but as an "open framework, continually in the making" (Chambers, 1990 p. 47). Hannerz (1992) is right: Our human passages leave traces "on the social organization of meaning in the world" (p. 247). C.L.R. James's reflections (1980) on the importance of movement and dynamism are also of value here.

> *Now one of the chief errors of thought is to continue to think in one set of forms, categories, ideas, etc.* when the object, the content, has moved on *(emphasis ours) has created or laid premises for an extension, a development of thought. (p. 15)*

Thus, what we think, feel, say, and do can be altered as a result of our passages (physical and cultural), or in some instances remain the same, depending on the extent and degree of our interpersonal encounters and our responses to them.

INFLUENCES ON ROOTS AND ROUTES

The way in which we communicate our roots is influenced by our culture (Gonzalez, Houston, & Chen, 1997). Although there are reportedly over 2,000 different definitions of *culture,* and we will provide one of our own in Chapter 3, we use the term here in an inclusive way.

We subsume under culture the music of Bach and Madonna, the plays of Shakespeare and August Wilson, the Bible and the Koran, blue jeans and high fashion; the writings of Ding Ling and Tolstoy; it is fine French wine, as well as muscadine wine grown in the hinterlands of Tennessee. The role of culture as we see it is to present a blueprint for individuals to use in the development and presentation of their roots. Although individuals learn a lot in the course of human development, they will not retain everything. Because it is not possible for individuals to participate in all aspects of their general culture, the rooting mechanism is designed to channel what an individual takes from his or her environment and considers important.

Our rooting mechanisms tell us to pay attention to A and not B, or to pay attention to A and B, and so on (Hall, 1976). For example, in African culture there is a general reverence for ancestors; however, the specific cultural activities that occur among the Yoruba in western Nigeria will be different from the ones that occur among the Igbo in southeastern Nigeria. In Igboland the annual yam festival that is held to honor the ancestors, because it is tied directly to the ancestral group referred to as Igbo, will make a tremendous difference in intercultural understanding (Uchendu, 1965). In this regard, cultural features that are learned and shared take on special meaning. One group will emphasize one aspect of culture while another group will em-

---

BOX 1-1

Rooting Involves	**Routing and Rerouting Involve**
Past histories and appeals to the past	Consideration of "others"
Traditions and customs	Recognition of difference
Generating meanings	Flow, fluidity, and dynamism
Sense of home	Rearranging elements (content) of communication
"Nesting"	
Tendency towards the local	Openness
Usually strong attachments and sentiments to home and country	Notion of "elsewhere"
	Tendency towards the universal
Binding and/or freeing experiences	Receiver orientation
Piety	Narrative/proverbial and other linguistic shifts
Tendency towards exclusion	
Sender orientation	Tendency towards inclusion

(Note: These traits are not meant to be bipolar)

---

phasize still other features. Once these cultural features are learned, however, they become rooted and take on special significance when members of a culture communicate with others.

At any moment during an intercultural encounter or route, an idea, thought, proverb, food, music, person, or animal will evoke in us memories of things that we hold dear—our roots. Remember our earlier example of how a man's experiences with the people of Borneo reminded him of the friendly people in his hometown of Bernice, Louisiana. That was an instance of a cultural event taking on special significance.

Sociocultural Influences

Recall from the incident that we recounted in the introduction to this chapter that the Ghanaians refused to support Appiah and his English friend's story concerning the traffic accident, although it was clear that the Ghanaian driver was legally at fault. We must recognize that the Ghanaians who witnessed the accident did not arrive at their decisions on guilt or innocence at the precise moment that the accident occurred. Rather, the decision was a cumulative result of years of cultural conditioning, of Ghanaians' observing, responding, valuing, and knowing when and how to act in specific situations.

There is a lesson here: Our roots are not developed in a vacuum, rather, they are shaped by our memberships in groups, which include family, friends, ethnic groups, sex, social class, and nationality. When people interact socially they "sort themselves into clusters" (Goodnough, 1981). This clustering becomes habitual if contact with others is frequent and ongoing. Consciousness of belonging to a specific group causes individuals to distinguish between members (in-group) and nonmembers (out-group). Because individuals derive meaning from the people with whom they associate, at-

---

BOX 1-2   An Interplay between Roots and Routes

Again, like Moore's oversubtle philosophers discoursing musefully on the real, anthropologists often spin notional complexities they then report as cultural facts through a failure to realize that much of what their informants are saying is, however strange it may sound to educated ears, meant literally. Some of the most crucial properties of the world are not regarded as concealed beneath a mask of deceptive appearances, things inferred from pale suggestions or riddled out of equivocal signs. They are conceived to be just there, where stones, hands, scoundrels, and erotic triangles are, invisible only to the clever. It takes a while (or, anyway, it took me a while) to absorb the fact that when the whole family of a Javanese boy tells me that the reason he has fallen out of a tree and broken his leg is that the spirit of his deceased grandfather pushed him out because some ritual duty toward the grandfather has been inadvertently overlooked, that, so far as they are concerned, is the beginning, the middle, and the end of the matter: It is precisely what they think has occurred, it is all that they think has occurred, and they are puzzled only at my puzzlement at their lack of puzzlement. And when, after listening to a long, complicated business from an old, illiterate, nononsense Javanese peasant woman— a classic type if ever there was one —about the role of "the snake of the day" in determining the wisdom of embarking on a journey, holding a feast, or contracting a marriage (the story was actually mostly loving accounts of the terrible things that happened—carriages overturning, tumors appearing, fortunes dissolving—when that role was ignored), I asked what this snake of the day looked like and was met with, "Don't be an idiot; you can't see Tuesday, can you?"

From: Clifford Geertz, *Local Knowledge: Further Essays in Interpretive Anthropology*, New York: Basic Books, 1983, p. 89.

tachments to in-group membership norms and behavior create endearing responses that are, in turn, anchored. It is in this sense that social structures become part of rooting behavior.

Symbolic Influences

Individuals who belong to particular groups are also susceptible to symbolic influences or language (Barnlund, 1989; Bradac, Hosman, & Tardy, 1978; Giles & Powesland, 1975; Gudykunst & Kim, 1992; Samovar & Porter, 1996). Because humans are symbol-using, symbol-building animals, as Kenneth Burke (1966) notes, they store an awful lot of attitudes that are expressed linguistically. And because so much of our culture is transmitted via language, language becomes the vehicle for depositing our noblest ambitions, our attachments to others, as well as our image of ourselves. Therefore, it is unbearable for some people to shed the language of their ancestors. What interests us here is that since so much of our feelings are intertwined with who we are and the language we speak, symbolic influences are part of all we do, and provide the blueprints for our interaction with others.

Historical Influences

Tuan (1977) notes that "All that we are we owe to the past" (p. 197). Our experiences, actions, attachments to home, family, and nation leave traces that we refer to here as historical memory. Whatever we have filled our time with constitutes our past, and at any moment these things can be "rescued," "called up," or "flashed to the surface," during an intercultural communication exchange and subsequently alter how we interact with others. This is a point to bear in mind. Another point is this: From our past, we develop a personal intellectual history that serves as a cultural storage bin for the interpretation of ideas and events. Into this bin we place knowledge of our ancestors, the old family home, a monument to a common hero, a picture album, a stroll down a country lane, the memory of sights and sounds and smells, and myriad other things.

At any point in our conversations with others, we can use these cultural data to embellish an argument, offer an example, clarify a point, or make our past accessible to others. In contrast, it is also the case that we can withhold our past from others, creating suspicion and mistrust, if that is the response that such withholding would engender.

It is worth noting as well that the cultural data of our historical memory need not be gained through direct experience or intimate knowledge. We also gain knowledge indirectly through newspapers, magazines, stories, and television. Indirect moments that are radical and full of meaning can nullify past events so that we are "ready to abandon home for the promised land," as

Tuan (1977) observes (p. 184). In this sense, then, historical memory changes depending upon whether our memory invites joy, pain, or indifference.

Time is also a factor in historical memory; indeed, it is the flow of time and what we add to it that allows us to reflect upon our past and determine what should be saved, deleted, or reinforced. To the extent that time modifies what we think, feel, or do, it plays a crucial role in intercultural interactions. Of course, cultures differ in the way in which they treat time, as you will learn in Chapter 9. For example, because Chinese culture promotes reverence for the ancestors, it also pays homage to the wisdom of the past in ways that North American culture, with its emphasis on the future, does not. It should be noted, however, that as a result of market and global forces, North Americans are becoming less future-oriented and Chinese less past-oriented, which are examples of the power of routing behaviors to alter our historical memory.

Our point in this section is to highlight the fact that what is rooted in the past can be swept away or retained, depending on the flow that energizes our routes. There is, then, an interplay between our roots and routes, which we will address in a later section.

THE LOCAL VERSUS THE GLOBAL

To this point we have defined roots and routes, discussed sociocultural and symbolic influences, and identified some of the consequences of historical memory, especially how events can change our attachments to home and ideas. Here we outline two basic ways that individuals can react to diversity in humans: locally (particularism) or globally (universalism). By the local we mean the tendency to emphasize specific differences in processing and interpreting data when interacting with others. In contrast, the global emphasizes likenesses in processing and interpreting data when interacting with others. It is also possible to interact at a level somewhere in between the global and the local.

Confronted with the apparent diversity in humans, locally focused individuals rely more heavily on their roots, tend to negate new information or ideas, and are relatively uncurious about the world around them. They treat their roots as the endpoint of communication about alien thoughts or ideas and can be dismissive when confronted with new, competing ideas and ways of behaving. One is likely to hear locally focused individuals make comments such as, "We don't do it that way," "What can the Japanese teach us about cars?" or "You cannot trust Germans." Instead of doubting the truth of their point of view, locally oriented persons can and do explain away why their world is better than the world of others. Locally focused thinkers rarely consult the other side because they are so convinced of the rightness of their own cause, and their roots are so deeply anchored as to bleach out other modes of thinking and behaving.

Here we do not mean to suggest that anyone who questions other points of view should be defined as having all of the characteristics that obtain in locally focused thought. Rather, we are suggesting that local and global communications are a matter of degree.

Globally focused individuals travel a different route, however. They believe there are enough similarities among humans to warrant identifying with others. Thus, their mode of thinking is more spacious in the sense that points of resemblances are manifested. For example, the ideas that most people are capable of thinking well, or that all people seek the truth, but in different ways, are characteristic of globally motivated individuals.

Thus, this global mode of thinking elevates the idea that people will be alike in some ways and different in other ways; however, the significant point driving this type of thinking is similarity. It is the notion that humans share common things around the globe. Iris Murdoch (1955), for example, has noted that there are more than 72 human traits that people share in common, ranging from concepts of beauty to political systems (pp. 123–142).

A tendency to see similarities means that in the course of their intercultural journey, globally focused individuals are aware that human constants can be cut up and rearranged in different places, among different people. For example, beauty in some cultures is highlighted by facial tatoos whereas in other cultures such markings are disdained. In each instance, however, there is some idea of what beauty means. The global way of thinking is also capable of transferring local habits and customs into a universal frame. In this regard, it is an accommodationist model, spacious enough to include our understanding of even the most rigid thinker, according to our definition of things.

THE INTERCONNECTEDNESS OF ROOTS AND ROUTES

Having distinguished between the local and the global, we now focus on the interrelationship between roots and routes. Our orientation is animated by the idea that communication relies on "rooting," "uprooting," " routing," and "rerouting" behaviors. The intersection comes when our roots criss-cross with the cultural routes that we take during the course of normal interaction with others. Daily we are confronted with ethnicity, gender, sex, class, thought patterns, and behaviors that challenge our histories, traditions, customs, and sense of place as we move into that zone we call *elsewhere*.

At the point that what has happened to us in the past (including whether we count time by using knotted rattan, consult the entrails of an animal for

future plans, or pray to Allah or to God), interacts with what flows up in tł
"here and now" (the opposite of using knotted rattan or worshipping Allał
an intersection occurs between our roots and routes.

Another way of looking at this crisscross is to say that a confrontation o
curs whenever there is a meeting between "then" (the past, our roots) ar
"now" (the present, our current passages or routes). When the two are co
joined by different conceptions of reality, these combinations suggest that
flow has occurred. Flow can be viewed as a body of water into which oth
cultural and communication streams or tributaries empty. Flow one equa
experience one, flow two, equals experience two, and so forth, until the boo
of water is altered much or little. In this regard, our roots and routes are eb
and flows between what we have been and done and what we encounter
we journey from one intercultural experience to another.

We also envision the intersection between roots and routes as either a f
cilitating or a retarding enterprise. Facilitating experiences move individua
in the direction of effective communication, whereas retarding experienc
create intense misunderstandings, tension, and conflict.

CONCLUSION

In this chapter we have defined roots and routes and examined aspects
rooting and routing behaviors: (1) cultural influences, (2) sociocultural inf
ences, (3) historical memory, (4) the local versus the global, and the interco
nectedness of roots and routes. These materials are building blocks for c
understanding of how the primary places that root our cultural experienc
help to shape what we think, feel, and do as we interact with others.

QUESTIONS

1. Do you agree with the authors that routes should be viewed as "int
   connections, back-and-forth passages, or exchanges linking past to p
   sent and future interactions with others"?   ·-
2. Can you think of ways that your own roots have interfered with yo
   ability to communicate interculturally?
3. How do the concepts of locally focused and globally focused individu
   help to explain the complexity of intercultural communication?
4. Why is it important to assess the interconnectedness between roots a
   routes?
5. Can you think of additional ways to approach the idea of communic
   ing interculturally?

ACTIVITIES

1. Develop a roots and routes chart showing how these two concepts influence your intercultural interactions with others. For example, you might identify your attitudes concerning family, equality, and happiness, charting how such attitudes have changed over the years based on your intercultural development. How many different factors are present in your cultural system? What facts about your culture do they reflect? What do they indicate about the possibility of change?
2. Interview two persons who are members of another culture. Ask these individuals what changes they have observed in their specific cultures. These may be changes in family relationships, belief systems, customs, or relationships toward nature. Next, ask the individuals what further changes are likely to occur and why.
3. The interaction between technology and people influence our intercultural roots and routes. Using some cultural innovation such as the automobile, television, medicine, or the alphabet, demonstrate how this invention has shaped our intercultural roots. For instance, the discovery of the bicycle make it easier for women to communicate with people in nearby villages and towns. The discovery of the bicycle, in turn, altered women's perception of independence.

REFERENCES

Appiah, K. (1992). *In my father's house*. New York: Oxford University Press.

Barnlund, D. (1989). *Communicative styles of Japanese and Americans: Images and realities*. Belmont, CA: Wadsworth.

Bradac, J., Hosman, L., & Tardy, C. H. (1978). Reciprocal disclosures and language intensity: Attributional consequences. *Communication Monographs, 45*, 1–17.

Burke, K. (1966). *Language as symbolic action: Essays on life, literature, and method*. Berkeley: University of California Press.

Castells, M. (1989). *The informational city: Information, technology, economic, restructuring, and the urban regional process*. Cambridge: Basil Blackwell.

Chambers, I. (1990). *Border dialogues*. London: Routledge.

Friedman, T. (1989). *From Beirut to Jerusalem*. New York: Farrar Straus Giroux.

Geertz, C. (1983). *Local knowledge: Further essays in interpretive anthropology*. New York: Basic Books.

Giles, P., & Powesland, P. (1975) *Speech style and social evaluation*. London: Academic Press.

Gilroy, P. (1993). *Small acts: Thoughts on the politics of culture*. London: Serpent's Tail.

Gilroy, P. (1993). *The black atlantic*. Cambridge, MA: Harvard University Press.

Goodnough, W. (1981). *Culture, language, and society*. Menlo Park, CA: The Benjamin/Cummings Publishing Company.

Gonzalez, A., Houston, M., & Chen, V. (Eds.). (1997). *Our voices: Essays in culture, ethnicity, and communication.* Los Angeles, CA: Roxbury.

Gudykunst, W., & Kim, Y. (1992). *Readings on communicating with strangers: An approach to intercultural communication.* New York: McGraw Hill.

Hall, E. (1976). *Beyond culture.* New York: Anchor Press/Doubleday.

Hannerz, U. (1992). *Cultural complexity: Studies in the social organization of meaning.* New York: Columbia University Press.

James, C. (1980). *Notes on dialetics* (p. 15). London: Allison & Busby.

Maugham, W. (1944). *The razor's edge.* Garden City, NY: Doran & Company.

Murdoch, I. (1955). Common denominator of cultures. In R. Linton (Ed.), *Science of man in the world crises.* New York: Columbia.

Pirsig, R. M. (1974). *Zen and the art of motorcycle maintenance: An inquiry into values.* Toronto: Bantam Books.

Samovar, L., & Porter, R. (1996). *Intercultural communication: A reader.* Belmont, CA: Wadsworth.

Sesser, S. (1993). *The lands of charm and cruelty.* New York: Vintage Books.

Shweder, R. (1991). *Thinking through cultures: Expeditions in cultural psychology.* Cambridge, MA: Harvard University Press.

Tuan, Y-F. (1977). *Space and place: The perspective of experience.* Minneapolis: University of Minnesota Press.

Uchendu, V. (1965). *The Igbo of southeast Nigeria.* New York: Holt, Rinehart and Winston.

2

COMMUNICATION
AND CONTEXT

Objectives

After reading this chapter and completing the activity, you should be able to:

1. Discuss the importance of context within intercultural communication settings.
2. Explain how the constituent elements in the communication process work in intercultural communication.
3. Discuss ways of reducing potential breakdown and misunderstanding in intercultural communication contexts.

Communication interactions are guided by contexts. This is to say that the contexts within which human beings communicate influence significantly the quality and quantity of the communication, the process that takes place during the interaction, and the eventual outcome of the encounter. In this chapter, we focus our attention on the need to understand contexts within intercultural communication settings by examining the constituent elements of the communication process. We also discuss how misunderstanding or misconstruing contexts can lead to communication breakdown. Through anecdotes, and our discussion of each element of the communication process, we look at ways of reducing the possibilities for breakdown in communication.

ROOTS AND CONTEXT

Contexts are particularly important in intercultural communication processes because of the mere fact that people from different cultural backgrounds have different notions of "context," which in turn dictate how they perform as the intercultural communication encounter progresses.

Because various cultures emerge from different roots, as communicators within an intercultural context, we should pay attention to the overriding importance of the fact that we do not all spring from the same cultural roots and that we go through several routes as we learn about the rules of the game in our cultures. We journey through life constantly learning about the cultural environment within which we survive daily. The learning takes place consciously and at times unconsciously. We obtain formal cultural training in institutions such as the family, schools, social clubs, churches, mosques, synagogues, temples, and other religious bodies that contribute to our upbringing. When we consider our roots and the routes that we take in learning about our culture, we should recognize the importance context has in intercultural communication settings.

SIGNIFICANCE OF CONTEXT

The significance of context is recognized by scholars who observe various cultures and develop classification systems of cultural behavior based on the nature of the context of given cultures. For instance, Edward T. Hall (1976) provides us an insight into his observations on two types of cultures he refers to as "high" and "low" contexts cultures. Among some of the differences between people from cultural contexts are that: people from high context cultures are less verbal, hence are more inclined to communicate nonverbally. People from low context cultures, on the other hand, value verbal expressions and are more talkative. For example, people from both contexts handle silence during intercultural encounters differently. Low context people usually feel uncomfortable, anxious to break the silence and continue to talk. High context people usually consider silence as a normal part of the communication interaction. In some African and Asian countries, when silence occurs during a conversation, people do not get edgy and try to break it. The conversation picks up naturally after the phase of silence. Hall classifies countries of Europe, North America, Australia, and New Zealand as low context cultures, whereas countries in Africa, Asia, and other non-Western areas of the world as high context cultures.

When we view culture within the above perspective, we can discern how "context" features during intercultural communication. It serves as a basis for explaining our attitudes when communicating, shaping our perceptions, and dictating our relationships within and outside of our respective cultures. As we engage in intercultural communication contexts, what we have learned about our culture provides the context and background for our interactions. People from other cultures with whom we interact also enter the communication context with all the information and knowledge they have also acquired about their culture, which provides for them the context within which they communicate. The challenge that we have in intercultural communication with regard to context is the extent to which we recognize the significance context plays in our interactions and the willingness to try as hard as possible to understand others who do not share our roots and have not used the same routes. Here is an anecdote that shows the importance of context in intercultural contacts and communication.

Context and Practice: An Anecdote

A Catholic priest is in an African country to preach the Christian gospel and convert Africans to Christianity. Upon his arrival in the African village, he observes that the inhabitants practice some from of African religion that teaches them about African values and morality and about life after death. In short, he observes first hand the "route" Africans in that village take in the socialization process, and how such process sets the context for their behavior. The priest experienced a different "route" in Europe, in going through the socialization process that eventually led him to a profession that required him to travel to foreign lands as a missionary.

We are confronted with a situation in which the priest and the potential converts have radically different roots and have gone through different routes in acquiring their respective cultural values. They are products of not just two different continents but also different ways of looking at the world. The communication context becomes charged with potential for misunderstandings, miscues, misperceptions, and misinterpretations. The priest, however, succeeds in converting the Africans.

With conversion to Christianity comes a name change. Each African is given a Christian name as he or she is baptized. The priest explains that conversion to Christianity requires a name change, from an African name to a Christian (European name) and that baptism is a major ceremony in the transformation process. Upon completing the baptism the priest informs the Africans that adopting the Christian faith as Catholics has certain laws. For example, Catholics (at that time) do not eat meat on Fridays, and Christians do not tell lies. He completes his work and goes on to the next village, promising to return periodically to check on the progress of the new converts and to see how best they are adhering to the laws of Christianity.

Several months later, the priest returns to the village on a Friday and meets an African man and his family eating meat. He gets annoyed and shouts at the converts reminding them about the laws regarding the eating of meat on Fridays. The African man calmly responds that he is doing nothing wrong. His response and calm attitude infuriate the priest who then accuses the African of breaking another law—lying! The African remains calm and denies that he is breaking any laws and tells the priest that he and his family are good Christians. The priest, still angry, asks the African how he can claim to be a good Christian while eating meat in front of him and then denying openly that he is not breaking the laws. The African responds calmly, telling the priest that he has an explanation for his actions.

He said that when he woke up he searched for food for his family but he could not get fish. So he went out of the village and hunted for a rabbit. He brought the rabbit home, poured water on its head and said, "as of now, you are no longer rabbit, but fish." He reminded the priest that when he became a Christian he was baptized with water and was told during the ceremony that he was no longer "Gbani" (his African name) but "John." As far as he was concerned, he was serving his "fish" to his family and was definitely not telling a lie!

A context that was charged with potential for conflict became one that forced the priest to "see" things from the perspective of the African. The African took the "route" to Christianity seriously based on Christian teachings that contained a significant number of miracles performed by Christ. The act of pouring water on the rabbit and changing its name was not that far removed from other acts in the gospel. The African himself was a living example. Not only did he "change" from Gbani to John, he crossed over into the Christian church from his African religion. Many times we tend not to realize that the way we approach people from different cultural backgrounds, experiences, and routes, can have communication outcomes that we least expect.

DIVERSITY AND CONTEXT

As many countries of the world become more and more culturally and linguistically diverse, the potential for misunderstandings between the various cultural groups will increase. In the United States for example, we must begin to pay closer attention to the fact that groups of immigrants that are coming from Southeast and East Asia (Cambodia, Vietnam, China, and several parts of South Asia), India, Sri Lanka, and so forth will make intercultural communication a basic skill to master. Immigrants are coming to the United States having gone through different routes and definitely coming from different roots. If not handled properly, intercultural communication experiences can become a nightmare. University education by itself without an understanding of the communication dynamics that take place between and among people of different cultural backgrounds is inadequate to prepare citizens for the twenty-first century.

Arizona, California, Florida, New Mexico, New York, and Texas are no longer the states in which one could easily find "ethnic enclaves" of Asians and Latin Americans that have a relatively long historical presence in the United States. The Midwest has its own significant share of immigrants from Asia and Latin America. The crisis in the former Soviet Union, the former Yugoslavia, and other Eastern European countries triggered by the collapse of communism and the subsequent wars in Bosnia and civil unrest in many parts of the former Soviet Union have resulted in an increase in the flow of immigrants. The immigrant population, however, is no longer one that manifests a preponderance of immigrants from Europe, Latin American, and Asia, but now we observe recent immigrants from Africa and others from the South Pacific.

All over the United States we observe many foreign-born professionals working in various contexts. They used different routes to get to America, coming with different expectations. There is, clearly, a major cultural and linguistic transformation that is occurring quite rapidly in America that makes it incumbent on all of us to become more and more sensitized on the issues of context and process as we engage in intercultural communication.

Complexity

Given all of the above, when we say that communication is influenced by context, we wish to stress that the context is complex, requiring participants in an intercultural communication encounter to be willing to spend a little more energy than usual, compared to situations in which we are communicating with people from the same roots and having gone through the same "routes" during the socialization process. The rate at which the emerging twenty-first century American society is growing more and more diverse, will create ever changing, complex, and indeed at times, a perplexing intercultural communication context. This phenomenon is not peculiar to America. Massive flows of people from various parts of the world are moving from one region to another because of political problems stemming from civil wars and economic hardship. Diversity concerns are prevalent in Africa, Asia, Australia, Europe, and New Zealand.

In order to avoid frustrations in intercultural communication encounters within such a complex context, we have to be ready to make the effort to work hard on recognizing ourselves and others as products of our respective cultures trying to communicate. Because this text is on communication, it is natural for us to stress the need to communicate rather than to walk away from an intercultural encounter that might be perceived as tedious, time-consuming, and irritating.

CONSTITUENT ELEMENTS OF COMMUNICATION

At this juncture, let us address the issue of *understanding* communication contexts. Intercultural communication like all other communication processes involves several elements that interact with each other. All communication processes have the following basic constituent elements at play during interactions: source, message, channel, receiver, and feedback. All these elements interact *within* a context and are *guided* by contexts. The interactive characteristic feature of communication makes us understand better that communication is a process. Being a process, it is dynamic and nonlinear. Sources encode messages—creating meaning for the receiver—and receivers decode messages—deciphering the meaning created by the source. It must be pointed out, however, that we do not restrict the use of the word "decode" to connote that only receivers carry out that act, and conversely, that only sources encode. Sources have to decode when receivers ask for clarification of meaning. The formulation of the questions by the receiver involves an act of encoding.

When we view communication as interactive, we recognize that it also could be purposeful or not, and intentional or unintentional. By the same token, even when we seek to communicate intentionally, we may *unintentionally* miscommunicate, resulting at times in conflict situations. This is particularly critical in intercultural communication interactions. As we shall see later, there are certain sociopsychological variables such as values, prejudice, beliefs, and stereotypes that play significant roles within the communication context. Certain stereotypes, for example, are ascribed to certain cultures. The stereotypes range from athletic abilities of certain ethnic groups to food preferences.

Having a Party

Take for instance a situation in which students at a university from various ethnic, national, and racial backgrounds are gathered at a party celebrating an event. A student from Israel walks up to an African American student at the party and observes that he is not dancing according to the rhythm of the Israeli music that is playing. In fact, he observes that the African American is completely off beat. He approaches him and makes a comment about his observations. The African American becomes very angry, thinking that the Israeli student is making assumptions based on stereotypes that portray African Americans as "good dancers." The Israeli student is surprised and tries to explain that paradoxically, he only wants to show the African American student how to dance to that particular Israeli song and that his comments have nothing to do with stereotyping. This anecdote shows how what we intend to communicate can result in unintentional messages as well.

What a Life!

Let us examine briefly another situation. A student from Mexico is relating how she feels about the death of her father and her deep sense of loss and emptiness following her father's passing. She states: "My dad used to tell me what to do. He made me feel needed. Now he is not here . . ." She stresses in her story the problems she encounters in her close-knit family when a caring father figure dies suddenly and there is no such figure anymore to "guide" the rest of the family. Her sentiments, she explains, are shared by the rest of her siblings and her mother.

Rooted in a culture that is dominated by a father figure, this student travels to the United States and attends a university. She has a sociology teacher who condemns outright patriarchal systems as "sexist" and "chauvinist." The student at first respects this teacher as a "source" with authority. She is the "receiver" of messages from a "source" that is becoming increasingly difficult to handle. The student becomes belligerent and confronts the teacher constantly, pointing out to her that she comes from a background that respects "patriarchal" systems.

Eventually, the exchanges between the student and the teacher become bitter. The student loses the battle and gets a failing grade because she could not bring herself to accept the approach of the teacher in the course, which in her view, is anti-Mexican and anti-male, having nothing to do with why she came to America to study.

Elements in Motion

We can discern several elements in the communication encounter between the Israeli student and the African American. There are animate (human) and inanimate elements in the communication context. The human elements are the two students who are involved in the interaction. Both represent the "source" and "receiver" interchangeably in the context. There are also inanimate elements such as the Israeli music.

In the case of the student and the professor interchanging their roles as "source" and receiver," they experience serious intercultural communication difficulties even though there is "feedback" going on consistently between the two. Neither manifests *openness* and *willingness* to empathize, which would have enabled them to understand why they relate to each other the way they do. Both parties come from different roots and have gone through different routes to the university. The context, therefore, requires a lot of willingness, openness, and empathy. Without the willingness to be open and to empathize, source and receiver cannot benefit from feedback. We have used several terms in the two examples given above, such as source, message, receiver, and feedback. Let us now examine the elements of the communication process in specific terms.

Source

The source is the person or institution that initiates the process of communication. In this sense, the source intentionally (at times unintentionally) creates a message for someone or an institution (the receiver). Both source and receiver can be as diverse as individuals and business corporations. They are influenced by their cultural roots, which form their respective contexts. The source is bombarded on a constant basis by numerous stimuli from the immediate environment or stimulus field, with varying levels of intensity.

These stimuli can be verbal or nonverbal: for example, our cultural background; stimuli like voices of individuals in our immediate vicinity; the sound from the heating/cooling system; the light in the room; pleasant and unpleasant odors; noises from construction crews; personal fantasies.

When the United States government initiates communication with Cubans (in Cuba) using the American government radio station called "The Voice of America" to condemn communism and socialism as instruments of governance and economic practice respectively, it is acting as a source. The authors of this book are sources initiating communication with you as readers of our messages. All of the sources mentioned above operate within the context of their stimulus field, which serves as the environment within which messages are generated.

As sources, people and institutions carry certain responsibilities, particularly in intercultural communication situations. The responsibilities include among others, communication competence—recognizing that intercultural communication encounters require a certain degree of knowledge of limitations and strengths of the source; the need to empathize with intended receivers; the need to manifest as best as possible, credibility and goodwill; and also ascertaining that codes (language) used in creating messages can be understood or decoded with the help of others if necessary. Basically, sources should always bear in mind that they are ultimately responsible for the communication they initiate. It behooves sources, therefore, to take intercultural communication encounters seriously, recognizing that the source is dealing with receivers who operate under different contextual circumstances.

Message

The source operates within an environment that is laden with stimuli. The source also selects and prioritize its response to the particular set of stimuli, which at the end of the process represents what is created in the form of a message. Hence, a "message" can be understood as that content the source creates by encoding from his or her stimulus field for a potential receiver(s). There are occasions, however that messages are not *consciously* organized by the source. This is particularly true of nonverbal communication and other forms of communication miscues that can be easily misunderstood by the receiver. One important element that has to be consistently kept in mind is that the message created is like a piece of personal property that has to be treated with care.

When messages are regarded as property, it makes the source more careful in structuring the content and in determining the most appropriate means (channel) of transmitting the message. This characteristic feature of messages—as property—is especially important in intercultural communication. We take responsibility for our property. When someone or an organization is given a message initiated by another source to deliver to a receiver, the initial source is responsible and not the person or organization requested to deliver the message.

Messages come in verbal and nonverbal forms. We elaborate on nonverbal communication in Chapter 9. We use the word "verbal" to connote not only spoken words, but also language used to create messages that have a "grammatic" structure. This is to say that braille is verbal to the extent that it conveys messages using the grammar or syntax of the language. Given this, the source has to be familiar or should learn to become familiar with the language or code of the intended receiver. The code that is used to structure the message should be one that is shared by the source and receiver or that could be *translated* or *interpreted* for the receiver. At international conferences at which participants come from different linguistic backgrounds, interpreters are used so that everyone understands the meanings and contexts of the words and ideas that are being communicated.

Blowing an Opportunity?

A source that fails to act responsibly in structuring an intended message could experience tremendous difficulties. For instance, Abdul, an African student at a major university tried to go out on a date with an American woman a few weeks after he arrived in the United States. He met the woman on time and they engaged in conversation on their way to the restaurant. Unknown to Abdul, she was very uncomfortable with the manner in which he kept touching her when speaking, particularly while emphasizing a point. For Abdul, touching a "friend" does not connote an unwanted sexual gesture or approach. Because he was going out with the woman he considered her a "friend" and felt comfortable relating to her as he would in his culture. The woman in turn did not want to tell him that she was uncomfortable because she felt she would hurt his feelings.

This was a clear case in which the African student was sending an unintended message on the one hand, and on the other, unknowingly creating a problem for himself in terms of missing out on another date. As would be expected, he found it difficult to have a date with that friend later. Furthermore, word went around quickly that he was a person that must be closely watched by women because he was too tactile. Inasmuch as people try to be responsible in sending messages, there are many instances in which sources fall prey to misperceptions and misinterpretations of messages both intended and unintended. People need to treat intercultural communication contexts with care and diligence.

Channel

As we move along with the discussion on the elements of the communication process, we have up to this point dealt with the generation and structuring of messages. After the message is developed, the source decides on the appropriate channel to use in order to convey it to the intended audience/receiver. Channels come in mechanical and human forms. Radio, telephones, television, and computer networks belong to the electronic media or channels. Newspapers, magazines, books, pamphlets, flyers, and other forms of printed matter belong to the print media or channels.

Oramedia

Beside the mechanical channels, there are channels that are regarded as "human" in the sense that they do not have the technical characteristics that the mechanical channels mentioned above have. For instance, in several African and Asian states, oral channels such as short stories and parables used by people are used to channel information to receivers. Frank Ugboajah (1982–83) refers to oral channels as *oramedia*. Drama, dance, song, myths, and legends represent vehicles by which information is channeled. The information can range from pedagogical content on the history and development of the given culture to socialization on the norms of that culture. There are techniques that need to be learned in the use of such channels. In the United States and in some other parts of the western world, people who believe that they can communicate with their departed friends and relatives through seance sessions rely on the medium—the person who serves as the link between the living and the dead.

Reaching the Beyond

Another media form that is not well known in Western nations is kola nuts. These nuts are used widely among an ethnic group in Sierra Leone as a means of communicating with the dead. When people visit grave sites of family members or friends, they "talk" to the departed and use the kola nuts as of means of obtaining responses from the dead.

Drums also are used in Africa and some parts of Asia to communicate within immediate and distant geographic locations. Native Americans used smoke signals as a means of transmitting messages among the various nations that constitute their community.

Mechanical Noise Factors

Stemming from the above, it is evident that the essential function of channels is that of a direct link between source and receiver. Given such a significant function, channels have to be as clear as possible. Shannon and Weaver (1949), in their research on telephone lines as channels, recognize "noise" as a major problem that affected the quality of the transmission. Noise comes in various forms. In telephone lines, it comes through as heavy static that leads to distortions of sound, which in turn affects our ability to hear what the person at the other end of the line is saying. Even with all the advances made in improving upon noise reduction, when using an ordinary cordless telephone, people experience static if they are far away from the base. A very good cordless phone has as a feature several channels to which a user can switch if static develops in the one being used. Such multiple channels provide accidental access to police patrol units talking to each other or to their base stations. Switching channels around may interfere with conversations going on by different users such as our neighbors.

When driving long distances, the farther away we get from our favorite station the more static we experience until we are no longer able to hear what the announcer is saying or to enjoy the music being played by the disc jockey.

Human Noise Factors

The noise referred to above has mainly been with mechanical devices. In the intercultural communication context, human noise is common. Such noise comes in the forms of sociopsychological variables such as prejudice, stereotype, beliefs, and attitudes. All societies develop an image of themselves and others. The worldviews of people differ from culture to culture. As people from diverse backgrounds meet, it is not uncommon for some of us to view other people from the perspective of our own worldview. This can create "noise" leading to communication breakdowns. So important are the worldviews of people and the impact of the various sociopsychological variables on day to day life that researchers spend considerable time working on projects and studies that might serve as a basis for reducing tensions and breakdown in communication among different cultural groups.

Laray Barna (1997) writing about the impact of sociopsychological variables in intercultural communication refers to them as stumbling blocks. Sitaram and Hapaanen (1979) also observe that ethnocentrism, based on how we view our values against those of others, creates major problems in intercultural communication encounters and can lead to failure to communicate. Channel selection in intercultural communication, therefore, requires close attention and an effort to reduce noise to its lowest possible level. The human noise factors that include prejudice and other forms of obstacles present the most challenging aspect in intercultural communication. We can learn a foreign language. It is very difficult to *unlearn* our prejudices, beliefs, attitudes, and stereotypes. It takes effort, willingness, and openness in intercultural communication contexts in order to succeed.

Channel Selection

Sources have to be careful in selecting appropriate channels so as to reach intended receivers with the least amount of difficulty. A source that intends to reach a largely illiterate audience cannot rely on books as channels. Take, for example, a situation in which a public health officer in a village in Thailand, where the villagers cannot write or read, decides to disseminate information on the rapidly spreading AIDS virus using data written in pamphlets and other forms of printed media. The audience will not get the content of the message unless there is someone there to read it to them. Various units in the oral channel—oramedia, referred to earlier—combined with printed material in the forms of posters carrying recognizable symbols such as pictures of AIDS victims before and after they become infected will be more useful. The officer may consider a combination of electronic media (radio and television) and the oral channels.

Bordenave (1971) reports that development workers in northeastern Brazil who selected print media paraphernalia to communicate innovations to rural dwellers failed in their efforts to reach their target audience. They had to resort to oramedia channels peculiar to the region. Appropriateness and noise reduction are two essential factors that require close attention in channel selection and use in intercultural communication contexts.

Receiver/Audience

We use "audience" and "receiver" interchangeably. When messages are encoded, the source has in mind an audience who would ultimately get them. There are occasions, however, when the encoded message reaches audiences unintentionally. The audience shares in many ways the same characteristic features of the source. They can be individuals, academic institutions, corporate bodies, and entire national entities. As with the source, the receivers operate within an environment laden with stimuli, peculiar to them. Inasmuch as the source is rooted in its environment, there is a need to recognize that receivers in intercultural contexts are also rooted in their environment, having been socialized to respond to and prioritize stimuli within that particular environment.

Because the source wishes to initiate contact with the receiver in the form of messages, it should ascertain that there is a degree of shared meaning in the content of the message(s) being transmitted. Without shared meaning, we cannot understand the content of the message. For instance, the expression "I love you" is used commonly in the United States among family members and friends. In some cultural contexts in Africa, for example, the expression may carry a more serious meaning and expectation than in America. If a woman friend tells a man friend that she "loves" him, the direct meaning is that she is *in love* with him. The context, therefore, has a lot to do with shared meaning. It is equally important to ensure that our word choice is congruent with that of the audience. Commonly shared meanings, therefore, are at the heart of the intercultural communication encounter. It goes beyond common language into the realm of nuances—a subtle distinction of verbal and non-verbal language that is not necessarily shared by a receiver. For example, a person may smile and wink at another person without recognizing that he or she can be misunderstood.

In addition to commonly shared meaning, the source has to have an idea of the makeup or profile of the intended target audience. If there is *adequate* information about the background of the receiver, intercultural communication becomes easier, because the source will structure the message in a manner that is consistent with the ability of the receiver to understand. Among some of the aspects that the source may require in a profile of the audience are demographic data, and as feasible, information on some of the basic sociopsychological variables already mentioned in the previous section.

On a one-to-one basis, and without the opportunity to prepare well, the source will have to make quick judgments through preliminary exchanges to determine the extent to which shared meaning can be achieved. It is at this point that the receiver and source switch roles rapidly through questions and answers, attempting to arrive at a common understanding of each other's message.

There are occasions, however, when such exchanges in the form of questions and responses do not take place. Recall the African student who miscommunicated during the course of a date by being too tactile, resulting in the receiver misunderstanding him and his motives. Some receivers within intercultural communication contexts get intimidated and do not seek clarification of what a source intends, creating an impression that they both understand each other only to discover later that a failure occurred in the communication interaction.

Misunderstandings between receiver and source are not just restricted to intercultural communication encounters. They happen in classrooms regularly between professors and students. They happen also among friends and relatives. Misunderstandings and breakdowns become more pronounced, however, in intercultural communication contexts for the obvious reason of basic cultural differences, hence the need to be open for questions that seek clarification and to be willing to provide responses in order to achieve shared meaning.

Feedback

The strategy referred to above as questioning the source in order to clarify an idea or an entire message is what we refer to as *feedback*. Feedback involves the process by which receivers get back to sources in the form of questions and/or responses in search of clarification. When a student does not understand what a professor is saying, he or she is obliged to ask questions. The professor who recognizes the importance of feedback solicits questions, hence feedback, from students. The professor may ask questions such as, "Does everybody understand what I am saying?" or "Are there any problems in seeing the point I am making?" Feedback links the source and receiver and creates the possibility of enriching the meaning of the communication transaction taking place.

There are sources that have built-in mechanisms in their message structures that allow for easy feedback. The *Larry King Live* program format is an example. Larry King brings in a guest whom he interviews, and members of the public make telephone calls and interact directly with the guest, debating or clarifying issues. People call in to *Larry King* from various parts of the world, providing immediate feedback to his program.

There are several radio talk shows that have the same format, allowing for interaction between the broadcaster and the audience at large. Corporations send out questionnaires to solicit feedback from the market on a new product to determine customer needs and satisfaction. At the end of the semester, teachers circulate teaching evaluation forms to students to get feedback on the quality and style of their teaching.

In conversational settings when we do not understand what a speaker is saying we ask for a repetition of what was said, or we request that the speaker use another way of stating what is intended to be communicated. We observe nonverbal forms of feedback by receivers of message by their facial expressions or bodily movement that may signify boredom or disagreement. In extreme circumstances, receivers use obscene gestures as feedback to speakers they strongly disagree with or dislike. Likewise, some people react negatively to other people who simply do not come from the same culture or are of a different race, religion, gender, or sexual orientation. We observe feedback in all forms—verbal and nonverbal.

The essential feature of the feedback element is that it creates a direct link between source and receiver, critical for intercultural encounters. At times we establish linkage with someone from another culture without realizing that we are not getting the reactions we anticipate. Feedback helps in reducing the possibility for communication breakdown or misunderstanding. Feedback, therefore, helps in clarifying issues resulting in the probable achievement of shared meaning. Finally, it gives both the source and receiver needed information that assists in improving upon the generation, handling, and management of new messages.

CONCLUSION

This chapter presents an introduction to the communication process in intercultural communication and the importance of understanding contexts. Even though the emphasis is on intercultural communication contexts, we emphasize that the notion of context is all pervasive in all communication encounters. Our roots shape our beings initially as people, and as we journey through life, we encounter en route several contexts that influence the outcome of communication interactions.

QUESTIONS

1. Discuss the importance of context in intercultural communication contexts.
2. How do the constituent elements of the communication process work in multicultural contexts? Select any three of the elements discussed in the text and apply them to an intercultural context of your choice.
3. Discuss the significance of openness, willingness, and empathy and their relationship to the reduction of potential for communication breakdown.

ACTIVITY

Divide the class into three or four groups. Each group is to develop a guide for people who are about to take a trip to a country with a different cultural tradition. The people traveling are being sent by an organization of your choice to introduce some technical innovation. Develop the guidelines on context and communication that would facilitate the interactions of the travelers and their hosts and present them in class. Discuss the differences and similarities in the approach taken by each group. At the end of the discussion, come up with an ideal prototype that could be used as a guideline for people interested in working in foreign countries. Please make sure that the groups work independently of each other.

REFERENCES

Barna, L. (1997). Stumbling blocks in intercultural communication. In L. Samovar & R. Porter (Eds.), *Intercultural communication: A reader*. Belmont, CA: Wadsworth.

Bordenave, J.D. (1971). *New approaches to communication training for developing nations*. Inter-American Institute of Agricultural Sciences.

Hall, E.T. (1976). *Beyond culture*. Garden City, NY: Anchor Press/Doubleday.

Shannon, C.E., & Weaver, W. (1949). *The mathematical theory of communication*. Urbana: University of Illinois Press.

Sitaram, K.S., & Hapaanen, A. (1979). In M. Asante, E. Newmark, & C. Blake (Eds.), *Handbook of intercultural communication*. Beverly Hills: Sage.

Ugboajah, F. (1982–83). 'Oramedia' or traditional media as effective communication options for rural development in Africa. In *Communication Studies Yearbook, 11*.

3

CULTURAL FOUNDATIONS

Objectives

After reading this chapter and completing the activity, you should be able to:

1. Discuss the central position of culture as the foundation of human behavior.
2. Discuss consequences arising from the meeting of cultures.
3. Define the concept of America as a potpourri of cultures.
4. Discuss cultural warrants and their functions.
5. Understand worldview and our perception of self and others.
6. Discuss the social implications of intercultural communication and relations.

In the Republic of Afghanistan various political factions and religious sects have been engaged in civil war for the past several years. Some factions are devoutly committed to the setting up of a theocratic state, with firm adherence to the traditional norms of the country. Such groups reject any attempt to introduce Western values or communism into Afghanistan. In September 1996 a revolutionary group called the Taliban, whose members espouse strict adherence to the *Sharia*, the laws of the *Holy Koran*, seized power in the country. Upon taking over from the government the leaders of the revolution executed a former president who was supported by the former Soviet Union. They commanded all women to dress strictly according to Islamic codes and all men to grow full beards within six weeks! The Taliban proclaimed a commitment to go back to their *cultural foundations.*

This chapter addresses the foundations of culture, focusing on some aspects of the meeting of different cultures, the emergence of co-cultural groups, management of cultural diversity, cultural warrants and how they serve as the bases for our reasoning, worldview, and the social implications of intercultural communication. Our treatment of culture is centered on its relationship with communication, as contrasted with an anthropological treatment. We show through our discussion of the subjects above how culture features in communicative interactions between and among different ethnic and racial groups and also how culture pertains to class and gender issues in communication.

THE ESSENCE

Culture is the essence of any community. There is no community on earth regardless of the level of social organization that does not have what we call culture. It is a phenomenon that is recognized in "small" social units such as corporate organizations as well. Given its locus in society, inhabitants of any given community are, in a way, "victims" of their culture. What therefore, is culture? A simple definition of culture is the composite set of patterns of behavior, language, mores, history, philosophy, values, belief structures, and religion that guide the day-to-day relations between inhabitants of a given community. Not only do the above facets facilitate human relations, they dictate to a significant extent people's relationship with their environment. Culture involves a diverse set of attributes that forms the foundation of human interactions. One important characteristic feature of culture is *patterned behavior*. This is to say that people in a given culture develop a pattern of behaving and responding to their environments. The pattern emerges out of consistent and repeated past actions and reactions and becomes a guideline for our behavior. In literate societies, the guidelines or rules are written and the written texts are used to instruct the young. Societies with oral traditions pass down the guidelines and rules through various channels such as short stories, dance, drama and song. In some West African societies, people are designated in communities to be the purveyors of the history of their respective communities. They are referred to as *Griots*.

We stress the importance of patterned behavior and responses to our environment because the patterns vary from culture to culture. And it is precisely because of the differences in patterns of behavior that people encounter cultural conflicts when they either fail to accept that cultures are different, or they simply believe that their pattern of behavior is "superior" to that of the culture they encounter. So critical is this issue of cultural differences that when cultures clash at various levels—ethnic wars, international wars, etc.—the victorious side quickly attempts to impose its own culture on the vanquished or, as has been the case in some conflicts, eliminate the vanquished. The Taliban in Afghanistan are an example of how the victorious side in cultural conflicts seek to eliminate their "enemies" or impose their values on the vanquished. The Taliban, no doubt, are determined to alter the pattern of behavior that existed before their successful revolution.

CULTURAL SOCIALIZATION

The concept of culture has been of interest to disciplines ranging from anthropology to psychology. Given its scope, scholars and researchers from various disciplines have contributed significantly to our understanding of how culture works and how it influences communication in our daily lives. Barrett (1991) observes, for example, that "Anthropologists are generally not interested in purely individual action or behavior that can be termed idiosyncratic but rather in how the behavior of individuals is influenced by their social and cultural milieu" (p. 55). In terms of intercultural communication, we are interested also in understanding how culture influences our interactions with people from different cultural backgrounds. Through our understanding of culture, we come to realize how pervasive the phenomenon is and how it impacts our communication.

There are various institutions within communities that orchestrate socialization, diffusion, and management of several elements that constitute culture. The family is the most direct channel of diffusing culture. Parents teach their children acceptable and unacceptable ways of behaving themselves. Schools (at all levels) instruct students about the native societal culture and its constituent elements and test students subsequently on the extent to which the instruction is absorbed, understood, and in some instances applied. Religious bodies instruct followers of the given religion about morality, the deity or deities, family values, and overall religious comportment. Social groups are organized around certain cultural norms to promote social cohesion among members during convivial occasions. All of the processes above constitute cultural socialization.

From the above, one could conclude that patterned behavior, mores, social, and environmental relations form the nexus of our understanding of culture. However, as societies emerge from small social units to larger and more complex units, cultural changes also take place. As societies open up their boundaries to other cultures, conflicts arise, and co-cultural communities form the resultant society. The emergence of such co-cultural groups is the direct result of the meeting of cultures. Let us discuss briefly, the idea of the "meeting of cultures."

WHEN CULTURES MEET

Before Europeans came to the shores of what is presently the United States, the indigenous population of the territories were comprised of several nations among which were the Cherokees, Apaches, Sioux, and many others. These were cultures markedly different from that of the strangers who were moving into the land that they were to subsequently occupy and call their own. The patterns of behavior of the indigenous populations was variously referred to as "savage" and "barbaric" by the Europeans who considered their culture and religion superior.

The American experience was not unique in terms of the meeting of different cultures and the subsequent establishment of an European cultural foundation in the lands that they colonized. Indigenous populations of many parts of the world experienced the same treatment. Jordan (1968) presents an authoritative account of the impact of cultural contacts between Europeans and Africans between 1550 and 1812 that serves as an important foundation in our understanding of relations between blacks and whites in the United States.

There are some basic lessons that can be learned from the meeting of cultures. First of all, cultures evolve over a long period of time as they form their foundations based on repeated actions and reactions. Secondly, the foundations of culture are so firm that people could go all out to resist any outside attempt to alter or destroy their roots. Thirdly, perceptions of superior/inferior relationships based on negative characterization of cultures with which we are not familiar do lead to undesirable circumstances. Fourthly, cultural encounters turn violent when other factors such as race creep in. It is therefore critical for students of intercultural communication to approach the subject with a sense of the historical roots and the processes involved in bringing about the formation of societies and cultures where they live. As a result of the meeting of cultures along the lines mentioned above and the subsequent setting up of national entities, the society becomes culturally diverse.

Such culturally diverse societies are comprised of co-cultural groups that have in many instances a fund of cultural practices and beliefs that influence their daily life. In essence, diverse cultural entities represent what we can call a potpourri of cultures. Like potpourri diners, culturally diverse societies can "taste" the flavor of its various co-cultural groups. In real life situations, however, some culturally diverse societies go through struggles to achieve harmony and social cohesion. Let us examine briefly the American experience as a potpourri of cultures and the implications for intercultural communication.

A POTPOURRI OF CULTURES

In countries such as the United States that represent a potpourri of co-cultures, the *dominant* white Anglo Saxon American Protestant (WASP) ethic formed the fundamental pillar of American culture. The "ethic" practically dictated every aspect of human conduct for centuries. By that ethic, co-cultural groups were judged. African Americans, for example, were told early in the days of the slavery institution that they lacked history and that slavery was a saving grace for them (Blake, 1990). Other co-cultural groups—Jews, Italians, Irish, Polish, and others—also did not meet the criteria for complete inclusion in the dominant structure. Hence, even though there is an apparent potpourri of cultures, one has stood out for many years as the dominant culture, influencing the direction of society and the relations between co-cultural groups.

The implication is direct: What existed for many years in the United States was an attempt to sustain a unicultural Eurocentric perspective against the background of a diverse society made up of co-cultural groups and immigrants with deep-rooted cultural foundations. It was difficult to maintain such a stance, which explains, in a way, the history of racial and ethnic tensions and struggles in the United States. The tensions have abated significantly, and the recognition of diversity as a real phenomenon in American society has helped tremendously in fostering a certain degree of effective intercultural communication.

From all indications, American society is rapidly moving away from one with a dominant culture that dictated to all others. The sheer numbers of some of the co-cultural groups and their ability to maintain to a significant extent their cultural foundations is presenting a different picture of the United States. Notably, the Latino population shows its adherence to its foundations by the use of Spanish on the airwaves and in several commercial settings. There are areas in Texas, California, New York, and Florida in which Spanish is the only language one hears people speaking in the street.

There is an African American caucus in the United States Congress. African Americans are to be found in all professions in the country. During the summer numerous cultural groups celebrate their origins and foundations during festivals and other convivial occasions. Kwanzaa, a ritual celebrating fruits of the harvest, invented by Professor M. Karenga, an African American, is widely celebrated throughout African American communities in the United States around the same time as Christmas. What is emerging is a true potpourri of cultures, with each contributing towards the larger American culture and strengthening the foundation of American culture.

What we have learned from the above is that: Cultures go through evolution and change, adapting to their environment in a consistent manner. The evolutionary process is slow, but discernible. With the pace of change occurring in the United States across racial, ethnic, and social lines, the need to become interculturally competent increases. The more the culture evolves, the more it becomes incumbent on citizens to respect each co-culture and benefit from the results of diversity. It would be naive not to expect resistance to change from those who had traditionally had the power to dictate to others.

The task at hand for the practice of effective intercultural communication is to provide the necessary training required to understand cultural diversity and how to manage and resolve tensions and conflict among co-cultural groups. In essence, managing cultural diversity is central to the realization of harmonious relations and communication among co-cultural groups. It is also a major contributing factor in the strengthening of cultural foundations of the newly emergent society. Let us turn our attention to some recent handling of the management of cultural diversity and the difficulties inherent in the task.

MANAGING THE ISSUES OF
CULTURAL DIVERSITY

The 1996 presidential elections marked a significant openness in the cultural makeup of the United States. Just prior to the launching of the campaign for the primary elections, California voted for a proposition that had a direct impact on cultural issues and intercultural communication. Proposition 187 called for several restrictions on access to medical care by children of illegal immigrants. The proposition sparked a national debate that found its way into the campaign rhetoric of candidates for the presidency. The most notable and outspoken candidate on the immigration issue was Pat Buchanan, who in a rally marking the end of his campaign on the eve of the Republican convention in California, practically called for a unicultural nation. In his speech delivered to his delegates in Escondido, California, Buchanan called for "one language" (English) and "one culture." Against the background of the existence of what we referred to earlier as a potpourri of cultures, the strategy of Pat Buchanan could be explained by making reference to the "resistance" to change in power relations as society evolves.

Buchanan's appeal demonstrates the fundamental hold "culture" has on people and how far individuals and nations will go to protect their culture from perceived "external" forces. Buchanan's attack was aimed at the increasing flow of immigrants across the Mexican American borders. The magnitude of the numbers of Latinos in the United States, and the reactions of the political superstructure, point towards the difficulties involved in managing a diverse community of legal immigrants, much more so when the illegal immigrant dimension is added.

Another example of the tasks involved in managing diversity can be seen in some of the deliberations of the 104th Congress that left a legacy students of intercultural communication would find interesting to study and on which to conduct research. Among its many laws passed is one on the issue of immigration—legal and illegal—as a means of redressing what the majority in Congress perceived as the immigration menace. The approach taken to manage diversity in this regard was to initiate legislation that provided guidelines on how to manage social and legal aspects of immigration. This went beyond California's Proposition 187 in the sense that their legislation has *national le-*

gitimacy. Hence, a major area in intercultural communication that will challenge students and scholars in the field as we approach the twenty-first century is the extent to which society can devise mechanisms that will facilitate
the management of diversity in a manner that will prevent violent intercultural conflicts.

In addition to the larger issues of cultural dominance and the management of diversity, societies that are multicultural in structure have to address
problems of distribution of resources and access to facilities such as education, health, and welfare. The 104th Congress and its actions on the immigration issue reflect the concern of who gets what resources and why.
Through legislation that denies, for example, access to education by children
of illegal immigrants and health and welfare resources for legal immigrants
in certain circumstances, the highest legislative body in the nation took a firm
stand on the issue of multiculturalism. Difficulties in managing diversity
push some right-wing politicians to polarize American society into the "us"
and "them" camps on the issue of immigration. The imperative, however,
seems to be the need to understand the complexities involved in managing
an increasingly diverse national entity. Let us, therefore, examine briefly the
issues involved in seeking an understanding of co-cultural groups, starting
with the "us" and "them" dichotomy.

UNDERSTANDING CO-CULTURAL GROUPS AND THE MANAGEMENT OF DIVERSITY

The "us" and "them" dichotomy provides a challenge that makes people
wonder why some co-cultures behave the way they do and challenge the resultant crises in providing resources to support a diverse population. Some
scholars have taken up the challenge in investigating the nature of race and
culture and their relationship to the makeup of individuals.

A group of social scientists and geneticists, however, have come out with
studies over the past twenty years that appear to explain why, for example,
African Americans continue to have difficulties in becoming fully accepted
and integrated into American society. For instance, Jensen (1969) fosters the
notion that African Americans are mentally inferior to whites. African Americans are variously referred to as "culturally deprived" and "culturally disadvantaged," which accounts for their status in society. Eitzen (1989)
presents an array of studies and hypotheses dating back to 1882 that articulate positions on what has been variously referred to as social Darwinism, a
culture of poverty, innate cultural inferiority and cultural deficiency in attempting to explain why African Americans find themselves in economically disadvantageous positions in American society. The controversial "bell
curve," which is an outgrowth of the Jensen claims, also adds to attempts by

scholars and researchers who attempt to explain why African Americans are the way they are.

Prior to the studies in contemporary times that focused on the genetic makeup of some co-cultural groups, linguists conducted studies to help society at large understand the worldview, for example, of the indigenous population of the United States. Their efforts were laudatory in the sense that their studies contributed to a fund a knowledge that facilitated a better understanding of a co-cultural group through an analysis of their language. The celebrated text by Hoijer (1954) presented an interesting treatment of the Sapir-Whorf analysis, which centered on the study of an indigenous language. Hoijer examined the works of Sapir and Whorf to highlight how the study of language helps us understand not just the linguistic aspects but also the social dimensions of the workings of language. Through language, we can have access to the life and workings of a community—its mores its worldview, and its initial formation. Hoijer's focus on language research was on the Navajo language, influenced by Whorf's study of the Hopi language. Given the background above, and the inherent controversy on the issue of culture and the management of diversity in multicultural societies, it is evident that an accurate understanding and appreciation of the complexities surrounding the phenomenon ought to be of concern for effective intercultural communication. Evident in the preceding section is the significance of roots and routes as they pertain to our understanding of cultural foundations and our perception as to what culture means and how it plays a role in communication in multiethnic and multiracial societies.

For instance, a young person who is of a conviction that cultures other than his are inferior would clearly hinder effective intercultural communication. Such a person demonstrates an inability to mange diversity and is a "prisoner" of his roots. If such an individual is sent to work in countries that do not manifest the facets of his culture, he would encounter serious communication problems that could even result in physical harm to him. Cultural awareness of self and others is, therefore, a fundamental prerequisite for successful intercultural transactions. Enroute to the "other" cultural setting, the would-be communicator is indeed "rooted" in his or her cultural milieu, but cognizant that the route to the "other" culture is not necessarily easy.

There is a famous text written by an African novelist, Amos Tutuola (1953), titled *The Palm Wine Drinkard*, in which he demonstrates the perils encountered enroute to other cultural settings. Tutuola's novel is full of mystical and supernatural anecdotes, in which he tries to understand why the "others" he encounters in lands far away from his home are the way they are. Even though mystical in tone and content, he presents a vivid story of "others" and the distinctions between his roots and the route he uses to enter the cultural domain of the "strange" characters he encounters in his journey.

In summing up this section, the overriding theme has been the management of diversity and the subsequent strengthening of our cultural foundations. The focus has been on the domestic front. There are, however, significant aspects of the theme in the international scene as well. Let us now turn our attention to an examination of the international dimensions.

INTERNATIONAL DIMENSIONS IN THE MANAGEMENT OF DIVERSITY

The crisis in management of cultural diversity is not peculiar to the United States. Conflicts surrounding cultural and racial preservation are also evident in Europe, notably in France, Britain, and Germany. European political leaders such as Enoch Powell of Britain and Jean-Marie Le Penn of France urge Britons and French citizens respectively to resist the flow of immigrants to their countries because they fear their cultures will suffer irreparable damages. These leaders fear the cultural foundations of the respective nations will weaken, resulting in the collapse and destruction of their societies.

On the other side of the debate on culture, dominant countries in the international system consistently seek to export their culture to other countries in the world, notably in the Southern Hemisphere, as a means of managing cultural diversity at the international level, believing theirs is the superior culture. The United States, for example, attaches the adoption of Western values and culture as a condition for foreign aid to countries in Africa, Asia, Latin America, and lately, the countries of the former Soviet Bloc of nations. Grenada was attacked and its prime minister and several Grenadans killed during President Reagan's term of office because of a perceived threat to American values and politics. The cold war that lasted for nearly fifty years was fought over the refusal to accept and manage ideological diversity at the global level. Contexts such as these point to the all pervasive influence of culture and how some countries perceive the strength and weaknesses of their culture and that of their perceived "enemies." Against that background, the management of diversity becomes reduced to aggression and loss of life and property. Millions of people in Africa, Asia, and Latin America, far removed from the capitals that spearheaded the cold war—Washington and Moscow—have died fighting over which of the two contending political ideologies grounded in alien soils is superior and appropriate for adoption.

KNOW YOURSELF

In concluding this section it is important to bear in mind the all-pervasive nature of culture on individuals in any given society. As human beings, we are essentially wrapped up within our peculiar cultural milieu. Hence, we are anchored within that milieu and we need to know that culture well before we can attempt to know or understand others coming from a different cultural milieu. Furthermore, being rooted in a culture allows an individual to have a frame of reference for day-to-day activities, relations with others within the same cultural milieu, attitude towards the "outsider," worldview, and normative structures peculiar to that given entity. The studies by Whorf, Sapir, and Hoijer reinforce the need to understand others through their language use and behavior in order to function well in a diverse society. Cultural awareness of self and others is an important prerequisite for handling and managing relationships with co-cultural groups. Knowledge of why people are the way they are is central to effective intercultural communication. Underlying all of the above is the need to understand the rules of the game. In this context, the rules of discourse that would facilitate intercultural encounters need to be understood. However, among the many rules of discourse is the need to justify why we adopt positions and provide reasons in support of them. Let us now examine a fundamental concept that people apply in justifying their actions and how it relates to our understanding of cultural foundations. The concept we examine is referred to as *cultural warrants*.

CULTURAL WARRANTS

The idea of cultural warrants is new. It is not a concept to be found in many sources. Blake (1993) first explained the concept of *cultural warrants* in discussing traditional African values and the right to communicate. Blake explains that cultural warrants are basically beliefs, laws, and customs that allow people within a given culture to justify their communicative actions and behavior. Such warrants are found in traditions, religious texts, traditional values, constitutions, important decisions by judicial bodies such as the Supreme Court, and in the general norms that guide the relationship between children and parents, the young and old, and authority figures and subordinates. Cultural warrants, in essence, give us the rationale to conduct affairs in a manner that society as a whole would accept with minimum resistance. One could argue that cultural warrants form the pillars, albeit the foundation, of culture upon which society depends to uphold the entity as an organic whole. Toulmin (1958) presents a detailed discussion of "warrants" (not cultural warrants) in his treatment of the nature of argument. The concept of "cultural warrants," as explained by Blake, has its roots in the Toulmin model.

Warrants support the evidence we use to substantiate our claims or propositions. In short, they provide a basis upon which we can ground our evidence, and in the process, strengthen and justify our case. The American Declaration of Independence presents a brilliant example of how warrants work. The drafters of the Declaration provide evidence on the specific abuses by the British Crown. The evidence is then grounded in a warrant that reads: "Whenever any form of government becomes destructive . . . it is the Right of the People to alter or abolish it, and to institute new Government . . . ." That statement serves as a justification for the revolution, which was based on the series of abuses by the king that prompted the revolt against the British Crown. It is a statement that can be generally accepted by a significant cross-section of the public. It is an essential aspect of the cultural foundation of American democracy. Warrants, therefore, help us to justify our positions, and they are generally accepted by people. Cultural warrants are those warrants such as traditions, values, beliefs, legends, and myths that are commonly shared and generally accepted in the societies in which they exist.

Viewed from this perspective, cultural warrants represent the foundations upon which human relations are carried out. So deeply rooted are our cultural warrants that they can be invoked even in circumstances that may appear to run contrary to what we expect, particularly in societies that are openly committed to justice and fair play. An example of such an anomaly could be seen in how biblical warrants were invoked during a critical period in American history.

SLAVERY AND BIBLICAL WARRANTS

An historical example of how cultural warrants in one society are invoked to support atrocities in distant and far removed cultures can be seen in the debate on slavery in the United States. Supporters of the institution of slavery in the United States and protagonists of racial inequality in the subsequent segregationist movement who depicted African Americans as amoral and normless, demonstrated the abuses of cultural warrants in intercultural communication contacts. An important cultural warrant—the Bible—was abused by supporters of slavery, to justify the institution by interpreting the curse on Ham in the Book of Genesis (9:27–29) as a curse on Africans.

The Bible as a cultural warrant in a country that is influenced by the Judeo-Christian tradition is a powerful source upon which an argument can be predicated. Cultural warrants are powerful tools we use in order to justify our actions. Cultural warrants provide the cover. They, therefore, represent, in a nutshell, "knowledge" of ourselves and about others derived from our traditions. The more we understand the central role and function of cultural warrants, the better are the prospects for positive intercultural contacts and exchanges.

Another characteristic feature of cultural warrants is that at times they remain at the declarative level for some people—usually the disfavored or disenfranchised in society. For example, among the most powerful cultural warrants in the United States is the Constitution. The Constitution declares among other issues that:

> *We hold these truths to be self-evident, that all men are created equal, that*
> *they are endowed by their Creator with certain unalienable rights, that*
> *among these are Life, Liberty and the pursuit of Happiness. That to serve*
> *these rights, Governments are instituted among, men, deriving their just*
> *powers from the consent of the governed.*

The quotation above is among the most powerful cultural warrants expressed by any society. Yet history teaches us that the warrant was celebrated in the midst of a situation in which men, women, and children were in bondage—slavery. It has taken several amendments to ascertain that an important warrant such as the constitution of the United States does not remain at the declarative level.

THE CASE OF A DEAD HUSBAND

Let us take another look at the centrality of cultural warrants in communication contexts in a different cultural context. Among the Luo, an ethnic group in western Kenya, when a husband dies, the ethnic community through a designated group assumes all responsibility for the burial ceremonies. The wife is relegated to a position in which she abides by the dictates of the norms of the Luo. In marriages that are intracultural, the warrants are clear and minimum controversies are experienced. If the marriage involves an interethnic partnership—a Luo married to someone from another ethnic group—the Kikuyu, for example, difficulties could arise. In a celebrated case in the Republic of Kenya, a Kikuyu woman lost her husband, a Luo. As a family, they had settled in Kikuyu land. When the husband died, the Luos moved in to take charge of the funeral arrangements according to their custom. The wife resisted and challenged the custom—built on a warrant that marks Luo obligations and rites in instances of death of married males. The body remained unburied for several months because the wife refused to release the corpse and sued the husband's clan. At the end of the adjudication, the court ruled in favor of the clan. The basic lesson derived from this anecdote is the centrality of warrants and how conflicting warrants result in breakdown in intercultural communications. In this anecdote, the judicial system was used to solve the dispute and repair the breakdown in communication. History teaches us that several wars have been fought over conflicting warrants.

Intercultural communication is deeply grounded in the understanding and management of cultural warrants. Attempts to impose one set of warrants on others result in conflicts. There are instances, however, when communities switch to alien cultural warrants or adopt external warrants while holding on to indigenous warrants. Chapter 7 addresses issues on religion and intercultural communication in which such adoptions occur. Let us now take a look at another element that is essential in building and sustaining cultural foundations. That element is worldview.

WORLDVIEW

Consider this short anecdote. An English man was sent to an island in the South Pacific to teach the Islanders western grain storage techniques. Upon arrival, he found a festival taking place and everyone was in a very happy mood. Food was in abundance and people were drinking copiously. He wandered around looking for signs of grain bins and silos that are customarily seen in agricultural areas. There was no visible evidence of what he considered to be food saved for the future or for emergencies. He shook his head in disgust and mumbled "Just as I thought! Living for the present. No consideration for the future! What a worldview!" He sat down quietly and observed the activities and ceremonies until dusk. As he walked towards the place he was staying, he mumbled again, "Just like those Africans I went to teach new sanitation practices. I'll never forget the death of the child and the attitude of the parents. They accepted the child's death as the desire of their God! Nothing, they said, could stop the Gods from doing whatever they wished! What a fatalistic worldview!"

The anecdote above por .rays the importance of worldview and how it influences our attitude towa ds life. The Englishman jumped to a hasty conclusion about his brief eⅰcounter with people who, he believed, had a different and inferior worldview to his. He had not inquired directly from the Islanders their concept of preparing for emergencies. He had encountered an African family that attributed the death of their child to the will of God. From the brief encounters, he rendered a judgment on the entire group.

Jain and Kussman (1997) explain that "worldview refers to a set of interrelated assumptions and beliefs about the nature of reality, the organization of the universe, the purposes of human life, God, and other philosophical issues that are concerned with the concept of being. A culture's worldview includes both implicit and explicit assumptions underlying the values, norms, myths, and behaviors of its people" (p. 79). Thus, worldview is the sum of all the facets of culture that we have discussed up to this point. Samovar and Porter (1991) note that worldview, "though somewhat abstract, is one of the most important [element] found in the perceptual aspects of intercultural communication" (p. 16). They continue, "worldview helps us locate our place and rank in the universe" (p. 16).

They observe further that "because worldview is so complex, it is often difficult to isolate during an intercultural interaction" (p. 16). This points to the significance that ought to be attached to it, if we are to become effective intercultural communicators. Worldview is not written on the faces of people. Individuals do not walk around daily with a banner proclaiming their worldview. It is not tangible and readily discernible. The requirement here is not that we should strive to master the worldview of co-cultural groups, but rather to recognize that people's behaviors are guided by their worldview and to attempt as best we can to not judge others based on the tenets of our own worldview. In essence, intercultural communication encounters are more demanding and require an open mind and empathy. This imperative is even more crucial as we move from multicultural societies such as the United States to countries in the Southern Hemisphere that share radically different worldviews.

ENVIRONMENT

We are guided also by our worldview when we try to understand people's relationships to their immediate environment. In the Southern Hemisphere, human–biosphere relationships portray a more harmonious co-existence with nature than what we observe in Western societies. In the latter, obsession with "development" of land and other resources in the biosphere tend to promote an aggressive expansion of human settlements into wildlife areas, reducing concurrently the wildlife population. Interestingly, the concept of having zoos could not be easily explained to inhabitants of some countries in the Southern Hemisphere because of the harmonious relationship between human beings and wildlife, each occupying their space in a common environment. Such contrasts reflect the differences in worldview in some aspects of human–biosphere relations.

MULTIPLE WORLDVIEWS

Inasmuch as we attach significance to the grip worldview has on us, people can exist with more than one worldview to guide their relations with others. Long-term exposure to other cultures and the recognition and acceptance of certain elements of an alien culture that bode well for our welfare lead us to adopt those elements of the alien worldview. Some people who come from cultures that are structured around a worldview that promotes social cohesion through an extended family and/or a communal form of social organization may find the concept of a nuclear family and rugged individualism unattractive but cost-effective. There are millions of Asians who are guided by a worldview influenced by Confucianism and who also adopt several elements of Western worldview. Adopting certain elements of a worldview that is alien to us does not, therefore, strip us of the strong and positive elements of our indigenous worldviews.

CONCLUSION

In concluding this section, it is noteworthy to observe how political leaders manipulate the concept of worldview to achieve their ambitions. In his acceptance speech at the Republican National Convention of 1996 at San Diego, California, the Republican presidential nominee, Senator Robert Dole, ridiculed Hillary Clinton's title to her book: *It Takes a Village to Raise a Child.* Senator Dole interpreted the title as one that promotes the interference of the state into an activity that is the sole responsibility of the family. He argued that it is *not* the responsibility of the village to raise a child but that of the child's parents. Dole's contention reflects his lack of understanding of an African proverb that Mrs. Clinton used as the title of her book, which promotes the idea that caring for the young is a communal responsibility to ensure maximum safety, inculcation of cultural norms, and the wholesome development of the child. Dole's parody on Mrs. Clinton's use of an African worldview demonstrates the difficulties that can be encountered in intercultural communication contexts.

To sum up our discussion on worldview, we must recognize that it provides the essential signals and rules of conduct on the cultural highway. Just as we are required to know all the traffic signs on the highway and rules for driving, we are equally required to understand the centrality of worldview in our cultural makeup. When we travel to foreign countries, we learn their traffic rules and regulations. When we encounter people from different cultures, it behooves us at least to recognize that we are on a cultural highway that requires excellent driving skills and safe driving attitudes in order to maintain harmony.

Finally, our cultural foundation is made up of several elements and the task at hand is to develop the necessary skills required to manage them within the context of culturally diverse societies. The extent to which we recognize the solid grounding we have in our cultural foundations will determine how best we can achieve effective intercultural communication.

QUESTIONS

1. Why should students of intercultural communication understand the importance of cultural foundations?
2. What are some of the problems that lead to cultural conflicts and their consequences when two different cultures meet?
3. How are cultural norms taught and through what contexts?
4. What do we mean by cultural warrants and how do they function in intercultural communication?

ACTIVITY

Conduct research on Proposition 187 and the 1996 laws on immigration passed by the 104th Congress, and prepare to debate in class how the proposition and the laws help or hinder intercultural relations and communication, and whether the idea of "one culture" is valid against the background of the laws and proposition on immigration.

REFERENCES

Barrett, R. (1991). *Culture and conduct*. Belmont, CA: Wadsworth.

Blake, C. (1990). *Through the prism of African nationalism: reflective and prospective essays*. Sierra Leone: W.D. Okrafo-Smart & Company.

Blake, C. (1993). Traditional African values and the right to communicate. *Africa Media Review*, 7 (3), 1–17.

Eitzen, D. (1989). *Social problems* (4th ed.). Boston: Allyn & Bacon.

Hoijer, H. (1954). *Language and culture*. Chicago: University of Chicago Press.

Jain, N., & Kussman, D. (1997). Dominant cultural patterns of Hindus in India. In L. Samovar & R. Porter (Eds.), *Intercultural communication, a reader* (8th ed., pp 89–97). Belmont, CA: Wadsworth.

Jensen, A. (1969). How much can we boost IQ and scholastic achievement? *Harvard Educational Review, 39* (Winter) 1–123.

Jordan, W. (1968). *White over black: American attitudes toward the Negro, 1550–1812*. Chapel Hill: University of North Carolina Press.

Samovar, L. & Porter, R. (1991) *International communication: A reader* (6th ed.). Belmont CA: Wadsworth.

Samovar, L., & Porter, R. (1997). *Intercultural communication, a reader* (8th ed.). Belmont: Wadsworth.

Toulmin, S. (1958). *The uses of argument*. Cambridge: Cambridge University Press.

Tutuola, A. (1953). *The palm wine drinkard*. New York: Grove Press.

4

RACE, ETHNICITY, AND GENDER

Objectives

After reading this chapter and completing the activities, you should be able to:

1. Explain how race and gender influence human perception.
2. Define the idea of racial ideology.
3. Explain the role of *nommo* in African American communication.
4. Describe in writing Weber's three styles of African American communication.
5. Explain sources of intercultural difficulty that stem from ethnic differences.
6. Describe the process of gender formation.
7. Give in writing some basic characteristics of male–female speech.

When designing a promotional brochure in February 1996, the Ford Motor Company in Europe decided to superimpose white faces on photos of its black and South Asian workers (Parker-Pope, 1996, p. A10). When the black, Indian, and Pakistani workers in Great Britain who had originally posed for the picture along with their white co-workers, saw a reprint of the original Ford brochure they were horrified. They all had been "turned into white people." Although the clothes they wore in the original photograph were the same, their faces, hands, and arms had been changed or lightened so that the once diverse-looking group looked like an all-white workforce. One worker who wore a turban and had facial hair in the original picture had been changed to a clean-shaven young white man.

Upon learning that this information had been printed in newspapers worldwide, the Ford Motor Company was embarrassed (Parker-Pope, 1996, p. B8). In explaining why they had changed the brochure, Ford argued that they had made the modification to reflect the ethnic makeup of Poland, which is basically an all-white country. Did Ford make the right decision? Was Ford wrong to have altered the photographs? And should race have played so prominent a role in the brochure?

In Japan some women walk a few steps behind their husbands in public. Once they have entered their homes, however, women control their husbands' allowances by giving them specific amounts of money for lunch, cigarettes, and even girlie magazines. Yet despite their power at home, only 2.3 percent of Japan's lower house of Parliament, the country's major governing body, consists of women (Kristof, 1996, p. A6). Why? What accounts for this apparent female control in the private sphere and a lack of it in the public sphere?

These two stories are by no means unusual. Race and gender are two of the greatest intellectual, moral, and behavioral factors in intercultural communication today, and they are played out against a backdrop of ever-changing attitudes toward and expectations of cultures worldwide. In this chapter we examine race and gender as a function of culture and suggest strategies and ways of thinking about these twin issues. Our purpose is to increase our awareness of and sensitivity to the impact of these variables on interpersonal communication.

RACE

Racial Formations

As part of our socialization, we are taught to categorize people based on their ethnic heritage, race, and color. This way of clustering people into groups around hereditary characteristics such as skin color, texture of hair, and general physical appearance can be found in sources as early as the Bible and ancient Greek history. Martin Bernal (1987) points out that Aristotle believed that Greeks were inherently superior to other peoples. For example, Aristotle classified people into three groups: races that lived in cold regions, Asiatic races, and his own race, the Hellenic race (Bernal, 1987, p. 202). Aristotle linked characteristics to each group claiming, for instance, that Asiatic races "have both brains and skill but are lacking in courage and willpower" (Bernal, 1987, p. 202).

By the end of the eighteenth century, Europeans had developed a line of argument that suggested that races might change their physical form over time but they always maintain immutable (unchanging) individual essences or tendencies. For example, at one time the racist pioneer, Comte de Gobineau, promoted ideas such as the Chinese were practical and could not dream and that all blacks occupied a restricted "intellectual zone" (Bernal, p. 241). Although racial classifications still occupy part of our thinking, rigid categorization of people is changing. This change is taking place because, as molecular biologists, geneticists, and anthropologists note, the nineteenth-century notion of race as being separate and discrete is false (Parker-Pope, 1996, p. A10). Of particular importance in understanding racial formation is to be aware of arbitrary, artificial, and false categories when defining people as, for instance, black, Chinese, Native American, or white.

For example, there is a movement among mixed-race individuals to outright reject *either-or* classification and move toward *both/and* classification; that is, one can be both black and white or Japanese and white. Some individuals might opt to develop a strategy similar to that of a Harvard University professor of Korean-Jewish identity: Since he was born in the United States, his practice is to reply Native American when asked for his racial genealogy! That is a whimsical response. The most sensible response when interacting with others is to learn—however discreetly—whether individuals wish to elevate one of their racial or ethnic backgrounds over another.

The Ideological Roots of Race

Previous research indicates not only that race plays a role in our interpersonal interactions with others, but also that its roots are ideologically grounded. Although ideology has a whole range of meanings (Eagleton, 1991), by "ideological roots" we mean ideas and beliefs that help to legitimate a dominant way of behaving and thinking about race. For example, in the United States during the nineteenth century, it was fashionable for white Americans to conceive of blacks and Native Americans as less than human, because this ideology helped to sustain a political, social, and economic way of life based on slavery and policies of extermination. Today, however, research indicates that "the 'modern' or 'symbolic' racist is unlikely to hold attitudes which outrightly demean black people as being racially inferior" (Billig, Condor, et al., 1992, p. 158).

Because we learn the rules of racial classification, our own racial identity, and what and how to think about matters of race without "obvious teaching or conscious inculcation," race becomes "common sense," "a way of comprehending, explaining, and acting in the world" (Omi & Winant, 1994, p. 60). In this way, our thoughts about race become routine. As Ulf Hannerz (1992) observes, common sense is cultural "business as usual," "standard operating procedure," "one's perspective at rest" (p. 127). As these phrases indicate, we become comfortable with such perceptions and scarcely know that we are acting or thinking racially.

Take, as an example, what happened during an exchange between one of the authors and her apartment mate at the University of Wisconsin. The author and her roommate, who was from New Zealand, were having a quiet, lovely dinner while discussing what had happened during the day, when the New Zealander exclaimed, "I worked like a nigger today." The author, quite taken aback, said, "Hilary, what did you say?" Hilary repeated her previous remark, unaware that she had conveyed a negative racial attitude. In reply, the author said, "Hilary, the word 'nigger' is considered to be an unflattering, inappropriate term." As expected, Hilary apologized profusely and the faux pas was forgiven. Hilary's heightened awareness ensured that she had learned enough to avoid using the word "nigger" again.

It should be noted here that, increasingly, people are changing their ideological frames concerning race. For example, Wetherell and Potter (1986) and McFadyen and Wetherell (1986) examined ways that middle-class New Zealanders talk about Maoris, the minority group in New Zealand. They found that there is no 'prototype' of the Maori as was typical years ago and that the way New Zealanders talk about Maoris has shifted from casting direct aspersions against the Maori to using a more "reasonable" and polite form of language.

These same researchers similarly found that Britons also avoid crudities of language when talking about nonwhites living in Britain (Billig et al., 1992, p. 161). Very real ideological differences in race, however, still play a critical role in intercultural communication. For example, despite shifts towards a more polite form, Britons still hold nonwhites to be "different from 'us'," and felt that the latter "would be better-off back in 'their' own countries . . ." (p. 161).

Look for ways in which different groups express their ideological orientations. At times these orientations will be expressed subtly. Much can be learned from knowing that during interpersonal interactions, individuals wish to present themselves in a favorable light and will therefore try to avoid extreme expressions of racist views (Van Dijk, 1984, p. 117).

Race as a Factor in Communication

A few years ago a black woman who was considered a splendid teacher was hired by a California high school. During her conversations with the other teachers, she made no comment about race. One day, however, during a heated discussion on housing, she said, "As a black woman, I feel that we must protect the right of every person to own or rent a home any place he or she wants." Her colleagues were stunned! And from that moment on, their ways of communicating with the black woman changed (Smith, 1973, p. 20). In fact, her colleagues began to consult her on all issues and matters pertaining to race.

In the above example, we see what can happen when race is introduced as an element of communication. One of the first things we notice about people when we meet them is their race and sex. We use race to give us some hint of whom a person is. As we can see from this discussion, race undoubtedly brings to the communication situation a different dynamic.

Communication, Credibility, and Race

A comment such as "you don't sound Japanese," a black business executive who is mistaken for a janitor, a Latino youngster who is followed by a sales clerk while shopping, and a store that classifies shoppers as W for white, H for Hispanic, and 07, a shorthand for black, all testify to the centrality of race as a way of shaping how we communicate with others (Williams, 1991, p. A9).

Michael Omi and Howard Winant (1994) capture how differences in skin tone color our social interaction:

> *Such diverse questions as our confidence and trust in others (for example, clerks or salespeople, media figures, neighbors), our sexual preferences and romantic images, our tastes in music, films, dance, or sports, and our very ways of talking, walking, eating, and dreaming become racially coded simply because we live in a society where racial awareness is so pervasive. (p. 60)*

Thus, believability, or trustworthiness, becomes especially important when race is a factor. Believability involves the extent to which we ascribe goodwill, character, and knowledge to individuals based solely on whether they are, for example, Chinese, Japanese, Indian, or white. The meanings and importance we assign to ideas and behavior can differ dramatically as ethnicity is imposed.

Race and Intercultural Accessibility

Accessibility in an interracial and intercultural context refers to our willingness to communicate with others regardless of race or ethnicity. An attitude such as "I don't want to communicate with Masami because she is Japanese and we have nothing in common" can act as a deterrent to accessibility and prevent us from becoming involved in interracial interactions. Professor Jack Daniel (1995) captures the reason we are reluctant to become available to a person of another race or culture: "Could it be that we are so comfortable with our homogenous subcultures that we don't wish to communicate across cultures?"

Physical proximity affects our potential to interact with others. The West Indian who lives in Bombay and the North American who lives in a small town in Indiana are both unlikely to interact with a Maori from New Zealand. Thus, we must consider both willingness and availability as keys to our ability to talk across cultures (Smith, 1973). The crucial test of our willingness and availability is whether we demonstrate an approach or avoidance attitude toward cultural others.

Race and Cultural Contacts

Race, Ethnicity, and Perception

When we consistently see race as a primary factor in our interaction with others, we color our perception of the "other." Perception is "the process by which people select, organize, and interpret sensory stimulation into a meaningful and coherent picture of the world" (Klopf, 1991, p. 48). Whether we feel joy at the sight of a snake or eat grasshoppers, for example, is influenced by the cultural meanings that we attach to the thought of "seeing" a snake or "eating" grasshoppers. Thus, our senses of hearing, tasting, smelling, seeing, and feeling are key to helping us not only to identify animals, objects, and events in the external world, but also to make sense of them based upon how our culture conditions us to respond to them.

Of particular interest to our discussion is the fact that perceptions of skin color are based upon differences of experiences. For example, Argentines are "hated" by many South Americans because they are considered to be "arrogant" and prideful of their European heritage (Sims, 1995, p. 4E). During the seventeenth century, when the Europeans first encountered the Incas, they characterized the Indians as people with "natural superior goodness," who needed "conversion to Christianity to become the most blessed souls" (Fagan, 1984, p. 88). Think of your experiences with the following groups: Chinese, Arabs, Japanese, African Americans, and white Americans. Then note the extent to which your perceptions have influenced your behavior toward these individuals.

A number of studies have provided evidence to support the observation that people's interactions in intercultural contexts are framed by their perceptions of reality and of the other person. The ways in which people react to skin color and accent provide examples of these influences on perceptions. Taijfel and Turner (1992) suggest that when we interact with members of another group, we compare ourselves to them on a number of important dimensions, such as emotional involvement and interdependent goals. These dimensions, in turn, lead us to differentiate ourselves (the in-group) favorably from the out-group.

Albert Vru and Frans Willem Winkel (1994) found evidence of the influence of skin on perception in their study of Dutch police officers' impressions of blacks, more specifically Surinamese. Vru and Winkel note, for example, that "typical Black nonverbal behavior displayed by Black citizens will be interpreted as suspicious, tense, and unpleasant behavior by White police officers" (p. 290). Vru and Winkel argue, however, that other factors in addition to skin color, such as our expectations of individuals who belong to specific social categories, may also influence our perceptions. For instance, in their study, black persons who dressed in a typical Dutch manner were perceived more positively by white persons.

Perceptions of race are also related to the *expectancy–violation theory*. This theory holds that if individuals deviate from the others' expectations, "evaluations will be in the direction of the deviation; that is, Black persons with positive traits will be assessed relatively positively (i.e., more positively than Whites exhibiting the same traits) and White persons with negative traits will be judged relatively negatively" (p. 292). This theory also helps to explain why we may have a good "white," "Arab," "black," or "Hispanic" friend, and yet still perceive other members of these specific races negatively. Such differences in perception can cause discomfort and misinterpretations. For example, comments, such as "You don't act French," or "You are so different from the others," while used interculturally to establish rapport, can offend a person and greatly damage interpersonal relationships.

The following story further illustrates the role of race and perception in interpersonal communication. As you read the story, consider the following questions: Are cultural variables other than race present? Are other, more subtle cues evident? If yes, what are they?

Twenty years ago a white woman and a black woman met in graduate school at Indiana University. They studied for their major Ph.D. examinations together and in many instances maintained similar schedules, including taking ice cream breaks together, sharing meals, and taking long restful walks together in the evenings. Following graduation, the white woman moved to Illinois and the black woman remained in Columbus, Ohio. From time to time, they exchanged cards, but soon contact between the two ceased. One day, about fifteen years later, the black woman decided to call her white colleague, who had by that time had retired from teaching. During the conversation, the white woman indicated that she had recently visited Columbus, Ohio, much to the surprise of the African American woman, who noted the matter privately. She wondered why she had not been paid a visit; however, she refrained from addressing the issue.

Four days following the telephone conversation, the African American woman received a card from her friend. As she took the card to her office, she was delighted and surmised that her friend was writing to thank her for her renewed contact after so long an absence. Instead, when she opened the card, she was horrified by its contents, which contained the following:

Dear Sarah: I felt surprised and delighted with your telephone call last week. I reflected most of the day upon our special relationship at IU. Do you remember telling me of your sister's surprise in discovering that I am white, since you had not mentioned it in speaking of our friendship?

What happened? For some time after I left IU, I continued to believe that our bond was for life. After several incidents, I concluded that you did not feel that depth of friendship. Namely, a couple of conventions at which you introduced me to your black friends as an acquaintance; your somewhat less than cordial reception when I visited you and John shortly after your marriage; your nonacceptance of my invitation for the 2 of you to visit Charles (her husband) and me; and finally, your failure to contact me until the end of my stay at Eigenmann (a halls of residence at IU) during the summer (1983 or 1984) even though I had written you that I would be there, and Mary Jane (her friend) had confirmed it with you the week of my arrival.

Of all people, we speech communication teachers understand the role perception *plays in our relationships. My* perception *is that the situation is one of reverse racial discrimination. Since* perception is not reality, maybe I have misinterpreted what happened between us. I would welcome your response. (emphasis added)

The African American woman sat in stony, unbelievable silence as she read those words. She could recall but one of the specific instances that her friend had cited in the card, and her interpretation was that although she still remembered her friend with affection, they had simply grown apart. She had attached no racial significance to the matter. When the African American woman had recovered from the *racial misconception*, she called her friend, and they had a marvelous conversation about the role of race and perception.

In this story, we see how *interpretation*, "the attribution of meaning to what we perceive" (Klopf, 1991, p. 53), plays a crucial role in communication between races. When communicating across cultures, *race* can have a strong impact upon *what* and *how* we feel, think, and act. Notice in our story that although the two women clearly held differing perceptions and definitions of friendship, race ultimately assumed overarching importance.

Race and Language

As Ribeau, Baldwin, and Hecht (1994) suggest:

African American communication is as complex as the culture from which it emerges. Taken from the shores of Africa, enslaved captives were forced to create a means of expression consistent with an African cultural tradition, yet responsive to life in slavery, and post-slavery experiences in the rural

South and North, created a unique ethnic culture for the group known as African Americans. (p. 140)

When discussing black language, it is important to remember the historical context in which it was derived. Weber (1994) suggests that the study of black language is, in reality, an examination of the African people and of their adjustment to the conditions of American slavery. Weber goes on to explain that in order to fully appreciate black language it is necessary to understand some general African philosophies about language and communication. One of the primary principles throughout African cultures is the belief that everything has a reason for being. Janheinz Jahn (1961) in his basic overview of African culture suggests four basic elements of life that are Muntu, mankind; Kintu, things; Hantu, place and time; and Kuntu, modality. Muntu is distinguished from the other three elements by his possession of *nommo*, the magical power of the word. According to Weber (1994):

Nommo is so powerful and respected in the black community that only those who are skillful users of the word become leaders. One of the main qualifications of leaders of black people is that they must be able to articulate the needs of the people in a most eloquent manner. And because Muntu is a force who controls Nommo, which has power and consequences, the speaker must generate and create movement and power within his listeners. One of the ways this is done is through the use of imaginative and vivid language . . . the analogies, stories, images, and so forth must be fresh, new, and alive. (p. 221)

In addition, nommo is the force that creates a sense of community among communicators, so much so that the speaker and the listener become one as senders and receivers of the message. Thus, the listeners who respond with "amen" and "right on" are just as important as the speaker, because without the listeners and their response, the speaker cannot be successful. Weber (1994) explains:

This interplay between speaker and listeners is called "call and response" and is a part of the African world view, which holds that all elements and forces are interrelated and indistinguishable because they work together to accomplish a common goal and to create a sense of community between the speaker and the listeners. (p. 222)

Finally, in addition to the speaker's verbal creativity and the dynamic nature of the communication environment, black speech is very rhythmic, flowing in a consonant–vowel–consonant–vowel pattern. Some syllables are held longer and accented differently from standard English in order to achieve this rhythm.

Weber (1994) describes three communication styles of African Americans. The first is *rappin*. It was originally used to describe the dialogue between a man and a woman wherein the man attempted to win the woman's admiration. His success depended on his ability to make imaginative and creative statements that generated the woman's interest. An unimaginative, nonrhythmical rap does not "win" the woman. Not all raps are sexual in nature. A nonsexual form is *running it down*. This style explains something in great detail. The speaker re-creates an event or concept so that the listener has complete understanding of the event or concept. The speaker describes in minute detail and vivid language every aspect of the thing being explained.

The *dozens* is a verbal battle of insults between speakers. The emphasis is not on the insult, but rather on which speaker can remain "the coolest" under pressure. When the dozens is played, there is usually a group of listeners who judge the creativity, originality, and humor of the comments. Weber (1994) provides the following example:

> *Say man, your girlfriend so ugly*
> *she had to sneak up on a glass to*
> *get a drink of water.*
>
> *Man, you so ugly you mamma had to put*
> *a sheet over your head so sleep could*
> *sneak up on you. (p. 223)*

Proverbial wisdom is often used in black language. These sayings, such as, "if you make your bed hard you gon lay on it," are used as teaching tools to impart values and truths. Proverbial wisdom is found on every socioeconomic level in the black community and makes the political statement that black people are African people and are determined to preserve an essential part of their culture—their language.

Often nonblacks judge black language by European language standards deeming the black language as "deficit." As Weber (1994) suggests:

> *The use of black language does not represent any pathology in blacks. It simply says that, as African people transplanted to America, they are a different flower whose aroma is just as sweet as other flowers. The beginning of racial understanding is the acceptance that difference is just what it is: different, not inferior. And equality does not mean sameness. (p. 225)*

Race, Language, and Ebonics

We have tried to demonstrate that language affects communication between people of different backgrounds. Recent discussions about the role of Ebon ics in shaping student learning and identity also illustrate the facilitating and retarding aspects of cultural roots that we outlined in Chapter 1. Recall that we underlined the point that some of our intercultural experiences can foster congenial communication while other experiences can create tensions between groups. In this section we explore the role of Ebonics in cultural relations. Our discussion of Ebonics is not intended to provide a historical rendering of the debate over Ebonics, however. Rather, we are interested in demonstrating the intersection between language, race, and culture.

Ebonics and *black language/English* are terms that are used interchangeably. Since the 1960s and 1970s (Baratz, 1970; Green, 1963), educators, linguists, and psychologists have argued about whether black children should speak Ebonics in the classroom. Some linguists (for example, Smitherman, 1977) maintain that young children benefit academically from studying the language of their roots, in this case, Ebonics.

In the past, some school districts, among them the Detroit city schools, had given teachers permission to teach Ebonics in the classroom, arguing that children should be permitted to learn in the language that they come to school speaking first, and then become proficient in standard English.

On December 18, 1996, the Oakland, California, Board of Education voted unanimously to require the teaching of Ebonics in the classroom. Members of the board reasoned that by requiring African American children to learn Ebonics, teachers could elevate students' test scores. The suggestion provoked much controversy (Sowell, 1996). Some of the controversy is traceable to school board members' use of the term, "a genetically based language structure," to define Ebonics. What was the nature of the controversy and what bearing does it have on our discussion of race and language?

First, the issue of Ebonics pushes to the foreground the importance of heritage and roots. Because language is such an integral part of people's identities, a great deal of emotion is attached to it. Language is like one's favorite armchair. It is the medium for binding people firmly to their ancestral history and land. Language evokes memories of home, hallowed shrines, neighborhoods, campfire meetings, stories, songs, land, and other factors that are associated with it. In this way, language promotes a keen sense of place. For this reason, people do not readily abandon the language that provides them with such meaningful attachments.

Diane Ravitch (1997), in commenting on the 1997 bilingual education initiative in New York City, identified the strong connection between language and roots. She observes, "Apparently, the purpose of this state initiative is not to help students learn English but to maintain their culture" (p. A21). Brent Staples (1997), in responding to the teaching of Ebonics, quotes Gerald Early as saying "the creation of this past (African) has in recent years become an all-consuming preoccupation," resulting in a "delusional dogma that tends toward claims of racial superiority" (p. 20Y). As these comments demonstrate, intense sentiments often are tied to Ebonics and race.

Second, the issue of Ebonics demonstrates the influence of language loyalty. Language serves as a means of fostering in-group loyalty. This means that some individuals choose to use their own language; such choices can lead to sharp differences between them and out-group members. A term that sociolinguists use for this behavior is language *divergence*, which is a shift away from a standard (national) form of language (Ryan, 1979). A shift away from the standard form increases the chances that a particular group will preserve its own speech. This orientation can be a source of in-group solidarity. In the case of Ebonics, the perception that teachers should teach black English in the classroom instead of standard English raises significant questions of

---

BOX 4-1   Key Considerations When Race Is a Factor

1. **Negative racial and ethnic interactions can be based on ignorance.** A rural Indiana farmer who has never seen a Native American is likely to be ignorant of communication issues that contribute to racism.

2. **Interact on the assumption of similarities and differences.** Shared meanings and experiences are very important; however, in those instances where common ground is not readily apparent, we can accept the "other's" fundamental humaneness as a starting point for genuine communication.

3. **Be flexible.** Few people find it easy to accept those who are different, whether the differences are of creed, ways of thinking, or color. When old, musty views of the racial "other" are challenged, be willing to act on the basis of new, factual information.

4. **Minimize the variable of race.** Adjust your messages to the personality, temperament, and mannerisms of specific individuals. For example, instead of assuming that all "Chinese" must be treated stereotypically, put forth the desire to create a new reality.

5. **Build trust.** Harry Triandis (1972) notes that "eco-system" distrust is a characteristic of groups that have had a series of negative experiences. For example, much distrust between blacks and whites is rooted in history of slavery and discrimination in the United States. This factor can increase tension between blacks and whites.

6. **Be aware of myths and legends!** As we understand it, most people and ideas have more than one side to them. The myth that all Latino Americans are both passive and emotional is a good example. Staying with such a stereotypical point of view "after the facts are in" is termed *prejudice*, which we will discuss in the next chapter.

linguistic and racial unity. For example, does the teaching of Ebonics and other languages undermine the notion of a common, civic culture? Can racial groups speak different languages and still operate harmoniously within the national culture? These are questions that lie at the heart of any discussion concerning Ebonics and race.

ETHNICITY

In 1992 the *New York Times* ("Ethnic Cleansing," p. 4E) reported that over two million people had been "driven from their homes or fled in fear" as a result of the fighting in the former Republic of Yugoslavia. Groups such as Croats, Serbs, and Macedonians struggled in bitter antagonism over the issue of ethnicity. Atrocities, attacks, mortar shellings, and maiming all occurred in the name of "ethnic cleansing." Ethnic cleansing refers to one group's systematic attempts to eliminate another group through intimidation, war, and physical violence. Yugoslavian neighbors who had once visited with each other, shared bread, and played games in the same community hall began to perceive of themselves differently. One soldier in the Muslin territory of former Yugoslavia noted that "for the Serbs, for the Croats and for Europe Muslim people are nothing; Muslim people are just dirt" (*New York Times*, 1992, p. 4E).

The war that took place among ethnic Yugoslavians, who had once lived in relative harmony with each other, raise crucial questions about the role of ethnicity in human communication. Why, for example, are people moved to commit heinous crimes in the name of a particular group? What role does ethnicity play in intercultural communication?

In this section we will discuss several aspects of ethnicity: conceptions of ethnicity and ethnic identity. An understanding of each component is central to the development of our abilities to perceive other people accurately.

Conceptions of Ethnicity

There are many definitions of ethnicity. For our purposes, however, an ethnic group is one whose members "entertain a subjective belief in their common descent because of similarities of physical type or of customs or both, or because of memories of colonization and migration" (Alba, 1990, p. 16). Weber notes that the matter of "objective blood relationship" is not as important as issues of rootedness and ancestry. Ethnicity is concerned with "real" or "presumed" ancestry, a common history that is apart from others, interaction among members who share a consciousness of kind, and an important attachment to the past (Alba, 1990).

A practical way of looking at ethnicity is to say that it involves a linguistic construction such as "I am Polish American," "Italian American," or "Mexican American," with an accompanying tie to the country of one's roots or origins. References to one's country of origin, as well as ethnic markers, serve as powerful ways of forging group identity. Later we will discuss how ethnic identity influences the nature of intercultural communication.

At this point, it is useful to note that there are basically two interdependent ways of viewing ethnicity: *social allocation* (Alba, 1990; Wilson, 1987; Yinger, 1981), which holds that individuals are situated in the social structure based on their ethnic characteristics (groups distinguished by occupation, educational level, and residence), and *social solidarity*, which provides keys for identifying people who interact with each other to achieve common purposes" (Asians who are members of the Asian American Center for Justice).

Some scholars note that *social allocation* is losing strength as a way of measuring or explaining ethnicity (Alba, 1990). Social solidarity, however, is gaining ground as a way of looking at ethnic membership.

There are three major sources of social solidarity. First, social solidarity signals a *consciousness of kind*. Individuals may, for example, interact with others because they are conscious of something such as distinctions between in-groups and out-groups. Social solidarity also may signal a consciousness that individuals share a common fate. For years, for example, Jews in Europe maintained a common bond because of the virulent forms of discrimination leveled against them. Based on unpleasant experiences, Jews inferred that they could advance their mutual interest by banding together. The notion of a common fate, however, is not characteristic of Jews exclusively. This type of behavior is evident among African Americans, Hispanics, and the male-dominated organization, Promise Keepers, which held a rally in Washington, DC, in October 1997.

A third way that groups signal social solidarity is through a *valued* heritage. Here the past assumes importance. Group solidarity is built around one's roots, ancestry, or descent. Notice that ancestry forces to the foreground one's background and the things that that background summons or evokes. For example, to say that one is Thai American is to declare that one shares with other like-minded individuals a series of activities, beliefs, and values that are *Thai-like*. These might include eating Thai food, visiting the graves of one's ancestors frequently, or wearing a special kind of jewelry. In these instances, the specific ethnic strands are rooted in ancestry, which, of course, is not the entire story of ethnic identity. We will now discuss ethnic identity, demonstrating its relevance to our multiethnic and multiracial society.

Ethnic Identity

In the Texas town of Amarillo, two women, fluent in both Spanish and English, lost their jobs because they chatted in Spanish (Verhovek, 1997, p. A10). Rosa Gonzales and Ester Hernandez were hired by an insurance company because they spoke Spanish. Later, the owner of the company asked that Gonzales and Hernandez speak only English while at work. In fact, he allegedly demanded that the women sign a pledge that they would not speak Spanish in the workplace, except to service their Hispanic customers. When Gonzales and Hernandez refused to sign a written agreement, expressing their intent to honor their owner's request, they were fired.

In refusing to sign the agreement, Mrs. Gonzales said, "I told him (the owner of the company) no. This is what I am; this is what I do. This is normal to me. I'm not doing it to offend anybody" (Verhovek, 1997, p. A10). As this story suggests, some people uphold their ethnic identity, whether the identity is expressed through language or customs. As Alba (1990; Taylor, 1992) and others indicate, ethnic identity is increasingly becoming an important dimension of intercultural interactions.

Scholars who study ethnic identity posit two alternative points of view about the concept. Ethnic identity is grounded in theories first developed by the noted psychoanalyst, Erik Erikson. Erikson (1980) observes that identity rests heavily on what he terms *the prototypes* that are available to individuals, based on their history and location. Erickson argues that we form our sense of identity because we find within our environment models (prototypes) of "good and evil." This means that during our formative years, our parents, extended family members, and significant others, exhibit modes of behavior (good and bad) that serve as frameworks for how we subsequently behave. These models, in turn, become linked to who we are, as well as to our membership in particular ethnic groups.

For example, children who grow up in Greek households learn early that their identity is formed on the basis of what Holden (quoted in Broome, 1997, p. 117) terms "truly double-born souls." The Greeks' struggle between opposites: "spirit and flesh," "ideal and reality," "triumph and despair," according to this view, leads Greeks to perceive of themselves to be constantly in a struggle between opposites. For this reason, Greeks see aspects of their universe in terms of the in-group over the out-group. This view, in turn, affects their intercultural interactions with others. Outgroup members are viewed more with suspicion and mistrust. In Greek society, therefore, family members, friends, and friends of friends, form tight identification circles. Using this model (prototype) of good and evil, Greeks develop an identity that is akin to something like the following: "Our sense of responsibility and obligation is to our family,"

"This is how we see ourselves," and "This is a good thing." Taken together, the communication activities we have outlined influence Greek perceptions of self and their ethnic identity.

Another example of how our cultural roots (ethnic identities) influence the way in which we communicate is found in the 1996 protests that accompanied the selection of a black Caribbean immigrant as Miss Italy (*New York Times*, "Italians contemplate beauty," September 10, 1996, p.3). The controversy centered around the issue of whether Miss Denny Mendez, a non-European Italian, could accurately represent Italy in a beauty pageant. Some Italians claimed that she did not have the physical features characteristic of Italian female beauty. Other Italians, however, recognized "Italy's changing identity" from a relatively homogenous culture to a more cosmopolitan one. Italy, like many countries worldwide, is increasingly becoming a place of immigrants. Along with these changing demographics should come a more heightened awareness of the tensions that can exist between people based on their physical attributes as well.

One must be careful, however, not to imply that membership in an ethnic group automatically promotes conscious identity. As Alba (1990, p. 22) notes, "individuals may be ethnic in their 'identities' and still consciously reject their ethnic backgrounds." This view suggests that sometimes we unconsciously hold fast to our ethnic roots because they have become "impregnated with influence." For example, one can exhibit traits of an Irish American even if one no longer consciously identifies as Irish. Another way of looking at this point is to say that one can publically and privately deny one's Irish roots and yet cling to forms of storytelling, which are manifestations of being Irish.

Another aspect of ethnic identity rests in the notion of self-concept and social recognition. This view holds that we gain a sense of who we are based not only on how we see ourselves, but also on how others see us. This conception of ethnic identity is often described as the *image* or *looking-glass theory*. The image theory also suggests that our membership categories help to define who we are. For example, to say that Idell is "female, white, a mother, and an author" is to suggest that these categories help to define who Idell is.

Subsumed under the conception of ethnic identity are two elements that are crucial: *commitment* and *salience*. Commitment (Alba, 1990, p. 23) refers to "the degree of investment in relationships to others that is premised on a specific identity, and thus the social cost of renouncing it," and *salience* is the "probability for a given person, of a given identity being invoked in a variety of situations." For example, a woman might identify herself as Chinese American simply as a way of noting that she has roots in China without making an issue of her ancestry.

In the context of intercultural communication, however, Charles Taylor (1992, p. 25) locates a central reason why there is tension and conflict among groups based on ethnic identity. Our "identity," Taylor argues, "is partly shaped by recognition or its absence." This suggests "that a person or group of people can suffer real damage, real distortion, if the people or society around them mirror back to them a confining or contemptible picture of themselves" (Taylor, 1992, p. 25). Herein lies the roots of some difficulty in the United States among ethnic groups and women. Women in the United States, for instance, maintain that a male-oriented (patriarchy) society has contributed to women's "depreciatory image" of themselves. Similarly, African Americans, Hispanics, and other ethnic groups claim that they are not being taken seriously by members of the larger society.

Asante (1987) and Dates and Barlow (1990) maintain that a negative portraiture derides, belittles, and robs African Americans of public virtue. Thus, minority group demands for recognition are deeply rooted in their claims to public virtue. Minorities' and women's search for recognition clearly undergird the cultural clash over ethnicity. The debate over the representation of women and ethnic groups in literary and historical texts is an example of individuals' search for identity.

The following example should give us a sense of the deep intersection between cultural roots and identity. The debate over the Western canon, once moved author Saul Bellow to say, "When the Zulus produce a Tolstoy we will read him," and Houston Baker to say that choosing between Pearl Buck and Virginia Woolf is "no different from choosing between a hoagy and a pizza" (quoted in Kimball, 1990).

These cultural tensions arise not from small disagreements or mundane matters. Rather they arise from strong notions (commitment) of who individuals are, as well as from one side's claim that recognition should not be based upon ethnic identity but upon individual achievement in keeping with the ideals of democracy. The other side argues for recognition, elevating (implicitly and/or explicitly) ethnic origins and identity. We saw evidence of the importance of identity in our earlier example of the Hernandez and Gonzales case.

Some critical questions that you should grapple with are the following: To what extent do claims to ethnic identity foster divisions among different groups? What relationship obtains between ethnic identities and the building of intercultural community? How important is ethnic identity to democracy? How will ethnicity influence intercultural communication in the coming twenty-first century?

However you answer these questions, it is important to remember that our ancestry, claims to ethnic identity, and the way we organize ourselves in relation to others profoundly influence our perceptions of others.

For example, once upon a time a professor at a major university presented a lively seminar presentation titled "Under Cherry Trees There Are No Strangers: Communicating Interculturally." Following the presentation, the professor invited her delightfully attentive audience to ask questions and make comments. Things proceeded as expected until a gentleman named Calvin made an observation that is of the greatest pertinence today: "I don't understand why people refer to themselves as African Americans, Asian American, or Hispanic American. We are all Americans!" Calvin's implied suggestion is that recognition of a person's ethnic identity is irrelevant to who we are as Americans. Is ethnicity irrelevant to improving intercultural communication?

THE GENDER FACTOR

We have shown in the preceding sections how race and ethnicity can greatly disadvantage and exclude certain groups from participating meaningfully in communication exchanges. Gender also plays a role in how we view people unlike ourselves. To understand fully the implications of gender's role in communication, we need to consider, for a moment, the importance of gender in culture.

Women traditionally have had a historical and cultural experience significantly different from that of men. Until recently men argued that such differences were based on biologically determined characteristics of women. Women were considered, for example, to be both emotional and nurturing, while men were considered to be rational and strong. Based on these differences, men assumed roles of ruler and protector and developed a family organizational structure known as *patriarchy* (Lerner, 1986).

Patriarchy

Patriarchy refers to a system of rule by men in which many of the groups they dominate exchange responsibilities and obligations for their protection. For example, men have historically dominated women in exchange for the responsibility of their economic support and protection. In some cultures, patriarchal structures have led women to be exchanged in marriage among tribes, denied an education, and excluded from participating in public talk.

Once men's dominance was established largely on the basis of sexual dominance, it lasted for nearly 2600 years and was incorporated into most cultures, including the Near East, Asia, Europe, Africa, and the United States. Today, however, men's dominance over women is being more openly challenged worldwide.

Gender and Gender Formation

We define gender formation as the sociocultural process by which female and male categories are created and transformed. From a gender-formation perspective, our conceptions of gender are influenced by both social structure and cultural development. All cultures differentiate between male and female behavior; once these behaviors are learned and categorized, they become associated with the characteristics of a specific sex. For example, in North America, the prevailing cultural view based on gender is that little girls play with dolls and little boys play with trucks. In playing with dolls, little girls begin to associate with role characteristics such as nurturing, caring, and childcare. Thus, by internalizing the characteristics of these roles, men and women begin to accept specific roles, causing them to become *natural* or *commonsensical* to both men and women.

Social construction is a term that refers to the way that gender develops. Julia T. Wood (1997, p. 165) notes that "Throughout our interaction with others, we receive constant messages that reinforce females' conformity to femininity and males' to masculinity. This reveals gender is a social creation, not an individual characteristic." In our previous example of little girls playing with dolls and little boys playing with trucks, gender is reinforced when parents and others teach children to associate one practice (playing with dolls) with girls and the other practice (playing with trucks) with boys. Soon, children learn that they should behave according to the norms prescribed by people in their group. In this way, one's cultural rootedness in families seem natural and therefore promote gender construction. Our cultural roots tell us how to be and act with others. Forms of persuasion outside the home also influence how we view gender. Think of television programs, movies, and other media activities that daily reinforce how we feel about the roles that men and women play. In those media cases that you can identify, how are men and women perceived? Note the relationship that exists between gender and media structures and practices.

Thus, we are not born with a tendency toward masculine or feminine behavior. We are taught and the lessons that we learn are internalized. This means that such lessons become a crucial part of our socialization and communication processes. Another way of stating this is to say that a child who is constantly reinforced for playing with dolls will soon believe that such behavior is not only appropriate but desirable. These social roles then lead men and women to view themselves as "different in their essence and their function" (Lerner, 1986). In this way, set ideas of gender are formed and normalized.

The significance of gender formation to intercultural communication is that it influences our feelings, beliefs, and behaviors in our relations to people unlike ourselves. For example, recall the interaction between Japanese men and women that we mentioned in the introduction to this section. Some

Japanese women tend to look weak in public; however, behind the scenes, privately, their publically demure behavior takes on an entirely different meaning. That gender is culturally based and created can be seen as well in the built-in gender differences in the Japanese language. For example, Kittredge Cherry (1987) notes the Japanese proverb, *onna sannin yhoreba kashimashii,* which means "Put three women together and you get noise." The character *kashimashii,* which means noisy is comprised of the female character repeated three times (p. 25). This female ideogram would imply that "noisiness" is a female characteristic and it is, according to Cherry (1987), "almost always the first example that springs to mind when linguistic sex discrimination is discussed" (pp. 25–26). Gender is also an important factor in intercultural communication when we consider Deborah Tannen's (1990) argument that men and women use different words and live in different worlds. Evidence is piling up that differences and approaches to communication are primary causes of tension and friction between the sexes. Next we focus on general differences between male–female interaction so that we can gain insight into how communication styles help to explain problems that arise between men and women.

Male–Female Communication

In 1988 Coates discussed how "the fact that women and men differ in terms of their communicative behavior is no established sociolinguistic fact. The problem remains of explaining such difference" (p. 65). Two conflicting views of how and why women and men possess different communicative norms is based on two conflicting views of women's status in society. The *dominance/deficit approach* views women as a minority group that is oppressed and marginalized. The *difference approach* sees women as simply different than men and argues that their language reflects that difference.

Dominant/Deficit Approach
The most widely known example of the dominance/deficit approach is Robin Lakoff's *Language and the Woman's Place* (1975). Lakoff outlines three areas of gender differences: lexical traits (word choice), phonological traits (sound), and syntactic–pragmatic characteristics (grammar and usage). Although Lakoff's work on women's language is based more on casual observation and introspection than on empirical research, it has been extremely influential and has made the study of women's language an important issue for all communication researchers.

Lexical Traits   Lakoff asserts that women use a larger number of words than men to describe things. For example, women use more words to describe color than men. In addition, both men and women use neutral adjectives such

---

BOX 4-2   Some Communication Differences between Men and Women

- Men talk more than women.
- Women tend to use more tag questions.
- Women use more qualifiers and intensifiers.
- Women communicate to build rapport.

- Men communicate to report factual information.
- Women use more cooperative language.
- Men use more competitive language.
- Women use more fillers.

---

as great and terrific. However, women are more likely to use adjectives such as adorable, charming, sweet, and lovely. Men are more likely to use terms such as nice, good, or pretty.

Phonological Traits   According to Lakoff, more stereotypically feminine people speak "in italics" by emphasizing some words more than others. For example, a feminine speaker might say, "I really *think* you should consider staying in school." Lakoff suggests because they are not sure they can convince listeners to do something, to compensate they use emphasis to make sure that their meaning is clear.

Syntactic–Pragmatic Characteristics   A common gender stereotype holds that women are expected to speak with more grammatical correctness than men. On the average, women's speech is closer to the norm of standard speech than men's, especially in formal situations (Smith, 1985).

Lakoff contends that women are more likely than men to end sentences with tag questions. Instead of saying "It's really hot," for example, a woman would be more likely to say, "It's really hot, isn't it?" Women also tend to use more hedges such as *well, you know,* and *kinda.* These words and phrases convey the impression that the speaker is unsure of the accuracy of his or her statements.

Research does not support Lakoff's observations about tag questions and hedges, however, because many researchers agree that men also use tag questions and hedges. In one study, men used thirty-three tag questions while women used none (Dubois & Crouch, 1975). What seems important in understanding tag questions is the gender composition of people talking to each other. Men and women use slightly different language patterns when talking to each other than when talking to people of their same sex. Females use more qualifying words such as *maybe* and *sort of* when talking to females than when talking to males. Males use more qualifying words (*maybe, guess, well, kinda of*) when talking to males than to females. Thus, some gender stereotypes are more prominent when females are talking to females or when males are talking to males.

In addition the same linguistic devices can be perceived differently depending on whether they are used by men or women. In one study of a small group situation, women who used tag questions and disclaimers (introductory expressions that excuse, explain, or request understanding or forbearance, such as, "I may be wrong, but . . .") were perceived less positively and were less influential than women who stated their views more directly. Males were viewed as intelligent and well informed even if they failed to support their arguments or if they used verbal disclaimers (Bradley, 1981).

There is still some support for Lakoff's dominance/deficit model. Carli (1990) finds women more tentative than men in mixed-sex conversations. Her study is based on the *expectations states theory,* which contends that inequalities in face-to-face interactions are a function of the relative status of the participants. This means that when people of different status interact, it is improper for the person of low status to communicate too aggressively because the behavior would be seen as an attempt to gain status at the expense of the other person.

Despite these differences in influence, however, both male and female speakers in Carli's study judged a woman who spoke tentatively as less competent and knowledgeable than a woman who spoke assertively. Carli concludes that the differences in the use of tag questions, disclaimers, and hedges are probably a function of status differences between women and men.

Difference Approach
According to Coates (1988) the difference approach to male/female language contends that

> *women and men talk differently, or behave differently in spoken interaction, because they are socialized in different sociolinguistic subcultures . . . [This approach] reflects a growing political awareness among linguists that by labeling men's language as "strong" and women's language as "weak," we were adopting an androcentric viewpoint. The difference . . . approach attempts to investigate sex differences in communicative competence, and in particular women's language, from a positive standpoint. (p. 69)*

One of the earliest conceptualizations of this approach is Maltz and Borker's (1982) list of women's and men's features of language. Unlike Lakoff, Maltz and Borker do not contend that these language differences reflect power imbalance between men and women, but rather that women and men have internalized different norms for conversation. They argue that communicative competence is developed in same-sex play groups and, consequently, communication problems may occur in mixed-sex interactions because women and men may have different expectations for interaction or may interpret specific aspects of language differently. Males are more likely to use a style of interaction based on power while females are more likely to use a style based on solidarity and support.

As a result of this difference, several problems may arise. For example, women use questions more than men and they use them as a conversational maintenance strategy, that is, to keep the conversation going. Men are more likely to interpret a question as a simple request for information.

Links between speaker's turns may also cause difficulties when men and women converse together. Women are more likely to start a speaking turn by directly acknowledging the contribution of the previous speaker ("I agree with Mark. Let's all meet at 7:00). Men are more likely not to acknowledge what has been said previously, making their point instead. Because of these differing styles, women may feel that their comments are being ignored while men may feel that switching the topic implicitly expresses agreement.

Topic shifts bring up similar problems. In all-male conversations, however, topic shifts may be very abrupt. Women, however, typically shift topics gradually. Men thus may be frustrated in mixed-sex interaction because they feel a topic has been "talked to death."

Perhaps the most widely known advocate of the difference approach is Deborah Tannen. Tannen (1991) argues that women tend to organize their talk cooperatively, while men are more likely to organize their talk competitively. She believes that "many women bond by talking about troubles, and many men bond by exchanging playful insults and put-downs, and other sorts of verbal sparring" (p. B1).

Tannen (1990) also notes that women tend to engage in "rapport talk," while men engage in "report talk." Rapport talk focuses on feelings or maintains rapport with others, while report talk focuses on factual information about what is going on, for example, in the world of sports.

Features of Communication Competence

Four variables of communication competence have received a large amount of research: verbosity, interruptions, conversational initiation, and argumentativeness. We will examine each variable briefly. (For an exhaustive review of this literature, see Stewart, Cooper, Stewart, & Friedley, 1996).

Verbosity Although the common stereotype is that women talk more than men, research does not bear this out. In fact, James and Drakich (1993), among others, show that men talk more than women. In 56 of the studies James and Drakich reviewed dealing with adult mixed-sex interaction, males talked more than females overall in 45 percent of the studies and talked more than females in some circumstances in another 18 percent of the studies. Only two studies found that females talk more than males.

Tannen (1990) contends that men may talk more in public situations while women may talk more in private situations. She argues that men talk more when they feel the need to establish or maintain their status in a group. Women view talk as crucial in maintaining close relationships, and they talk more in private settings.

Interruptions   James and Clarke (1993) review thirty-two studies that have examined interruptions in mixed-sex conversation. Seventeen of these studies find no significant gender differences in interruptions. In ten studies men produce more interruptions than women. A similar range of results is produced in studies of same-sex interaction. Seventeen of the twenty-two studies in this category report no gender differences.

Interruptions can be used for a variety of purposes. They can communicate enthusiastic assent, elaboration of another person's idea, participation in an ongoing topic, or a desire to take control of the speaking turn. James and Clarke note that "no clear conclusion . . . can be drawn . . . as to whether males' interruptions are more likely to constitute attempts to seize the floor than are those of females, or as to whether females are more likely than males to have dominance related interruptions directed at them" (p. 258).

Conversation Initiation   Topics introduced by men tend to be noticed and carried on by their conversational partners, while topics introduced by women more often may die a sudden death in spite of the fact that women initiate more topics than men. As Smith (1985) notes, "there is considerable evidence that the norms of femininity and masculinity encourage women and men to control communication situations and the goals of interaction somewhat differently" (p. 135). The traditional concept of masculinity is associated with the control dimension, the extent to which a person can exert active control over the process and outcomes of an interaction. The affiliative dimension—the tendency to elicit warmth and approach—is associated with the traditional norms of femininity. Thus, men may be more concerned with controlling a conversation while women are more concerned with establishing connections through conversation.

This conclusion is supported by Mulac and colleagues (Mulac, Wiemann, Widenmann, & Gibson, 1988), who find that men are more likely to use direct control tactics such as directives ("you should write down your answers") and to maintain speaking turns by using fillers to begin sentences ("and another thing . . ."). Women are more likely to use indirect control strategies such as questions ("What next?") and to express interest in others through the use of personal pronouns such as we.

Argumentativeness   Argumentativeness is a stable trait that predisposes an individual in communication situations to advocate positions on controversial issues and to attack verbally the positions that other people take on these issues (Infante & Rancer, 1982). Males have been found to score higher than females in both argumentativeness and verbal aggression (Nicotera & Rancer, 1994). Women are more likely to believe that arguing is a hostile, aggressive, and combative form of communication. They are more likely than men to believe that arguing is a strategy for dominating and controlling another person.

Sexist Language
A great deal of research on language has examined sexism in vocabulary and the structure of language itself. Sexism is discrimination against individuals or groups on the basis of their gender. Sexist language perpetuates negative stereotypes. Ayim (1993) points out that "our language fosters and perpetuates racist and classist bigotry as well as sexism" (p. 3).

Colwill (1993) maintains that the status differential between men and women continues to be maintained by sexist language. She claims that language negatively affects our communication in the following four ways:

1. Using masculine words to refer to females and males (e.g., countrymen)
2. Using titles of different levels for women and men (a woman is greeted as Betty, while a man is called Mr. Smith)
3. Using different words to describe women and men doing the same thing (nurse vs. male nurse, writer vs. female writer)
4. Reinforcing gender stereotypes ("When a manager hires a secretary, he should choose her with care.) (p. 4)

Because language use is a reflection of the society in which we live, as long as society defines men and women in terms of gender stereotypes, gendered language will persist.

CONCLUSION

This chapter considered two important differences that play a major role in human interaction and have played a major role in the history of humankind: race and gender. Because groups interact on the basis of racially coded categories—through hair color, facial features, and skin tones, for example—we tend to put an ethnic label on people. These labels often become enormously important, sometimes disturbing normal communication with others. Factors such as perception, ideology, credibility, and accessibility affect communication with perhaps the clearest and strongest indications racial categorization.

Gender formation, the differences between male and female commu cation, features of communication competence, and sexism were also e plored. For us to contribute to human understanding, we must search fo way out of the limiting and confining aspects of both race and gender.

QUESTIONS

1. How do perceptions of race and gender hinder effective intercultu communication?
2. In what sense can one say that men and women live in two differe worlds?
3. If you were invited to give a talk to a group of futurists on the to "Under Cherry Trees There Are No Strangers: Improving Race Relatic in the Twenty-First Century," where would you begin? What then would you include? Why? What solutions would you suggest?

ACTIVITIES

1. Collect a list of terms (vocabulary) that African Americans from all wa of life use that relate specifically to the Black Church and the urban co munity. What is the importance of these terms in understanding Afric American culture and history? What facts about the creative nature black talk do these terms reflect? What do such terms indicate abe African Americans' relationship to the larger society?
2. Author John Gray (1994) uses the phrase, "Men are from Mars a women are from Venus" to highlight linguistic and cultural differen between men and women. Interview a person who is accustomed to teracting with both males and females. Ask this person what changes or she has observed in language usage between males and females. Th may be changes in terminology (vocabulary) or changes in patterns speaking (who speaks to whom, different topics of conversation). W accounts for these changes?
3. Analyze the interaction between race and gender, using your favo television program or movie as a model. What assumptions does writer or director make about the nature of interactions between race a gender? Note the attitudes that are reflected in the characters. How v does the writer's perspective accord with your own perspective?

REFERENCES

Alba, R. (1990). *Ethnic identity: The transformation of white America*. New Haven, CT: Yale University Press.

Asante, M. (1987). *The Afrocentric idea*. Philadelphia: Temple University Press.

Ayim, M. (1993). Issues in language and gender: An annotated bibliography. *Resources for Feminist Research, 22* (1/2), 1–35.

Baratz, J. (1970). Should black children learn white dialect? *ASHA, 12,* 415–417.

Bernal, M. (1987). Black athena: The Afroasiatic roots of classical civilization, vol, 1. The fabrication of ancient Greece 1785-1985. New Brunswick, NJ: Rutgers University Press.

Billig, M., Condor, S. Edwards, D., Gave, M., Middleton, D., & Radley, J. (1992). Prejudice and tolerance. In W. Gudykunst & K. Young (Eds.), *Readings on communicating with strangers: An approach to intercultural communication* (pp. 158–169). New York: McGraw-Hill.

Bradley, P. (1981). The folk-linguistics of women's speech: An empirical examination. *Communication Monographs, 48,* 141–148.

Broome, B. (1997). Palevome: Foundations of struggle and conflict in Greek interpersonal communication. In L. Samavor & R. Porter (Eds.), *Intercultural communication: A reader* (pp. 116–124). Belmont, CA: Wadsworth.

Carli, L. (1990). Gender, language, and influence. *Journal of Personality and Social Psychology, 59,* 941–951.

Cherry, K. (1987). *Womansword: What Japanese words say about women*. Tokyo: Koansha International.

Coates, J. (1988). Introduction. In J. Coates & D. Cameron (Eds.), *Women in their communities: New perspectives on language and sex* (pp. 63–73). New York: Longman.

Colwin, N. (1993). Sexist language revisited (and revisited and revisited . . .). *Women in Management, 3* (4), 4.

Daniel, J. (1995, April 18) Speech delivered at the Central States Communication Association, Indianapolis, IN.

Dates, J., & Barlow, W. (Eds.) (1990). *Split image: African Americans in the mass media*. Washington, DC: Howard University Press.

Dubois, B.L., & Crouch, I. (1975), The question of tag questions in women's speech: They don't really use more of them, do they? *Language in Society, 4,* 289–294.

Eagleton, T. (1991). *Ideology: An introduction*. London: Verso.

Erikson, E. (1980). *Identity and the life cycle*. New York: W.W. Norton.

'Ethnic cleansing.' Europe's old horror, with new victims. (1992, August 2). *The New York Times*, p. 4E.

Fagan, B. (1984). *Clash of cultures*. New York: W. H. Freeman.

Gray, J. (1994). *Men are from mars, women are from venus: A practical guide for improving communication and getting what you want in relationships*. New York: Harper/Collins.

Green, G. (1963). Section B: Negro dialect, the last barrier to integration. *The Journal of Negro Education, 32,* 81–83.

Hannerz, U. (1992). *Cultural complexity: Studies in the social organization of meaning.* New York: Columbia University Press.

Harris, M. (1985). *Good to eat: Riddles of food and culture.* New York: Simon and Schuster.

Infante, D.A., & Rancer, A. S. (1982). A conceptualization and measure of argumentativeness. *Journal of Personality and Assessment, 46,* 159–170.

Italians contemplate beauty in a Caribbean brow. (1996, September 10). *The New York Times,* p. A3.

Jahn, J. (1961). *Muntu.* New York: Grove Press.

James, D. & Clarke, S. (1993). Women, men and interruptions: A critical review. In D. Tannen (Ed.), *Gender and conversation interaction* (pp. 231–180). New York: Oxford University Press.

James, D., & Drakich, J. (1993). Understanding gender differences in amount of talk: A critical review of research. In D. Tannen (Ed.), *Gender and conversational interaction* (pp. 281–312). New York: Oxford University Press.

Kimball, R. (1990). *Tenured radicals: How politics has corrupted our higher education.* New York: Harper & Row.

Klopf, D. (1991). *Intercultural encounters: The fundamentals of intercultural communication.* Englewood, CO: Morton Publishing Company.

Kristof, N.D. (1996, June 19). Japan is a woman's world once the front door is shut. *The New York Times,* p. A6.

Lakoff, R. (1975). *Language and the woman's place.* New York: Harper & Row.

Lerner, G. (1986). *The creation of patriarchy.* New York: Oxford University Press.

Maltz, D., & Borker, R. (1982). A cultural approach to male-female miscommunication. In J.J. Gumperz (Ed.), *Language and social identity* (pp. 196–216). New York: Cambridge University Press.

McFadyen, R., & Wetherell, M. (1986). Categories in discourse. Cited in W. Gudykunst & Y. Kim (Eds.), *Readings on communicating with strangers: An approach to intercultural communication* (p. 161). New York: McGraw-Hill.

Mulac, A., Wiemann, J., Widenmann, S., & Gibson, T. (1988). Male/female language differences and effects in same-sex and mixed-sex dyads: The gender-linked language effect. *Communication Monographs, 55,* 315–335.

Nicotera, A., & Rancer, A. (1994). The influence of sex on self-perceptions and social stereotyping of aggressive communication predispositions. *Western Journal of Communication 58,* 283–307.

Omi, M., & Winant, H. (1994). *Racial formation in the United States from the 1960s to the 1990s.* New York: Routledge.

Parker-Pope, T. (1996, February 2). Ford puts blacks in whiteface, turns red. *The Wall Street Journal,* p. B8.

Ravitch, D. (1997, September 5). First teach them English. *The New York Times,* p. A21.

Ribeau, S., Baldwin, J., & Hecht, M. (1994). An African-American communication perspective. In L. Samovar & R. Porter (Eds), *Intercultural communication: A reader* (pp. 140–148). Belmont, CA: Wadsworth.

Ryan, B. (1979). Why do low-prestige language varieties persist? In H. Giles and R. St. Clair (Eds), *Language and social psychology* (pp. 145-155). Oxford: B. Blackwell.

Sims, C. (1995, July 30). The South American art of name-calling. *The New York Times,* p. 4E.

Smith, A. (1973). *Transracial communication.* Englewood Cliffs, NJ: Prentice-Hall.

Smith, P. (1985). *Language, the sexes and society.* Oxford, England: Basil Blackwell.

Smitherman, G. (1977) *Talkin and testifin.* Boston: Houghton Mifflin.

Sowell, T. (1996, December 26). 'Ebonics' seen as another tragic chapter in racial self-destruction. *The Herald-Times,* p. A10.

Staples, B. (1997, January 4). The trap of ethnic identity. *The New York Times,* p. 20Y.

Stewart, L., Cooper, P., Stewart, A., & Friedley, S. (1996). *Communication and gender.* Scottsdale, AZ: Gorsuch Scarisbrick.

Taijfel, H., & Turner, J. (1992). The social identity theory of intergroup behavior. In W. Gudykunst & Y. Kim (Eds.), *Readings on communicating with strangers.* New York: McGraw-Hill.

Tannen, D. (1990). *You just don't understand: Women and men in conversation.* New York: Ballantine Books.

Tannen, D. (1991, June 19). Teachers' classroom strategies should recognize that men and women use language differently. *The Chronicle of Higher Education,* pp. B1, B3.

Taylor, C. (1992). *Multiculturalism and "the politics of recognition."* Princeton, NJ: Princeton University Press.

Triandis, H. (1972). The analysis of subjective culture. New York: Wiley-Interscience.

Trump the race card. (1996, February 23). *The Wall Street Journal,* p. A10.

Van Dijk, T.A. (1984). *Prejudice in discourse: An analysis of ethnic prejudice in cognition and conversation.* Amsterdam: J. Benjamins.

Verhovek, S.H. (1997, September 30). Clash of cultures tears Texas city. *The New York Times,* p. A10.

Vru, A., & Winkel, F. (1994). Perceptual distortions in cross-cultural interrogations: The impact of skin color, accent, speech style, and spoken fluency on impression formation. *Journal of Cross-Cultural Psychology, 25*(2), 284–295.

Weber, S. (1994). The need to be: The socio-cultural significance of black language. In L. Samovar & R. Porter (Eds.), *Intercultural communication: A reader* (pp. 220–225). Belmont, CA: Wadsworth.

Wetherell, M., & Potter, J. (1986). Discourse analysis and the social psychology of racism. *Newsletter of the Social Psychology Section of the British Psychological Society, 15,* 24–29.

Wilson, J. (1987). The truly disadvantaged: The inner city, the underclass, and public policy. Chicago: University of Chicago Press.

Williams, L. (1991, April 30). When blacks shop, bias often accompanies sale. *The New York Times,* pp. 1, A9.

Wood, J. (1997). Gender, communication, and culture. In L. Samavor & R. Porter (Eds.), *Intercultural communication: A reader* (pp. 164–173). Belmont, CA: Wadsworth.

Yinger, M. (1981). Towards a theory of assimilation and dissimilation. *Ethnic and Racial Studies, 4* (July), 249–264.

5

STEREOTYPES AND PREJUDICE

Objectives

After reading this chapter and completing the activities, you should be able to:

1. List the five steps in the perception process.
2. Give an example from your own experience of the three components of perception.
3. Explain ethnocentrism and cultural relativism and their relationship to perception.
4. Explain the social cognition process.
5. Give an example of the self-fulfilling prophecy.
6. Define five types of attribution error.
7. Explain techniques used to help make accurate attributions.
8. Explain the relationship between stereotypes and prejudice and how they affect intercultural communication.

> *"Are you all moved into your new apartment now?"* Teresita asked.
> *"Yes, I think I'll like it a lot,"* Sylvia replied.
> *"What do you do when you finish work?"* Teresita continued.
> *"Oh, lots of things,"* Sylvia was becoming annoyed.
> *"And does your family approve of your living alone?"*
> *"They don't mind."* Sylvia searched for a way to end the conversation quickly.
> *"Excuse me, I must help this customer,"* she said, and hurried to the front of the bank.

Sylvia had been at work only two days since transferring from the U.S. to the Philippine branch of the bank she worked for. She was doing the same job she'd done in America, though there were some variations in procedure. She was glad to learn the new techniques and have errors pointed out by Teresita, her superior. But every conversation they had about some problem seemed to go on and on and ultimately got very personal, with Teresita asking questions and discussing subject that had nothing to do with their work at the bank. "I hardly know her, and she is prying into everything I do," Sylvia thought angrily. "I'll just have to tell her next time that it's none of her business."

(Kohls & Knight, 1994, p. 112)

To make sense of the previous interaction, communication scholars suggest you ask yourself the following four questions:

1. How does each individual view the situation?
2. What impressions do the individuals have of one another?
3. How do each of the individuals view the relationship, such as, friends, acquaintances, employer–employee, etc.?
4. How do individuals explain their own and each other's behavior in the interaction?

These four questions are concerned with the processes that influence our perceptions of people and social events—our social cognitions, which enable us to categorize people and events and thereby "make sense" of our social interactions. For example, it might have helped Sylvia to know several important things (Kohls & Knight, 1994):

Actually, by asking personal questions Teresita meant to show her concern for Sylvia. Filipinos highly value pakikisama*—the art of smooth interpersonal relationships. Ideally one accomplishes his or her purposes without conflict, direct confrontation, or injury to another's* amor propio.

One way Filipinos attempt to minimize hurt and unpleasantness is by inquiring into another person's private life. After giving some form of criticism, the Filipino boss may follow with questions about an employee's family and personal affairs. This relieves the employee and makes her feel she still belongs and is accepted.

Sometimes a personal question is asked merely as a matter of courtesy— a hotel clerk, for example, may ask a guest "Where are you going?" every time he leaves the hotel. Such an inquiry is simply a greeting—couched in more personal terms than Americans are used to—and carries no more significance than the American question, "How are you?"

(p. 112)

In this chapter we will be concerned with social cognitions and how they relate to the intercultural communication process, particularly in terms of stereotypes and prejudices. However, before we discuss social cognitions, we'll briefly examine the perception process—how it "works" in general and how it relates to intercultural communication.

PERCEPTION PROCESS

Why might two people, such as Sylvia and Teresita, have such different views of the same situation? The answer is that we select, organize, and interpret the stimuli we receive through our senses into a meaningful picture of the world around us. This process is called perception and is the basis of our communication with others. However, as Singer (1987) indicates, "We experience everything in the world not as it is—but only as the world comes to us through our sensory receptors" (p. 9). In other words, we each construct our own reality. Thus, my reality may not be the same as yours.

Each of us goes through the process of perception as we come into contact with others.

1. We observe the available data in our environment.
2. We choose what data we see/hear/feel/smell/taste and process it (selective perception).
3. We define the person or event and build expectations of future behavior.
4. Our expectations help determine our behavior toward the person.
5. Our behavior affects the other person's perceptions.

Obviously, the data we select from all the available data is affected by our personal experiences, our psychological states, our values, our culture, and many other factors. Perception affects our communication. We make judgments on others based on those perceptions and we communicate accordingly. If people interpret reality differently, communication problems may result.

Three components are involved in our interpretation of our reality: the attributive, the expectative, and the affective. The *attributive component* consists of those characteristics we attribute to the person or object or event. These characteristics may or may not be present. However, based on our experiences, we perceive them as being there. We may view foreigners as hardworking, eager, and intelligent. Or, we may view them as lazy, unmotivated, and unintelligent.

The *expectative component* consists of the expectations we have of the things we perceive. In American culture, we expect a college professor to read different kinds of books than a construction worker. We also expect them to dress differently. Based on the characteristics you attribute to others, you'll expect certain behaviors. For example, if you view foreigners as hard-working, eager, and intelligent, you'll expect them to be good employees.

Finally, we have feelings about the objects and people we perceive—the *affective component* of perception. The feelings are derived from our experiences with whatever we're perceiving, the characteristics we attribute to whatever we're perceiving, and from our expectations concerning whatever we're perceiving. If you have the first view of foreigners presented above, you'll probably feel positively toward them. If you have the second view, you'll no doubt dislike foreigners.

This whole process is, of course, reciprocal. So, for example, Americans tend to believe that opinions should be stated clearly and forcefully. Japanese tend to believe that opinions should be stated more indirectly and humbly. Thus, Americans might perceive Japanese as "wishy-washy," while Japanese might perceive Americans as "pushy."

CULTURE AND PERCEPTION

Our culture plays a key role in structuring our perceptions. We are all taught ways of perceiving people, objects, and events. As the song from the musical *South Pacific* so aptly states, "You have to be carefully taught." This teaching may lead to ethnocentrism. Summer (1950) defines ethnocentrism as "the view of things in which one's own group is the center of everything, and all others are scaled and rated with reference to it" (p. 13).

Everyone is ethnocentric to some degree. As we have suggested throughout this text, we cannot escape our roots. Since our culture teaches us what the world is "really like," we believe that the values of our culture are the best. Thus, we may consider people from other cultures who do things differently "wrong," "odd," or "strange." If we are highly ethnocentric, we see our in-group (our culture) as virtuous and superior and our values as universals (applying to everyone). We see out-groups (those outside of our in-group that we encounter on our routes) as contemptible and inferior and we reject their values (Gudykunst, 1994). Thus, our tendency is to evaluate the patterns of out-group behavior negatively rather than to try to understand the behavior of out-group members.

The opposite of ethnocentrism is cultural relativism—trying to understand others' behavior in the context of the culture or group of the person engaging in the behavior (Gudykunst, 1994, p. 78). If we try to interpret other's behaviors from her or his own cultural frame of reference, we have a better chance of communicating effectively.

So how might ethnocentrism and cultural relativism relate to communication? In 1978 Lukens wrote about the concept of ethnocentric speech in which we use our speech patterns to create a feeling of communication distance between us and the people with whom we communicate. Using Lukens' analysis, Gudykunst and Kim (1997) extended Lukens' idea of ethnocentric speech to include cultural relativism. If we combine these two concepts we can place them on five positions on a continuum: very low cultural relativism/very high ethnocentrism, high ethnocentrism/low cultural relativism, moderate ethnocentrism/moderate cultural relativism, low ethnocentrism/high cultural relativism, and very high cultural relativism/very low ethnocentrism.

What happens to communication as we move along this continuum? What happens is that communication distances are created by the distances between these positions. For example, the distance of disparagement involves very high levels of ethnocentrism and very low levels of cultural relativism. The in-group has animosity towards the out-group. This level of communication is characterized by the use of pejorative expressions about the out-group and the use of name calling. Imitation and mockery of speech styles are also frequent.

The distance of avoidance minimizes contact with members of an out-group. A technique often used to accomplish this is an in-group dialect. For example, the use of "black pride" or other in-group jargon might be used to show solidarity of the in-group and exclusion of the out-group.

The distance of indifference is the speech form used to "reflect the view that one's own [group] is the center of everything" (Lukens, 1978, p. 42). This distance reflects an insensitivity to the other group's perspective. As Gudykunst (1994) suggests:

One example of the speech use at this distance is "foreigner talk," the form of speech used when talking to people who are not native speakers of a language. It usually takes the form of loud and slow speech patterns, exaggerated pronunciation, and simplification (e.g., deletion of articles) (p. 79).

The distance of sensitivity reveals, as its name implies, a sensitivity to group differences and reflects a desire to decrease communicative distance between people. When communicating at this level, we would, for example, use the term for the other person's ethnic group that she or he prefers (e.g., African American rather than Black American or Negro).

Finally, the distance of equality reflects our desire to minimize the distance between ourselves and others. We have an attitude of equality. At this level we strive to avoid evaluations of the other. We use speech that reflects our desire for equality. For example, we would not use the generic pronoun "he," but the more reflective of equality phrase "he or she" (Gudykunst, 1994, p. 80).

SOCIAL COGNITION

Now that we understand how the perception process works and its relationship to intercultural communication, let's return to the four questions with which we began this chapter and examine them more closely.

The Situation

First, we "size up" the situation—what is going on? In order to communicate effectively, we need to understand "where we are"—the physical setting as well as the social setting. The social setting involves social episodes—"internal cognitive representations about common, recurring interaction routines within a defined cultural milieu" (Forgas, 1981). In other words, each culture has its own social episodes. Thus, the social episode of Chinese New Year celebrations differ from our American New Year celebration. Although both cultures celebrate the new year, we do so in different ways. For example, our new year begins with the first day of January on the calendar. The beginning of the Chinese New Year varies from year to year. In addition, Chinese traditions include paying off all debts, both financial and moral, incurred in the previous year, putting up luck-bringing papers, buying flowers and plants (the favorite plant is the peach tree just coming into bloom since the wood is a potent enemy of demons and the peach itself is symbolic of longevity), feeding the kitchen god sweets before he ascends to heaven to report to the Jade Emperor about the family's activities during the previous year, and giving children bright red "lucky money" envelopes with money inside. The celebrations last for two weeks and the focus of activities is the family.

The People

We also need to size up the other individuals in the social episode. Trenholm and Jensen (1996) suggest four factors to consider: personal constructs, implicit personality theory, self-fulfilling prophecies, and cognitive complexity. Let's briefly examine each one.

Personal constructs are the mental yardsticks for evaluating objects, events, and people. These constructs are of four types (Duck, 1976):

Physical constructs (tall-short, ugly-beautiful)—These are generally the constructs we use to form first impressions.

Role constructs (buyer-seller, student-teacher)—We try to understand each person's position in the social situation.

Interaction constructs (friendly-hostile, polite-rude)—We try to understand the other person's style of communication.

Psychological constructs (motivated-lazy, kind-cruel)—We use all the other three constructs to understand what kind of people the other inter-actants are.

Implicit personality theory suggests we organize our individual percep-tions into a cluster, filling in missing data. Thus, individual traits are related to other traits and when we "see" an individual trait, we assume the person possesses the other traits in the cluster. For example, Kelley (1950) conducted research that suggests that "intelligent," "quiet," and "friendly" cluster to-gether. So, if we view someone as friendly, we also view them as quiet and intelligent. Interestingly, once we've formed an impression of someone (which is formed during the first four minutes of interaction [Zunin, 1972]), we ignore other cues that are not consistent with our original first impression.

This relates to another perceptual tendency—the self-fulfilling prophecy. One of the most famous examples of self-fulfilling prophecy occurred in classrooms. In their research, Rosenthal and Jacobson (1968) randomly la-beled some elementary school children as high achievers and others as low achievers. This information was given to teachers. Students who were labeled as high achievers had raised their IQ scores significantly from the beginning of the school year to the end. Rosenthal and Jacobson suggest the role non-verbal communication may have played:

> We may say that by what she [the teacher] said, by how and when she said it, her facial expressions, postures, and perhaps her touch, the teacher may have communicated to the children of the experimental group that she ex-pected improved intellectual performance. Such communication . . . may have helped the child learn (p. 181).

This finding is substantial in research study after research study (Cooper, 1995). A self-fulfilling prophecy occurs when one person (the observer) be-lieves something to be true about another person (the target). The observer behaves toward the target as if the belief is fact. This behavior prompts the target to behave as the observer expected. For example, if a teacher believes all Japanese are hard working and studious, he or she will treat them as such (call on them more often, ask them higher level questions) and they will be-have intelligently in that classroom. They will self-fulfill the prophecy for them.

Finally, we differ in the complexity of our cognitions. We differ in both the number (differentiation) and quality (abstraction) as well as the ways we integrate these cognitions in evaluating others. If we are cognitively complex, we use a larger number of personal constructs, use more abstract psycholog-ical constructs, and have more elaborate ways of relating these constructs. In contrast, if we are less cognitively complex, we use fewer constructs, less abstract constructs, and the constructs are more isolated impressions (Delia, 1977).

So what does this mean in terms of intercultural communication? In general, less cognitively complex people are unable to integrate the constructs they use to form a more complete image. Thus, they ignore contradictory information or are unable to use new information to change their initial impression (Delia, Clark, & Switzer, 1979). More cognitively complex people are more accurate in processing information about others, probably because they weigh more evidence before formulating a complete impression. In addition, they are better able to put themselves in the role of the other person (Crockett, 1965). It is likely that people who are more cognitively complex are better able to adapt to cultures different from their own than are less cognitively complex people.

Culture affects the variables that people use to explain others' behavior. Collectivist cultures make greater references to situational factors and less references to personality factors than individualistic cultures (Gudykunst & Ting-Toomey, 1988). Ehrenhaus (1983) notes:

> high-context culture . . . members are attributionally sensitive and predisposed toward situational features and situationally based explanations. Low-context culture . . . members are attributionally sensitive to and predisposed toward dispositional characteristic and dispositionally based explanations (p. 263)

In addition, culture seems to affect what information people emphasize when making attributions. Okabe (1983) indicates that verbal skills are more necessary and more prized in low-context, individualistic cultures than in high-context, collectivist cultures. In high context cultures, verbal skills are considered suspect. Thus, confidence is placed in the nonverbal aspects of the interaction. For example, Tsujimura (1987) examines four characteristics of Japanese communication: (1) ishin-denshin ("traditional mental telepathy"), (2) taciturnity, (3) kuki (mood or atmosphere), and (4) respect for indirect communication. Thus, the emphasis for Japanese people is primarily on nonverbal communication.

The Relationship

After sizing up the people and the situation, we size up the relationship. In order to do this we label the relationship—parent/child, spouse, friend, acquaintance, co-worker, business partner, and so on. Whatever level we assign determines our perception of the appropriate behavior in the relationship. As the relationship develops, we will "work out" a master contract with the other person that guides our recurring interaction (Carson, 1969).

One variable that determines how we do this is self—what aspects of our self-perception fit into the relationship. Our ability to be aware of and adapt our self-image to the current situation is referred to as a self-monitoring (Snyder, 1974). Snyder suggests that, in a given situation:

> The high self-monitor asks, "Who does this situation want me to be and how can I be that person?" In so doing, the high self-monitoring individual reads the character of the situation to identify the type of person called for by that type of situation, constructs a mental image or representation of a person who best exemplifies that type of person, and uses the prototypic person's self-presentation and expressive behavior as a set of guidelines for monitoring his or her own verbal and nonverbal actions. [The low self-monitor asks] "Who am I and how can I be in this situation?" (p. 89)

Thus, the low self-monitor presents a consistent image regardless of the situation, whereas the high self-monitor "reads" the situation and adapts his or her self-image appropriately (Snyder, 1979). In terms of intercultural communication, this awareness and adaptation becomes extremely important. If we cannot "read" the new situation and adapt to it, we will not be effective in our intercultural interactions.

Explaining Behavior

Finally we explain the behavior both we and the other individuals in the situation have engaged in. Theories that deal with the ways people infer the causes of behavior are called *attribution theories*.

Attribution has three general principles (Littlejohn, 1996). First, people attempt to determine the causes of behavior. Second, people assign causes systematically. Third, the attributed cause affects our perception and our behavior. We'll discuss each of these briefly.

Heider (1958) suggests that people try to figure out whether an observed behavior has been caused by personal or situational factors. Whenever we explain someone's behavior in terms of her or his personality, motivation, or personal preferences, we are using personal attributes. When we explain someone's behavior in terms of unusual circumstances, social pressure, or physical forces beyond the person's control, we are using situational attributes.

Kelley (1967) presents covariance theory—another theory that attempts to explain the types of information we use to make our attributions. According to Kelley, we attribute another's behavior to one of four variables:

- The actor (the person who performed the behavior)
- The target (the stimulus object or person the behavior is aimed at)

- The circumstances (the physical setting or social context)
- The relationship (the master contract governing actor and target when they interact)

We make our attributions to one of the above based on three types of information:

Consensus—Does the actor typically behave the same way in similar situations? If so, we have information leading to high consensus.

Consistency—Does the actor behave the same way across a wide range of situations? If so, we have information leading to high consistency.

Distinctiveness—Does the actor behave this way only towards the target? If so, we have information leading to high distinctiveness.

Table 5-1 outlines how we use consensus, consistency, and distinctiveness to make our attributions (Trenholm & Jensen, 1993, p. 82).

When we make our attributions, we are prone to several biases. When we explain another's behavior in terms of personality and underestimate the influence of situational factors, we engage in personality error. As Littlejohn (1996) suggests:

One of the most persistent findings in attribution research is the fundamental attribution error. This is the tendency to attribute the cause of events to personal action, the feeling that people are personally to blame for what happens to them. This tendency results from the insensitivity to many circumstantial factors causing events. Many of us tend to overlook causes of behavior that may not be the person's fault. This tendency, however, is reduced in the case of one's own responsibility. In other words, you tend to blame other people for what happens to them, but you blame the situation for what happens to you. If your roommate fails a test, you are apt to claim that he did not study hard enough, but if you fail the test, you will probably say that the test was too hard. (p. 137)

We also might engage in group bias. We tend·to attribute positive behavior by in-group members (our own friends, family, ethnic group) to their personality and their negative behavior to situational variables. In contrast, we tend to attribute positive behavior by out-group members (groups to which we don't belong) to situational variables and negative behavior to personality variables (Jaspers & Hewstone, 1982).

Differences in cultural attributions can create misunderstanding. For example, Yum (1988) contends that silence and the use of indirect forms of communication are used widely in Korean cultures. Hall (1976), Hsu (1981), and

TABLE 5-1   A Model of Attribution Theory Outcomes, Based on the Work of Harold H. Kelley

When	We are most likely to attribute responsibility to
CONSENSUS is low CONSISTENCY is high DISTINCTIVENESS is low	THE ACTOR: The person who performed the behavior
CONSENSUS is high CONSISTENCY is high DISTINCTIVENESS is high	THE TARGET: The person toward whom the behavior is directed
CONSENSUS is high CONSISTENCY is low DISTINCTIVENESS is low	THE SITUATION: The setting or circumstances outside the control of either person
CONSENSUS is low CONSISTENCY is low DISTINCTIVENESS is high	THE RELATIONSHIP: Behavior pattern negotiated implicitly or explicitly by both parties

From: Sarah Trenholm and Arthur Jensen, *Interpersonal Communication*, Second Edition, p. 82. © 1992 by Wadworth Publishing Co., Belmont, CA. Used by permission.

Bond (1994) make similar observations about Chinese culture. If we come from a culture in which those are not used widely, we may attribute the wrong reasons to a behavior.

For example, the Chinese are reluctant to say "no," especially to a foreigner because this might upset harmony. Thus, they are more indirect. When asked a question to which the answer is "no," they might say, "maybe." A Westerner assumes that this "maybe" means that there is a possibility of "yes." When the Westerner finds out the answer is, and always was, "no," she or he may think the Chinese person is a liar, unethical, or even immoral. However, the fact is that the Chinese person's response was entirely appropriate within his or her culture. Another Chinese person would realize that "maybe" is an indirect way of say "no."

A male graduate student from Saudi Arabia who is studying in the United States has a term paper assigned to him by a professor. The student turns in a paper, but the professor makes it "F" and writes "plagiarized" on the front page. Plagiarism is a problem that demands disciplinary action at American universities, but given that the student is from overseas, the professor calls the foreign student adviser on campus rather than the college dean. The professor asks, "Is there something going on here that I don't know about? I don't want to see this student expelled from school." The action of the professor indicates attribution ambiguity concerning the cause of the student's behavior. He doesn't know whether (a) the attribution should be one he might use for an American student, such as "He got caught—he's a cheat," or (b) there is another, as yet unknown, attribution that would make interpretation of the problem less severe. This professor, incidentally, should be applauded for calling the foreign student adviser. Some professors, behaving quite reasonably according to widely accepted norms in academia, would go to the dean, and the student would face a major disciplinary hearing (Cushner & Brislin, 1996, p. 343).

Cushner and Brislin go on to explain:

The good foreign student adviser, however, knows that there are situational factors at work in this plagiarism incident. Many foreign students have grown up in cultures where knowledge is not necessarily always attributed to developers of knowledge. In contrast, Euro-American students are trained to credit the developers of knowledge when discussing their work (e.g., if one is discussing the theory of relativity, one must mention Einstein). Knowledge in many cultures is considered to be open, usable by anyone, without constant reference to the scholars who developed that knowledge. Thus when his foreign student writes a paper without citing his scholarly sources, he is employing a familiar strategy. But writing without citation is considered plagiarism by Euro-American professors. When the situating factors in this case are taken into account, and it is understood that the student is behaving according to his previous training, the attribution is quite different from "he is a cheat." (p. 244)

As indicated earlier, when we make attributions of others, we often do so using trait labels ("He is a cheater"). We are less likely to consider situational factors (factors outside the individual and not a permanent part of the individual's personality).

Triandis, Kurowski, and Gelfand (1994) suggest we use "isomorphic" attributions. These are shared attributions about people or events that take cultural differences into account. How do we do this? Bond (1994) suggests that vivid, personalized incidents overwhelm our attention and, therefore, carry more weight than they should in our final attributions. Cushner and Brislin (1996) provide the following example and solution to the problem Bond cites:

John is searching for housing in the country to which he has been assigned. He buys a guidebook put out by a group of concerned sojourners who want to help newcomers make their way in the host country. The developers of the guide sampled the opinions of 200 sojourners concerning good housing possibilities, and the book specifies several good neighborhoods. John then hap-

pens to name one of these neighborhoods to a person he has recently met and who has been helpful in John's adjustment. The friends say: "I know that area. My wife's cousin lived there and didn't like it. This person found that it had poor bus service and was too far from stores." What does John do?

There is a strong tendency, which all of us have, to place a great deal of weight on personal input. This input is given to John orally, probably with some colorful gestures, in contrast to the dull manner in which information is presented in the guidebook. But examine the situation more closely. The cousin is 1 person, and the guidebook was developed based on a survey of 200 people. So John now has input from 201 people, and the weight of the evidence is still strongly in favor of the neighborhood he was considering. However, the vivid, personalized input is likely to have more impact than simply 1 of 201 pieces of information. This tendency to react to vivid events is especially common among sojourners because they are exposed to many new and exciting events, but what is new and exiting is not necessarily important. Sojourners should keep this point in mind and ask themselves, am I overacting to a vivid incident directed at me, personally? Is there other information I might use before coming to a conclusion? (p. 345)

In addition to personality and group bias error, three other attribution errors are possible: egocentric bias (the tendency to see our own behavior as normal and appropriate [Kelley, 1967]), premature closure (the tendency to stop searching for explanations of behavior once we have a reasonable and relevant explanation [Taylor & Fiske, 1978]), and the principle of negativity (the tendency to overemphasize negative information about others' behavior [Kanhouse & Hanson, 1972]). If we engage in any of these, our intercultural communication will probably not be as effective as it would be if we did not engage in them.

Our own personalities influence our attributions. Gudykunst (1994) suggests two of these personality factors—category width and uncertainty orientation. Remember we said that when we perceive, we place our perceptions into categories. Category width is "the range of instances included in a cognitive category" (Pettigrew, 1982, p. 200).

Detweiler (1975) studied how category width influences the attributions European Americans use about people who are culturally similar and those who are culturally different (a person from Haiti). He found that narrow categorizers:

assume that the effects of behavior of a person from another culture tell all about the person, even though he [or she] in fact knows nothing about the actor's [or actress's] cultural background. He [or she] seems to make strong judgments based on the positivity or negativity of the effects of the behavior as evaluated from his [or her] own cultural viewpoint. Contrarily, when making attributions to a person who is culturally similar, the narrow [categorizer] seems to view the similarity as overshadowing the behavior. Thus, positive effects are seen as intended, and negative effects are confidently seen as unintended. (p. 600)

In contrast, a wide categorizer

seems to assume that he [or she] in fact doesn't know enough to make "usual" attributions. Thus, behaviors with negative effect result in less confident and generally more neutral attributions when judgments are made about a person from a different culture. Conversely, the culturally similar person who causes a negative outcome is rated relatively more negatively with greater confidence by the wide categorized since the behavior from one's own cultural background is meaningful. (p. 600)

Thus wide categorizers are more likely to search for appropriate interpretations of a culturally dissimilar persons' behavior than are narrow categorizers.

Sorrentino and Short (1986) explain the second personality factor that affects our perceptions, uncertainty orientation:

There are many people who simply are not interested in finding out information about themselves or the world, who do not conduct causal searches, who could not care less about comparing themselves with others, and who "don't give a hoot" for resolving discrepancies or inconsistencies about the self. Indeed, such people (we call them certainty oriented) will go out of their way not to perform activities such as these (we call people who do go out of their way to do such things uncertainty oriented). (pp. 379–380)

In general, uncertainty-oriented people evaluate ideas on their own merit and do not necessarily compare them with others, want to understand themselves and their environment, are more likely to question their own behavior and its appropriateness when communicating with strangers, and are likely to try to gather information about strangers so they can communicate more effectively with them. In contrast, certainty-oriented people hold onto traditional beliefs, have a tendency to reject ideas that are different from their own, and do not examine themselves or their behavior.

Making Accurate Attributions

If we want to improve the accuracy of our attributions in order to be more effective intercultural communicators, we can use three techniques: perception checking, active listening, and feedback.

Perception checking helps us make sure that our interpretation of another's behavior is what she or he meant. A perception check consists of stating three things: describing what you have heard and seen, the conclusion you have drawn, and a question that asks the other person whether your perception is accurate. For example, you might say, "I saw you are frowning and your eyes are red. You look like you were crying. Were you?" Note that the perception check has no evaluative element to it. In other words, you aren't saying, "You're always crying." That would be passing judgment and perception checks are void of judgment. One note of caution here. As Gudykunst (1994) suggests, if you are an individualist communicating with a collectivist, it is important to keep in mind that collectivists may not feel comfortable answering direct questions. In that case, you have to ask your perception checking questions indirectly.

A second technique for improving the accuracy of attributions is *active listening*. The underlying assumption of active listening is that listening is not a passive activity. We need to become actively involved in the listening process. We can do this by attending to the other person (leaning forward and facing the speaker, maintaining eye contact, giving the other person our undivided attention) and using perception checking. We also can use paraphrasing to make sure we understand the other person's ideas and perspective. Paraphrasing is restating what the other person says in our own words to make sure we have interpreted the other person's ideas as he or she intended.

Finally, we can seek *feedback* from others and provide feedback on their communication. Feedback is "the response listeners give to others about their behavior . . . Feedback from others enables us to understand how our behavior affects them, and allows us to modify our behavior to achieve our desired goals" (Haslett & Ogilvie, 1988, p. 385). When we give feedback, we need to use "I" statements, which give our thoughts and feelings, and avoid "you" statements, which can only be our perceptions of another's thoughts and feelings. We need also to keep in the "here and now." Bringing up old issues, resentments, or concerns can only "cloud the issue" presently being discussed. In terms of intercultural communication, we need to also consider how feedback is given in the other person's culture. As Gudykunst (1994) suggests:

> To illustrate, assume that I (a European American male) want to present feedback to a Japanese male friend with whom I am communicating in Japan. If I am direct in the feedback that I give my friend, he may perceive my feedback as a threat to his public image (i.e., it may threaten his face). The reason for this is that Japanese try to preserve harmony in relations with friends. To accomplish this, they use an indirect style of communication. If I am direct and he perceives this as a threat, my feedback will be ineffective. To provide culturally sensitive feedback, I have to be indirect in the way I

give it. If we are in the United States speaking English, I can be more direct than if we are in Japan speaking Japanese. (p. 236)

The cultural norms of our roots can cause misunderstandings when we meet people along our routes. Much of this misunderstanding is a result of the attributions we have for another's behavior. As Gudykunst (1994) indicates:

consider how uncertainty is reduced in the United States and Japan. In the European American middle-class subculture, people try to obtain information about others' attitudes, feelings, and beliefs to reduce uncertainty. In Japan, where high-context messages are emphasized, on the other hand, people must know others' status and background in order to reduce uncertainty and know which version of the language to use (there are different ways to speak to people who are "superiors," "equals", and "inferiors"). This leads Japanese to introduce themselves by saying things like "'I belong to Mitsubishi Bank,' and immediately asking . . . "What is your job?", "How old are you?", and "What is the name of your company?"' (Loveday, 1982, pp. 4–5). *These questions are designed to gather the information necessary for a Japanese to communicate with a stranger. They are, however, perceived as "rude" and "nosy" by middle-class European Americans.* (p. 128–129)

STEREOTYPES

Stereotypes influence the way we process information. A stereotype is a generalization about a group of people. When we stereotype we take a category of people and make assertions about the characteristics of all people who belong to that category, such that the differences among the members of the group aren't taken into account. Hamilton, Sherman, and Ruvolo (1992) write that we need to remember that

"stereotypes" are certain generalizations reached by individuals. They derive in large measure from, or are an instance of, the general cognitive process of categorizing. The main function of the process is to simplify or systematize, for purposes of cognitive and behavioral adaptation, the abundance and complexity of the information received from its environment by the human organism. . . . But such stereotypes can become social only when they are shared by large numbers of people within social groups. (pp. 146–147)

Miles Hewstone and Rupert Brown (1986) outline three essential aspects of stereotypes:

1. We categorize others based on easily identifiable characteristics.
2. We assume that certain attributes apply to most or all of the people in the category.
3. We assume that individual members of the category have the attributes associated with the group.

Stereotypes can be individual or social. In other words, we have stereotypes that (Taijfel, 1981, p. 142):

operate as a source of expectancies about what a group as a whole is like (e.g., Hispanics) as well as about what attributes individual group members are likely to posses (e.g., Juan Garcia). Their influence can be pervasive, affecting the perceiver's attention to, encoding of, inferences about, and judgments based on that information. And the resulting interpretations, inferences, and judgments typically are made so as to be consistent with preexistent beliefs that guided them.

Often stereotypes serve as self-fulfilling prophecies—the tendency to see behavior that confirms our expectations, even when the behavior is absent. Hamilton and his colleagues (1992) explain that

perceivers can influence a person with whom they interact by constraining the person's behavior. However, perceivers typically do not recognize this influence or take it into consideration when interpreting the target's behavior. Although a target person's behavior may be affected by perceiver-induced constraints, it is often interpreted by the perceiver as a manifestation of the target's personality. (p. 149)

How do stereotypes affect our intercultural communication? When we stereotype we often make errors in the interpretation of others' behavior. We also make assumptions about how these people will behave and we make judgments about that behavior. Kunta and Sherman-Williams (1993) write:

Consider, for example, the umambiguous act of failing a test. Ethnic stereotypes may lead perceivers to attribute such failure to laziness if the actor is Asian but to low ability if the actor is Black. Thus stereotypes will affect judgments of the targets' ability even if subjects base these judgments only on the act, because the stereotypes will determine the meaning of the act. (p. 97)

If we are to be more effective intercultural communicators, we need to increase the complexity of our stereotypes (i.e., we need to include a large number of traits in the stereotype and differentiate subgroups within the group being stereotyped) and question our unconscious assumption that most, if not all, members of a group fit a single stereotype (Stephan & Rosenfeld, 1982).

In addition, we should cultivate what psychologist Ellen Langer (1989) calls mindfulness—the state of "alert and lively awareness" (p. 140) and avoid mindlessness, a state of reduced attention. Langer outlines three characteristics of mindfulness. The first of these is the creation of new categories. According to Langer, we need to create more, not fewer distinctions (categories). Langer uses the example in the category "cripple." If we treat all people in this category the same, we begin to treat the category in which we place a person (in this case, "cripple") as her or his identity. If, on the other hand, we make more distinctions within this category (create new categories), we stop treating the person as a category. If we see someone with a broken leg, or a broken arm, or on crutches, we do not necessarily treat that person as a "cripple."

In addition to the creation of new categories, Langer suggests that mindfulness involves openness to new information and awareness of more than one perspective. These two characteristics are related to the idea that we need to focus on the process of communication, not the outcome. Langer explains:

> an outcome orientation in social situations can induce mindlessness. If we think we know how to handle a situation, we don't feel a need to pay attention. If we respond to the situation as very familiar (as a result, for example, of over-learning), we notice only minimal cues necessary to carry out the proper scenarios. If, on the other hand, the situation is strange, we might be so preoccupied with the thought of failure ("What if I make a fool of myself?") that we miss nuances of our own and others' behavior. In this sense, we are mindless with respect to the immediate situation, although we may be thinking quite actively about outcome related issues. (p. 34)

Thus, according to Langer, focusing on the process of communication (i.e., how we communicate), forces us to be mindful of our behavior in the situations in which we find ourselves.

Before we leave the discussion of stereotyping, it's important to point out that we all have stereotypes. It is a part of human interaction—a way we categorize data in order to communicate. However, we need to be aware of and move beyond our stereotypes to communicate with each individual as an individual, not as a group member.

It's also important to remember that all cultures stereotype people from other cultures. Below are some examples of how people from other cultures stereotype Americans (Kohls, 1996, pp. 43–45).

1. India:
   Americans seem to be in a perpetual hurry. Just watch the way they walk down the street. They never allow themselves the leisure to enjoy life; there are too many things to do . . .

2. Australia:
   I am impressed by the fact that American teachers never seem to stop going to school themselves.

3. Turkey:
   Once we were out in a rural area in the middle of nowhere and saw an American come to a stop sign. Though he could see in both directions for miles and no traffic was coming, he still stopped!

4. Colombia:
   The tendency in the U.S. to think that life is only work hits you in the face. Work seems to be the one type of motivation . . .

5. Japan:
   Americans seem to feel like they have to say something instead of having silence—even when what they say is so well known that it sounds stupid. They say things that are so obvious. Japanese people realize that we have all observed these things so it is unnecessary to talk about them.

6. Vietnam:
   Americans are handy people. They do almost everything in the house by themselves, from painting walls and doors to putting glass in their windows. Most of them showed me the pretty tables and bookshelves they made by themselves in their spare time.

7. Iran:
   The first time . . . my [American] professor told me, "I don't know the answer, I will have to look it up," I was shocked. I asked myself, "Why is he teaching me?" In my country a professor would give a wrong answer rather than admit ignorance.

8. Japan:
   Unfortunately, I was given a bad impression by some American students who speak of their own country very poorly, especially of its foreign policy. I knew all the foreign policy of America was not good, but I did not want to be told so by a native. I hate people who speak badly of their own land, even if they speak the truth.

9. Colombia:
I was surprised in the United States to find so many young people who were not living with their parents, although they were not yet married. Also, I was surprised to see so many single people of all ages living alone, eating alone, and walking the streets alone. The United States must be the loneliest country in the world.

10. The Netherlands:
Imagine my astonishment when I went to the supermarket and looked at eggs. You know, there are no small eggs in America; they just don't exist. They tend to be jumbo, extra large, large, or medium. It doesn't matter that the medium are little. Small eggs don't exist [in America] because, I guess, they think that might be bad or denigrating.

PREJUDICE, DISCRIMINATION, AND RACISM

Prejudice

Prejudice consists of negative attitudes toward others based on faulty and inflexible stereotypes. It is helpful to break down the term. *Pre* means beforehand; *judice* comes from the same root as judge. Thus, prejudice is a form of prejudgment, or judging based on particular knowledge, without any previous thought or concern (Cushner & Brislin, 1996). Gordon Allport (1954) suggests that prejudiced people (1) ignore evidence that is inconsistent with their biased viewpoint or (2) distort the evidence to fit their prejudice.

Van Dijk (1987) in his analysis of prejudices suggests several characteristics:

1. Prejudices are attitudes—generalized evaluations about a person, object or action that are the result of individual experience, interpersonal communication, or media influence.
2. Prejudices are group-based—developed through communication with in-group members and used to describe out-group members.
3. Prejudices fulfill social functions for in-groups—support the power and dominance of in-group members.
4. Prejudices are negative evaluations—we devalue others for not being like us, for competing for scarce resources, and for threatening the in-group's way of life.
5. Prejudices are based on cognitive models:

When in-group members interpret "ethnic encounters," their goal in doing so is not primarily to establish a truthful and reliable representation of

*"what is really going on." Rather, just as in the interpretation of other en-
counters, people construct a model that is subjectively plausible . . . is
coherent with previous models of ethnic encounters, and is a partial instan-
tiation of general knowledge and attitude schemata.* (p. 235–236)

It is possible that the cognitive model is biased. Table 5-2 outlines the
major types of cognitive bias.

If prejudice is destructive, why do people have prejudices? Brislin (1991)
suggests that prejudice serves several functions, and he outlines four. The
first is utilitarian or adjustment function. We need to adjust to a complex
world. If holding certain prejudices helps us to adjust, we are likely to maintain those prejudices. The second function is the ego-defensive function. Prejudices can protect our self-esteem. If I am unsuccessful, I may be prejudiced
against successful people. In this way, I protect myself by not having to examine the reasons for my lack of success. The third function is a value expressive function. This function serves to protect my self-image. If I believe
my group members have certain qualities that are unique, valuable, or highly
desirable, my prejudicial attitude towards others not in my group is a way to
express the value I feel those qualities have. As Brislin suggests, the value-
expressive function of prejudice can complement the ego-defensive function.
The value-expressive function projects an image to the world; the ego-
defensive function protects that image through attitudes that shift the blame
for difficulties to others. Finally, prejudices can serve a knowledge function.
We may hold certain prejudices because of our proclivity to neatly organize
and categorize the world. In this sense, our prejudices can provide security
and increase predictability.

TABLE 5-2   Major Types of Cognitive Bias

Cognitive Bias	Definition
Negative interpretations	Interpreting everything the out-group does as negative
Discounting	Dismissing information that doesn't fit the preconceived schemata
Fundamental attribution error	Interpreting another's negative behavior as dispositional (personality) rather than situational
Exaggeration	Exaggerating negative character of out-group actions
Polarization	Tendency to perceive minor differences between in-group and out-groups as major

Discrimination

Prejudice often leads to discrimination. While prejudice refers to people's attitudes, discrimination refers to the behaviors exhibited as a result of the prejudice. This discrimination leads to unequal treatment of certain individuals based on their membership in a certain group.

Teun Van Dijk (1987) studied people's everyday conversations as they discussed different racial and cultural groups. Based on these studies, Van Dijk suggests that when people make prejudiced comments, share negative stereotypes about others, and/or tell jokes that belittle and dehumanize others, they establish and legitimize the existence of their prejudices. This laying of "communication groundwork" makes it acceptable for people to perform discriminatory acts.

Racism

Prejudice can lead to discrimination and discrimination often leads to racism. Because we discussed this in the chapter on gender and race, we will not discuss it here. Suffice it to say that racism is distinguished from prejudice and discrimination by oppression and power. Thus, racism is the tendency by groups of institutional and cultural power to use that power to oppress members of groups who do not have access to the same kinds of power. Racism oppresses groups of people and makes it difficult, if not impossible, for their members to have political, economic, and social power.

CONCLUSION

In this chapter we have discussed social cognitions and how they relate to the intercultural communication process—particularly in terms of stereotypes and prejudices. Basic to our discussion has been the process of perception. We would leave this chapter with a quote from Kenneth Burke (1935). As you move along your intercultural routes, remember:

> A way of seeing is also a way of not seeing—a focus on object A involves a neglect of object B. (p. 70)

QUESTIONS

1. We all have prejudices and stereotypes. Think about yours and how they will affect your intercultural communication effectiveness.
2. Describe an incident in which your ethnocentrism caused an intercultural misunderstanding.

3. Are you a high self-monitor of a low self-monitor? How do these two affect intercultural communication?

ACTIVITIES

1. Try perception checking for a week. Report to the class how this technique affected your communication effectiveness.
2. With two to three classmates attend a foreign film or cultural activity. Observe people and events closely. Discuss with one another what you saw and heard. What attributions did you make? What is the effect of these attributions?
3. Try to be mindful during the next week. Discuss with a classmate or small group the effect of this mindfulness.

REFERENCES

Allport, G. (1954). *The nature of prejudice.* New York: Macmillan.

Bond, M.H. (1994). Continuing encounters with Hong Kong. In D. Sloan (Ed.), *Education and values.* New York: Teachers College Press.

Brislin, R. (1991). *Cross-cultural encounters: Face-to-face interaction.* New York: Pergamon.

Burke, K. Permanence and change. *New Republic,* 1935, p. 70.

Carson, R. (1969). *Interaction concepts of personality.* Chicago: Aldin.

Cooper, H., & Tom, D. (1984). Teacher expectation research: A review with implications for classroom instruction. *The Elementary School Journal,* 85, 77–89.

Cooper, P. (1995). *Communication for the classroom teacher* (5th ed.) Boston: Allyn & Bacon.

Crockett, W. (1985). Cognitive complexity and impression formation. In B.A. Mather (Ed.), *Progress in experimental psychology research* (2nd ed.). New York: Academic Press.

Cushner, K., & Brislin, R. (1996). *Intercultural interactions: A practical guide* (2nd ed.). Thousand Oaks, CA: Sage.

Delia, J. (1977). Constructivism and the study of human communication. *Quarterly Journal of Speech,* 63, 68–83.

Delia, J., Clark, R., & Switzer, D. (1979). Cognitive complexity and impression formation in informal social interaction. *Speech Monographs,* 41, 299–308.

Detweiler, R. (1975). On inferring the intentions of a person from another culture. *Journal of Personality,* 43, 591–611.

Detweiler, R. (1978). Culture, category width, and attributions. *Journal of Cross-Cultural Psychology,* 11, 101–124.

Duck, S. (1976). Interpersonal communication in developing acquaintances. In G.R. Miller (Ed.), *Explorations in interpersonal communication* (pp. 127–147). Beverly Hills, CA: Sage.

Ehrenhaus, P. (1983). Culture and the attribution process. In W. Gudykunst (Ed.), *Intercultural communication theory.* Beverly Hills: Sage.

Forgas, J. (1981). Affective and emotional influences on episode representations. In J. Forgas (Ed.), *Social cognition: Perspectives on everyday understanding* (pp. 165–180). London: Academic Press.

Gudykunst, W.B. (1988). Uncertainty and anxiety. In Y. Kim & W. Gudykunst (Eds.), *Theories in intercultural communication.* Newbury Park, CA: Sage.

Gudykunst, W.B. (1994). *Bridging differences: Effective intergroup communication* (2nd ed.). Thousand Oaks, CA: Sage.

Gudykunst, W.B., & Kim, Y.Y. (1984). *Communicating with strangers: An approach to intercultural communication.* New York: McGraw-Hill.

Gudykunst, W.B., & Kim, Y.Y. (1997). *Communicating with strangers: An approach to intercultural communication* (3rd ed.). New York: McGraw-Hill.

Gudykunst, W.B., & Ting-Toomey, S., with Chua, E. (1988). *Culture and interpersonal communication.* Newbury Park, CA: Sage.

Hall, E.T. (1976). *Beyond culture.* New York: Doubleday.

Hamilton, D., Sherman, S., & Ruvolo, C. (1992). Stereotyped based expectancies. In W.B. Gudykunst & Y.Y. Kim (Eds.), *Readings on communicating with strangers.* New York: McGraw-Hill. (Originally published in *Journal of Social Issues*, 1990, 46 [2], 35–60).

Haslett, B., & Ogilvie, J. (1988). Feedback processes in small groups. In R. Cathcart & L. Samovar (Eds.), *Small group communication: A reader* (5th ed.). Dubuque, IA: William C. Brown.

Heider, F. (1958). *The psychology of interpersonal relations.* New York: John Wiley & Sons.

Hewstone, M., & Brown, R. (1986). Contact is not enough. In M. Hewstone & R. Brown (Eds.), *Contact and conflict in intergroup encounters.* Oxford, United Kingdom: Blackwell.

Hsu, F. (1981), *Americans and Chinese* (3rd ed.). Honolulu: University of Hawaii Press.

Jaspers, J., & Hewstone, M. (1982). Cross-cultural interaction, social attribution, and intergroup relations. In S. Bochner (Ed.). *Cultures in contact.* Elmsford, NY: Pergamon Press.

Kanhouse, D., & Hanson, L. (1972). Negativity in evaluations. In E. Jonmes, D. Kanouse, H.H. Kelley, R. Nisbett, S. Valins, & L. Petrullo (Eds.), *Attribution: Perceiving the causes of behavior.* Morristown, NJ: General Learning Press.

Kelley, H.H. (1950). The warm-cold variable in first impressions of persons. *Journal of Personality, 18,* 431–439.

Kelley, H.H. (1967). Attribution theory in social psychology. *Nebraska Symposium on Motivation, 15,* 192–238.

Kohls, L.R. (1996). *Survival kit for overseas living* (3rd ed.). Yarmouth, ME: Intercultural Press.

Kohls, L.R., & Knight, J.M. (1994). *Developing intercultural awareness.* Yarmouth, ME: Intercultural Press.

Kunta, Q., & Sherman-Williams, B. (1993). Stereotypes and the construal of individuating information. *Personality and Social Psychology Bulletin, 19,* 12–17.

Langer, E. (1989). *Mindfulness.* Reading, MA: Addison-Wesley.

Littlejohn, S. (1996). *Theories of human communication* (5th ed.). Belmont, CA: Wadsworth.

Loveday, L. (1982). Communicative interference. *International Review of Applied Linguistics in Language Teaching, 20,* 1–16.

Lukens, J. (1978). Ethnocentric speech. *Ethnic Groups, 2*, 35–53.

Lustig, M., & Koester, J. (1996). *Intercultural competence: Interpersonal communication across cultures.* New York: Harper Collins.

Okabe, R. (1983). Cultural assumptions of east and west: Japan and the United States. In W.B. Gundykunst (Ed.), *Intercultural communication theory.* Beverly Hills, CA: Sage.

Pettigrew, T.F. (1982). Cognitive styles and social behavior. In L. Wheeler (Ed.), *Review of personality and social psychology* (vol. 3). Beverly Hills, CA: Sage.

Rosenthal, R., & Jacobson, L. (1968). *Pygmalion in the classroom.* New York: Holt, Rinehart and Winston.

Singer, M. (1987). *Intercultural communication: A perceptual approach.* Englewood Cliffs, NJ: Prentice Hall.

Snyder, M. (1974). Self-monitoring of expressive behavior. *Journal of Personality and Social Psychology, 30*, 526–537.

Snyder, M. (1979). Self-monitoring processes. In L. Berkowitz (Ed.), *Advances in experimental social psychology, 12* (pp. 86–131). New York: Academic Press.

Sorrentino, R.M., & Short, J.A. (1986). Uncertainty orientation, motivation, and cognition. In E.T. Higgins & L.M. Sorrentino (Eds.), *Handbook of motivation and cognition.* New York: Guilford Press.

Stephan, W.G., & Rosenfield, D. (1982). Racial and ethnic stereotying. In A. Millar (Ed.), *In the eye of the beholder.* New York: Praeger.

Summer, W.G. (1950). *Folkways.* Boston: Ginn.

Taijfel, H. (1978). Social categorization, social identity, and social comparisons. In H. Taijfel (Ed.), *Differentiation between social groups.* London: Academic Press.

Taijfel, H. (1981). Social stereotypes and social groups. In J. Turner & H. Giles (Eds.), *Intergroup behavior.* Chicago: University of Chicago Press.

Taylor, S., & Fiske, S. (1978). Salience, attention, and attribution. In L. Berkowitz (Ed.), *Advances in experimental social psychology* (Vol. 11). New York: Academic Press.

Ting-Toomey, S. (1988). A face negotiation theory. In Y. Kim & W. Gudykunst (Eds.), *Theories in intercultural communication.* Newbury Park, CA: Sage.

Trenholm, S., & Jensen, A. (1993). *Interpersonal communication* (2nd ed.). Belmont, CA: Wadsworth.

Trenholm, S., & Jensen, A. (1996). *Interpersonal communication* (3rd ed.). Belmont, CA: Wadsworth.

Triandis, H.C., Kurowski, L., & Gelfand, M. (1994). Workplace diversity. In H. C. Triandis, M. Dunnette, & L. Hough (Eds.), *Handbook of industrial and organizational psychology* (2nd ed., Vol. 4, pp. 769–827). Palo Alto, CA: Consulting Psychologists Press.

Tsujimura, A. (1987). Some characteristics of the Japanese way of communication. In D. Kinkaid (Ed.), *Communication theory from Eastern and Western perspectives.* New York: Academic Press.

Van Dijk, T. (1987). *Communicating racism: Ethnic prejudice in thought and talk.* Newbury Park, CA: Sage.

Yum, J.O. (1988). The impact of Confucianism in interpersonal relationships and communication in East Asia. *Communication Monographs, 55*, 374–388.

Zunin, L. (1972). *Contact: The first four minutes.* Los Angeles: Nash.

6

THE ETHICAL SENSE

Objectives:

After reading this chapter and completing the activities, you should be able to:

1. Explain how an ethical sense influences intercultural interactions.
2. Demonstrate in writing how the six stages of moral reasoning proposed by Kohlberg operate.
3. Explain the difference between shame and guilt cultures.
4. Define the relationship among the various forms of a moral sense.
5. Define individualism and collectivism.

Shanika Jones of Spearsville, Louisiana tells the story of Nikki, a black student who, some years ago, joined the African American Shanu Club at a major American university. Following her initiation into the club, the president of the club appointed Nikki to the Fundraising Committee, which sponsored a community raffle to raise funds for needy children. When the members of the Fundraising Committee met in private to determine the winner of the raffle, the first name to be pulled from the raffle box was that of a white student who was well-known by members of the Fundraising Committee. "Let us draw another name," said one member of the Fundraising Committee, whose suggestion was supported by other members of the Fundraising Committee. Nikki, feeling a deep sense of moral responsibility, responded firmly to the Committee's suggestion. "To draw another name from the raffle box would be wrong. Let us honor our moral contract with the individuals to whom we sold raffle tickets in good faith," Nikki argued.

Our ethical sense helps to explain a great deal about why we behave as we do. Because we are rarely indifferent to our environment, we are called upon to make judgments about what we "ought" to do as opposed to what "we want to do" in specific situations. To understand why we behave as we do, and under what circumstances, it is necessary for us to learn about moral sentiments, the wellsprings of human emotions. Scholars argue that although all people remote in time and space share basic emotions in common, the rules for determining when and where to feel joy, pain, and other emotions are rooted in families and culture (Morris, 1994). In this chapter we consider the fact that there is diversity in conceptions of ethics, although much of what we do can be explained individually. We also examine how once we choose to act a certain way based upon our moral codes, such codes can also lead to love or hate, indifference or antagonism (Wright, 1994).

Two comments are, perhaps, called for at the outset. First, we will use the terms *moral sense* and *ethical sense* interchangeably, because there is not much etymological difference between the two. In philosophical thought, for example, the ancient Greeks used the term *ethical* to refer to a general sense of the good. Scholars and philosophers of the Christian tradition later adopted the term *morality* as a basis for discussion about the right and the good (Larmore, 1996). Second, we trust the reader will not wrongly assume that we are being prescriptive about categories of moral thought and behavior.

EMPATHY AND SYMPATHY

Of all the sentiments that have the potential to alter what we do interculturally, none are more important than empathy and sympathy. Although both sympathy and empathy are crucial in human morality, empathy is the bedrock of intercultural communication. Sympathy "is the human capacity for being affected by the feelings and experiences of others" (Wilson, 1993, p. 30). It is considered to be the bedrock for understanding people whose values may be different from our own. Feeling sorrow for individuals who lose their homes in an earthquake, grieving for children affected by cholera in India, feeling joy over the high school team winning a soccer game, or cheering when the villain in a motion picture is wounded are among the countless ways that we express sympathy. A feeling of pleasure or distress, then, is not limited to those close to us. It extends to strangers, animals, and even fictional characters in our favorite novel.

Adam Smith was one of the first moral philosophers to help us understand the universal dimensions of moral sentiments. According to Smith each human being has "some principles in his nature, which interest him in the fortune of others, and render their happiness necessary to him, though he derives nothing from it except the pleasure of seeing it" (Wilson, 1993, p. 31). For our purposes, the ability to imagine the feelings of others is a key com ponent in intercultural understanding. It is what we mean by empathy. Although sympathy and empathy are closely related, empathy extends beyond the realm of sharing the feelings of another who is in sorrow or trouble. Empathy is more spacious. By spacious we mean that individuals who are empathic "can by the force of imaginative insight" (empathy), understand . . . the values, the ideals, the forms of life of another culture or society, even those remote in time and space" (Berlin, 1991, p. 10).

Let us focus for a moment on what is meant by "imagining the feelings of others." This means that we understand the behavior of others better when we are able to enter their world and "see it" through their eyes. If we accept the proposition that people's "behavior and . . . words can be interpreted as intelligible responses to the natural conditions in which they find themselves and which they seek to understand," we are better equipped to deal with diversity. Of course, attempting to "see through the eyes of others" does not mean that we can duplicate others' actual feelings, but rather that we can suspend judgment and seek to enter their minds and feelings through "imaginative participation," which we will develop more fully later.

For example, upon the sight of a homeless child in Copenhagen, Denmark, we might think, " I can imagine what it would be like for a child to be without food or shelter." We then accompany this mental image with an emotional response in the form of sadness, horror, pain, and similar emotions. Such empathetic reactions follow a "rule of correspondence," meaning that feeling sympathy should invite a response proportionate to the plight of the object of our sympathy. Our observations of a spoiled boy feeling very distraught over losing a penny would not, for example, bring a feeling of sympathy but derision, because his feeling and the content of his situation do not accord. By the same token, a daughter's indifference to the death of her mother would not bring sympathy, but likely disdain. The point we need to remember is that we approve the conduct of others when we feel sympathy and when our feelings correspond to the feelings that we think motivate the object of our sympathy (Wilson, 1993, p. 32).

The origins of sympathy are very complex. Wilson supposes that the sources of sympathy are rooted partially in a sense of kinship that grows out of our natural inclination to be generous towards those with whom we have close ties. These innate inclinations are then helped along by the instructions and actions of primary social role givers such as our parents, teachers, relatives, and neighbors. For example, young children soon learn that they cannot act simply on the basis of what makes them feel good, but that they must be mindful of the feelings of others. This *other-regarding behavior* translates into the notion that our happiness is related to the happiness of others. Later, instructions in the form of stories, fables, proverbs and other *sympathy-giving forms* help a child to master the art of sympathy.

An important point to remember here, however, is that sometimes sympathy for others is limited to one's kin or immediate friendship circles. We learn very early that "likes attract likes," which suggests that in general, we are more prone to "enter" the minds of those whom we are most like. For example, Sunni Muslim women of Hama—a city on the central Syrian plains—are more likely to sympathize with individuals who speak and dress as they do. Underwood and Moore (1982) have found, however, that the more we take on the roles of others, the more likely it is that we can imaginatively enter the feelings and thoughts of others. This information is valuable to intercultural communication because it suggests that those whose roots are not inclined toward sympathy can learn to grasp it through attempting to take on the roles of others.

MORAL REASONING

Kohlberg (1976, 1984) argues that our ability to make moral judgments consists of six stages, which are basic to all cultures. According to Kohlberg, we move through these stages in sequence, although the manner and rate of progression vary across cultures. We will consider each stage of moral reasoning in turn.

Stage one: Obedience and punishment orientation. This stage involves avoiding breaking rules, obeying them for the sake of obeying them, and avoiding physical harm to persons and property. For example, a child realizes, "If I steal cookies from the cookie jar, I will be punished."

Stage two: Instrumental purpose and exchange. During this stage we learn when it is in our interest and the interest of others to abide by specific rules. We follow these rules using an "only then and when" orientation: "If I refrain from stealing cookies from the cookie jar, then will I get a brand new bag for school."

Stage three: Interpersonal accord and conformity. Here we learn that "being good is important," so we live up to the expectations of others: "When I refrain from stealing cookies from the cookie jar, I am being virtuous and I also make my mother and others very happy."

Stage four: Social accord and system maintenance. During this stage, we move to fulfilling the actual duties obligated by laws and that our social contract with others obligate, except in extreme cases where these duties conflict with other important values. We learn as well that we are contributing to a social group, or social organization: "Refraining from stealing promotes the common welfare and establishes a system of trust among people."

Stage five: Social contract, utility, and individual rights. According to Kohlberg, by the time we arrive at stage five we are aware of the fact that people hold a variety of beliefs and opinions, and that although most values are relative to our group, they should usually be upheld because they are part of the social contract. We also learn that some values should be upheld in any society regardless of majority opinion. Refraining from stealing is normally such an overarching value.

Stage six: Universal ethical principles. Following ethical principles, we reason that there are certain universal principles, such as justice, the equality of human rights, and respect for the dignity of human beings. We uphold these principles because of our personal sense of commitment to these values.

The important contribution of Kohlberg's research is that it is universally based. For example, Kohlberg and his colleagues studied children in the United States and other countries, including India, Turkey, and Israel. Using a research strategy that elicited responses to hypothetical situations that pose issues of moral choice, Kohlberg concluded that "Major aspects of moral development are culturally universal because all cultures have common sources of social interaction, role-taking, and social conflict which require moral integration" (1984, p. 196). Kohlberg's findings are also significant to intercultural understanding because they reveal much about the human capacity to participate in rule-governed, organized social activities that sustain much harmonious and cooperative social behavior around the globe. As Kohlberg notes, the desire to be known as "good" and "nice" is universal because all socially adjusted people want others to see them as someone with the potential for a "profitable" and "decent" relationship. This point of view is indeed attractive; it is the foundation of much confidence we have in interacting well with others.

Fairness

When we interact with others, we try to determine whether we are being treated fairly by them. Because various ways of defining fairness exist, we can expect cultural differences in these conceptions. In some sense, all people for whom there is necessary information in an exchange have methods for judging notions of fairness in these exchanges, which comes down to the idea that "I helped you, so you ought to help me" (Wilson, 1993, p. 60). The sociological term for this in fair exchange is the *norm of reciprocity*. Its principal role is to teach cooperation, on which much of human behavior relies. The norm of reciprocity is crucial to intercultural behavior, because once a favor is extended, return of the favor or the failure to return it can determine the nature and quality of subsequent interactions with others. The key to reciprocity is trying to strike a balance between expectation and behavior, which can be difficult to reconcile in intercultural communication.

Reciprocity, however, can be interpreted entirely differently, depending upon how it is rooted in a particular culture. For example, in Nigeria, the Igbo are expected to uphold the principle of *direct reciprocity*. This concept is illustrated by a song they have that states, "The drinker of other people's liquor, when shall we drink your own liquor" (Uchendu, 1965, p. 71). Similarly, any guests who receive free lodging and food are expected to provide *indirect reciprocity* some time in the future to another traveler in a situation similar to theirs.

We should not, of course, expect all parties to reciprocity to see the worth of exchange in the same way. For example, Charles Darwin, in exchanging goods with the Fuegian Indians, wrote of "both parties laughing, wondering, gaping at each other; we pitying them, for giving us good fish and crabs for rags, etc.; they grasping at the chance of finding people so foolish as to exchange such splendid ornaments for a good supper" (Wright, 1994, p. 194).

It is also important to remember that rules governing reciprocity may not be abstract in some countries as they are in North America, where there is a high value placed on abstract principles such as truth and justice even when these principles are stripped of their context. For example, in North America one can enforce principles such as truth and justice largely removed from the concrete situation in which they occur. In fact, according to Goodell (Wilson, 1993), Western notions of justice are found to be "excessively legalistic, depersonalized, and devoid of a vitally important sense of context" in countries such as Korea and Singapore (p. 72).

While these rules do vary interculturally, it is comforting to know that humans of all cultures can at least start out with the same sentiments necessary to building common ground and empathy, which are essential ingredients for *other-regarding behavior*. To say through words and deeds, "I see you and I take you and your ethical codes seriously," is to provide a means for promoting ties of kinship and communication.

Shame and Guilt

Some cultures are referred to as guilt cultures while others are considered to be shame cultures. A guideline that helps to determine whether our roots are in a shame culture or a guilt culture is the degree of obligation to others that we feel when things go wrong. Because shame can be unbearable in most Asian cultures, people are careful to meet obligations and to be considerate of others. For example, because Koreans value their elders, the worst thing that could happen would be for them to bring shame on their family. The fear of shaming one's family and friends helps to explain Asians' and others' attachment to kin.

Nicholas Kristof (1997, p. E3) argues that the Japanese instill notions of propriety through "a culture of shame." He notes, for example, that because Japanese belong to a culture that values shame, parents cannot wear "an old T-shirt when taking their kids to school." People who live in guilt cultures do not have such "rigorous notions of propriety," and therefore are less likely to feel the same social pressure regarding the wearing of an old T-shirt! There is a lesson here: Our cultural roots influence the direction and character of our behavior.

Self-Control and Etiquette

Ethical sense is also related to etiquette and self-control. As young children, we tend to express our inner feelings freely. However, once we become young adults we quickly learn that our culture has rules about civility to which we must adhere. These rules for curbing self-indulgence (Wilson, 1993, p.80) are referred to as *etiquette* or *politeness.*

Margaret Visser's (1991) vision of etiquette pervades everyday life: "Politeness forces us to pause, to take extra time, to behave in pre-set, pre-structured ways, to 'fall in' with society's expectations" (p. 40). Every culture has developed manners to assist its members in controlling not only what they are supposed to say and do, but when and how they speak and act. For example, even though it might be awfully tempting after a tantalizing meal of roast suckling pig to pick one's teeth at the table, in North American culture it would be the height of poor taste and bad manners to do so. We use some of our harshest language to judge those who fail to abide by the rules of etiquette. Observing rules of etiquette is important because through them we help to persuade others that we are decent individuals who act appropriately. Because the precise content of these deeply rooted rules of behavior differ interculturally, we should learn a culture's rules so that we can better manage our intercultural relationships in that culture.

For example, an East Indian from childhood knows at least 24 castes or levels of being and worth in their culture. They also know what the correct hierarchical pattern is for each caste, as well as how to relate to members of other castes. Food rituals provide an example of such etiquette, because East Indians must know who can eat from the hand of whom (Visser, 1991). In Japan there are exacting rules governing courtesy. For instance, younger people bow first and bow deeper than their elders; women defer to men in polite situations; business cards are accepted with both hands while bowing; and a slight bow is used in everyday encounters. Another example of etiquette centered around food is that African children must eat dinner after the adults have been served. Rules of etiquette and self-control abound throughout cultures.

Honesty, Honor, and Duty

Honesty is a perception of the confidence we place in individuals' promises. The general rule across cultures is there should be consistency between what an individual promises and what he or she delivers. For example, Wilson notes that many businesspeople prefer Mormons as employees because they are considered to be more honest than non-Mormons (1993). Perceptions of honesty vary across cultures and can interact with other communication factors. In Mexico, for instance, such heavy reliance is placed on interpersonal relationships that these relationships are valued over North American conceptions of honesty. Mexicans are inclined to "tell people what they want to hear" in order to preserve interpersonal relationships, but some visitors to Mexico perceive this custom as "stretching the facts." Klopf (1991) distinguishes between two views of Mexican reality: an *objective reality* and an *interpersonal reality*. In the United States, we are inclined instead to view interpersonal communication in terms of objective reality, embracing George Washington's principle, "I cannot tell a lie."

Honor is another factor that regulates interpersonal interactions. Honor relates to one's character and reputation, and some cultures go to great extremes to preserve these attributes. In North America, for example, in the culture of the early South preserving one's honor was considered more important than preserving the United States Constitution. In Middle Eastern countries, as Thomas L. Friedman (1989, p. 87) notes, "tribe-like" honor and "intense primordial or kin-groups" create loyalties and govern people's attitudes. "Defending one's honor" helps to explain why some cultures "go all the way in exacting a price from those who dared to tread on them" (p. 88). Similarly, in Scotland, there is a motto above the thistle that says: "Nobody hurts me unharmed" (Friedman, 1989, p. 88).

Deeply rooted values of honor are often linked to how we behave toward others. Whenever we find cultural groups with a keen sense of fundamental identity, difficulties can arise.

By *duty* we mean the ability of people to act on the virtues of fidelity and obligation. Thus far, researchers have found these traits common to all cultures. Another way of looking at these twin characteristics, duty and honor, is to note that both are expected to govern our behavior in the "absence of coercion" (Wilson, 1993, p. 115). A sense of duty carries with it a strong conscience, by which we mean a keen ability to "internalize anxieties" (p. 107). Our eagerness to "earn praise and avoid blame" helps to shape our human conscience, which in turn leads to dutiful behavior.

In most cultures, great honor is bestowed upon those who exhibit a strong sense of duty. Honor and duty are vital to a culture's way of living because they act as internal guides, providing ways for individuals to behave. In a sense, were the virtues of duty and honor absent from cultures, there would be no way to pass on values from one generation to the next. This helps to explain why cultures have some public way of acknowledging those who go "beyond the call of duty," to use a North American expression. Duty becomes part of the glue that causes the mores and folkways of cultures to remain intact. In fact, wars have been fought between clashing cultures because of each culture's extreme sense of duty. For example, Friedman (1989) notes that "a spirit of solidarity, a total obligation" to others, helps to explain battles that have been fought in the Middle East among rival ethnic groups (p. 87).

ETHICAL SENTIMENTS: PATHS TO INTERCULTURAL BEHAVIOR

Individualism

To understand the impact of ethical sentiments on interpersonal interactions, we should recognize that individualism lies at the core of some cultures. By individualism, we mean a person's belief in "the dignity" and "sacredness of the individual" over the community (Bellah, Madsen, Sullivan, Swidler, & Tipton, 1985, p. 142). Cultures that stress individualism tend to emphasize the ability to think, judge, and speak for oneself; to make one's own decisions and live pretty much autonomously. These traits are so ingrained in the average North American and in some Westerners that to violate them would be a serious breach of moral etiquette. Thus, some of the deepest conflicts that occur among groups interculturally can be traced to a belief in individualism that conflicts with a belief in community. The United States, Australia, Great Britain, Canada, and the Netherlands are examples of cultures that value individualism. Along with individualism come certain communication traits, such as directness, objectivity, and a drive to complete projects. One must be careful, however, not to assume that everyone from these Western cultures will and must exhibit such characteristics.

Aspects of individualism are deeply rooted in the history, literature, and fables of North American culture. For example, individualism is embedded in the image of the lonely cowboy who roamed the Great Plains and in the myth of the self-made man as revealed in the life of Abraham Lincoln. So the idea of placing the efforts of a group above those of an individual is not an easy concept for most North Americans to grasp. Knowing this, as Hofstede (1980) points out, we can expect persons who subscribe to individualism to be more expressive and assertive and to advance themselves and disclose more about themselves than individuals who come from collectivistic cultures.

Our point is that an individualistic orientation governs North Americans' expectations of others and, by extension, influences their communication style. Thus, a person from an individualistic culture might be perceived to be more honest by members of his or her culture. The crucial thing to remember, however, is that our ethical judgments guide our interactions with others.

Collectivism

People who believe in collectivism make greater distinctions between in-groups and out-groups, and their concept of the "other" is stronger and more diverse than that of the individualist. These persons place great value on community, groupness, harmony, and maintaining face. Colombia, Venezuela, Pakistan, Peru, Chile, and Hong Kong are examples of collectivistic cultures. In these cultures, individuals expect loyalty to be given in exchange for commitment to group norms (Hofstede, 1980).

These moral moorings influence the nature and kind of communication that emanates from members of collectivistic societies. As Cohen (1991) observes, communally oriented people are most concerned about how they will be perceived by others. Group disapproval and loss of face must be avoided. It should be noted as well that members of such societies place a great deal of value on interpersonal relations. Oliver (1962) points out that one of the defining differences between Western religions and the Confucianism that rules much of the Far East is the latter's emphasis on social relations. For example, Confucianism prescribes five hierarchical groups for members of its societies; each group must adhere to precise modes of behaving. According to these forms of human relations, "younger children owe affectionate obedience to their elder brothers, all the children to their parents, the wife to her husband, neighbors to neighbors, and citizens to the King" (Oliver, 1962, p. 106). This five-fold code is based on subordination, creating a hierarchical mechanism through which orderliness and responsibilities can be enforced.

Similarly, Poranee Natadecha-Sponsel (1993) notes that in Thailand, "Family relations provide one of the most important contexts for being a morally good person, which is traditionally the principal concern in the Buddhist society" (p. 51). The lesson here is that one would expect unequal relationships to obtain between parent and child, worker and boss, and teacher and student.

One of the authors experienced first-hand the difference in the teacher-student relationship in an exchange with a Korean woman enrolled in her cross-cultural communication class at an American university. As the two were leaving the classroom during one of those precious moments when the interaction between teacher and student is at its height, the author noticed that the student was walking a few paces behind. Acknowledging the fact and wishing to find out the reason, the author remarked, "Am I walking too fast?" The student replied, "No, in my country students are expected to walk behind the teacher." At that point the author knew that it was time for a lesson on appropriate ways for Korean students studying in America to behave toward North American professors!

COLLECTIVE MORALITY: SOME EFFECTS ON HUMAN BEHAVIOR

Rules against eating certain foods further demonstrate the hold that moral edicts have on collectivistic individuals. Marvin Harris (1985) notes that around the globe people in need of vitamins, proteins, and minerals that meats provide refuse to eat certain kinds of animal flesh because of their moral and religious beliefs. In India, for example, some Hindus, in keeping with their most sacred beliefs, choose to deny themselves certain kinds of food rather than violate their religious and moral principles.

The moral norms seem obviously correct to the members of that group. In order to remain a member in good standing with the community, one must act appropriately and hold to these norms.

Wilson (1993) points out, significantly, that the power of moral laws is that one will obey them even in the absence of a parent or any other specific lawgiver. If, for example, Jewish Americans have been taught not to eat certain foods, they will sometimes not eat them regardless of whether there is anyone around to administer punishment. The point of these stories is to demonstrate the tyrannical hold that the ethical sense has on human behavior. In subsequent chapters, we will talk a great deal about how we can interpret aspects of behavior in order to promote competent communication with others.

CONCLUSION

In this chapter we have discussed aspects of the moral sensibilities that shape human realities and experiences. Sympathy, fairness, honor, honesty, duty, shame and guilt, self-control, and etiquette provide the rules of conduct that help us to determine how we should act in specific intercultural situations.

To be an effective and competent intercultural communicator includes acting appropriately on ethical beliefs, attitudes, and prescriptions. These orientations, in turn, give us the capacity to exercise self-control, experience empathy, feel appropriate guilt or shame, and follow an assigned course of

conduct. The ability to communicate competently will also be determined b
our conception of the importance of moral reasoning.

QUESTIONS

1. Why is the concept of empathy important to our understanding of inte
   cultural communication?
2. How do scholars account for the development of an ethical sense? 1
   what extent does knowledge of a universal moral sense foster better i
   tercultural relationships?
3. Why are some cultures considered to be shame cultures and others gu
   cultures?
4. If you were required to defend or destroy the following thesis, which p
   sition would you take and why? Thesis: "Our deepest moral sentimen
   are the products of the culture in which we have been raised and a
   therefore relative."

ACTIVITIES

1. Observe a rite of passage that occurs in your culture. This may be a cl
   initiation, graduation, an academic honors ceremony, a wedding, or
   promotion. Assume that this rite of passage reflects important moral v.
   ues. Then make a list of the values that that rite of passage reflects. Y
   might also explain how the rite of passage helps to maintain the soc
   order.
2. Collect at least three stories from a culture different from your own. Bre
   them down into categories based upon themes such as *duty and hon*
   fairness, and *self-control.* Next, examine how the authors of the stories tl
   you selected developed their arguments. Were examples used? Stat
   tics? What do the forms of argument reveal about the culture that y
   chose?
3. Interview a student, doctor, teacher, policeman, judge, or religious lead
   Ask the person the following questions:
   a. How do questions of morality influence the decisions that you ma
      daily?
   b. Can you think of an instance in which your own sense of morality d
      fered from the moral principles of a person from another culture?
      yes, how did you manage the moral difficulty? What was the natu
      of that difficulty?
   c. What is new or different about issues of morality in the 1990s as c
      posed to the 1980s?

REFERENCES

Bellah, R., Madsen, R., Sullivan, W.M., Swidler, A. & Tipton, S.M. (1985). *Habits of the heart: Individualism and commitment in American life.* New York: Harper & Row.

Berlin, I. (1991). *The crooked timber of humanity: Chapters in the history of ideas.* New York: Knopf.

Cohen, R. (1991). *Negotiating across cultures: Communication obstacles in international diplomacy.* Washington DC: Institute of Peace.

Friedman, T. (1989). *From Beirut to Jerusalem.* New York: Farrar Straus Giroux.

Harris, M. (1985). *Good to eat: Riddles of food and culture.* New York: Simon and Schuster.

Hofstede, G. (1980). *Culture's consequences.* Newbury Park, CA: Sage.

Kristof, N. (1997, August 31). Introducing a child to the culture of shame. *The New York Times,* p. E3.

Klopf, D. (1991). *Intercultural encounters.* Englewood CO: Morton.

Kohlberg, L. (1976). Moral stages and moralization. In T. Lickona (Ed.), *Moral development and behavior: Theory research and social issues* (pp. 31–53). New York: Holt, Rinehart and Winston.

Kohlberg, L. (1984). *Essays on moral development: Vol 2. The psychology of moral development.* San Francisco: Harper & Row.

Larmore, C. (1996) *The morals of modernity.* New York: Cambridge University Press.

Morris, D. (1994). *The human animal: A personal view of the human species.* New York: Crown.

Natadecha-Sponsel, P. (1993). The young, the rich, and the famous: Individualism as an American cultural value. In P. DeVita & J. D. Armstrong (Eds.), *America as a foreign culture* (pp. 46–53). Belmont, CA: Wadsworth.

Oliver, R. (1962). *Culture and communication.* Springfield, IL: Charles C. Thomas.

Snarey, J. R. (1985). Cross-cultural universality of social-moral development: A critical review of Kohlbergian research. *Psychological Bulletin, 97,* 202–232.

Uchendu, V. (1965). *The Igbo of Southeast Nigeria.* New York: Holt, Rinehart and Winston.

Underwood, B., & Moore, B. (1982). Perspective-taking and altruism. *Psychological Bulletin* 91: 141–73.

Visser, M. (1991). *The rituals of dinner: The origins, evolution, eccentricities, and meaning of table manners.* New York: Grove Weidenfeld.

Wilson, J. (1993). *The moral sense.* New York: The Free Press.

Wright, R. (1994). *The moral animal: The new science of evolutionary psychology.* New York: Pantheon Books.

7

RELIGION AND INTERCULTURAL COMMUNICATION

Objectives

After reading this chapter and completing the activity, you should be able to:

1. Discuss the role and impact of religion in intercultural communication contexts.
2. Discuss religion as a facilitator of intercultural communication situations.
3. Explain how some groups use religion negatively in their communication with other cultures.
4. Explain how religion performs a galvanizing role in intercultural encounters.
5. Discuss pacifism and intercultural communication.

Religion is defined as "a set of beliefs concerning the cause, nature and purpose of the universe, [especially] when considered as the creation of a superhuman agency or agencies, usually involving devotional and ritual observances, and often containing a moral code governing the conduct of human affairs" (*Random House Dictionary*, 1993, p. 1628). The dictionary goes on further to define religion as "a specific fundamental set of beliefs and practices generally agreed upon by a number of persons or sects." The dictionary definition is neutral and allows us to encapsulate the wide spectrum that "religion" as a human and yet private phenomenon occupies. We are also informed that religion is "something a person believes in and follows devoutly." All societies manifest some form of religion, and in numerous instances *religions*. Religion is a human phenomenon that plays a significant role in setting up belief systems usually regarding the supernatural and on issues pertaining to life after death. Furthermore, religion forms the core element in value systems that dictate ethical behavior and also sets the standards of judgment for good and bad acts and moral and immoral relationships between and among people.

In this chapter, we will examine several contexts within which religions and religious beliefs play a central role in intercultural communication in the United States and a few countries in the rest of the world. We will look at two major dimensions: the negative aspects of religion as a factor in intercultural communication, and religion as galvanizer in the promotion of intercultural communication and understanding. The specific details on the practices, dogmas, and rituals of the various religious faiths are not treated in this chapter.

It is tempting to make broad generalizations on the essential tenets of the multifarious religions that exist. The problem, however, is linking unilaterally the tenets of each faith with the communication/behavioral patterns of individuals. Jain (1991) describes Hinduism, a widely practiced religion in India, as "an amorphous body of beliefs, philosophies, worship practices, and codes of conduct." He also cautions, however, that Hinduism is "hard to define . . . or to say precisely whether it is a religion or not in the usual sense . . . [adherents, however] tend to believe that the highest divine powers complement each other for the well-being of humanity and the world" (p. 78).

Although it is interesting to note such general characteristic features, they may not be confined solely to the faiths to which they are ascribed. They are not necessarily mutually exclusive. The tenets of the "Oriental" faiths are to be found also in several African societies as well. Of more importance is the temptation to assess an individual's action and communication behavior on the basis of his or her religious convictions. Such an assessment is tantamount to stereotyping. The focus on this chapter, therefore, is on religion as a factor and how it functions within intercultural communication contexts.

It is important to grasp the fundamental characteristic feature of religion as defined earlier: It is the source within which individuals who adhere to the precepts of their given religions ground their belief and value systems. Religion becomes for some the ultimate warrant. So strong are religious warrants that societies have mounted large-scale invasions of foreign countries in efforts to impose their religious beliefs upon others they consider "pagans," as in the Christian crusades, or "infidels" as in the Islamic jihads (holy wars).

In addition to the extensive invasions mentioned above, disagreements over the interpretation of the tenets of a given religion have resulted in divisions and schisms, bringing about the formation of different denominations within the same religion. In 1543 Christians had a major rift in the church over the activities of the Pope, which led Martin Luther of Germany to attack, through his Ninety Nine Theses, some of the fundamental assumptions of the papacy. His attack led to the formation of the Protestant denomination that broke away from the Catholic fold and that later on suffered schisms that resulted in the emergence of several Protestant denominations. The Islamic religion also experienced disputes that resulted in the emergence of several Islamic denominations or sects variously referred to as the Sunni, Shiite, Ahmadhia, and other groups all in the name of Islam.

Disputes such as those that have occurred within major religious groups that span the globe have created severe difficulties in intercultural and international communications. The Islamic jihads that contributed to the spread of Islam in Africa, for example, involved the imposition of Islamic belief systems, practices, and rituals on Africans. Christianity also was imposed on several cultures worldwide, with missionaries glorifying Christian belief systems and values and denigrating others. Christianity and Islam sought to uproot the belief systems of their converts as far as the deity and religious rituals were concerned and to replace them with Christian and Islamic beliefs and values.

RELIGIOUS WARRANTS AND INTERCULTURAL COMMUNICATION

In Chapter 3 we examined the concept of cultural warrants and the use of such warrants in intercultural communication. Warrants assist us in rationalizing the claims and data we use on issues over which we argue and debate. Blake (1997) identified several types of warrants that serve as basis for justification of actions of individuals, groups, and even nations, among which are religious warrants. Hence, in our efforts to persuade someone or a group, we rely on the strength of our warrants. In this section, we will discuss religious warrants and how they function in communication contexts, with an emphasis on intercultural communication.

For instance, if we are engaged in a dispute on the issue of abortion, religious warrants appear somehow in the conversation particularly if we are talking with Christians who believe in the Biblical commandment: "Thou shalt not kill." That commandment is among warrants that are used to justify their position against abortion.

Christian pro-life protagonists invoke the above warrant passionately. So attached are they to this religious warrant that no other reasons can convince them to modify their position or change their minds. For example, pro-abortion groups with members who are also Christians argue that reasons other than the religious warrant we cite above—"thou shalt not kill," which also serves as a warrant for them—should be considered in making a decision about abortion. They provide some of the following reasons: abortions that are necessary to protect the health of the mother, particularly in situations where the pregnancy is causing difficulties for both fetus and mother; abortions that are necessary because the mother became pregnant as a result of rape or incest. Some pro-life groups dismiss such reasons, relying mainly on the Biblical warrant that forbids the taking of life. What is important to recognize with the abortion example is that even within the same culture—one guided by the same religious warrants—different groups of people interpret differently the same warrants that are deeply rooted in religion. Such religious debates have deteriorated into violence against group members who fail to share the same meaning and interpretation of a religious warrant, or who attempt to deviate from the strict interpretation of a warrant, or who seek to circumvent it. Examples of such breakdowns in communication can be seen in the fatal attacks against medical personnel and individuals associated with institutions that provide counseling and assistance for would-be abortion patients.

Another area in which disputes arise over the same warrant is doctor-assisted suicide. The most notable figure in the doctor-assisted suicide dispute is Dr. Jack Kervorkian. He dismisses the fundamental religious warrant couched in the commandment mentioned above. He argues consistently during radio and television interviews that religious reasons should not feature in the decision of a person to end his or her own life with the assistance of a doctor. His antagonists, he argues, use the wrong warrants. His antagonists, on the other hand, use religious warrants and positive laws to counter Dr. Kervorkian. The complexities involved in the questioning of warrants used by protagonists and antagonists in the doctor-assisted suicide debate are evident when one recognizes that Dr. Kervorkian won three cases levied against him by the state of Michigan. The prosecution relied on positive law as warrant. The religious warrant could not be used to render a decision on the guilt or innocence of an individual in the courts of law in the United States. Interestingly, in Islamic republics where the Sharia (religious laws) is the law of the land, religious warrants play a key role in supporting arguments in the law courts.

RELIGIOUS WARRANTS IN
PLURALISTIC SETTINGS

In the United States there are numerous religious groups—Christians, Jews and Muslims—numbering in the millions. Besides the different religious groups, the ethnic composition of the country makes it crucial to understand the central locus of religion and religious warrants in a pluralistic setting like the United States. The largest religious denomination in the United States the Catholic Church, yet one cannot conclude that all Catholics adhere to the precepts of the religious warrants articulated by the church. In terms of ethnic affiliation, there are more Catholics in the Latino population than Protestants. But that does not mean that we can make a blanket assumption that all Latinos adhere to all the precepts and warrants espoused by the church. There are differences of opinions ranging from abortion to celibacy of the clergy.

The above examples indicate that even though religious warrants are always to be found in societies that practice such religions, perceptions on the manner in which such warrants are invoked during interpersonal, group, and intercultural communication vary from individual to individual. Individuals who share closely the same orientation towards a given religious warrant form groups reflecting their like-minded attitude to the interpretation and meaning of such warrants. This explains why we have groups such as the pro-life movement that bases its raison d'etre mainly on religious grounds, and the Christian Coalition that bases its raison d'etre *entirely* on the teachings of the Bible—their ultimate warrant.

What we can derive from the discussion above is that religious warrants are grounded in the cultural heritage of a nation and that its strong place in society gives it a powerful role in influencing how individuals and groups in diverse societies perceive each other and the world at large. Furthermore, when we consider the diverse nature of American society, we should consistently bear in mind the influence of religious beliefs and concomitant warrants in the day to day life of Americans who claim to be followers of one religion or another. In the same vein, Americans who do not profess any religious beliefs should be cognizant of the power and influence of religion on people who may wish to rely on their religious values as they engage in discourse. Diversity in religious values and warrants is not just peculiar to America. Many countries in the world have religiously diverse populations as well.

ETHNICITY AND RELIGION

The combination of ethnicity and religion in intercultural contexts presents an interesting interaction for students of intercultural communication. In this section, we examine the interplay between ethnicity and religion within communication contexts in certain cultural settings and how religion influences behavior patterns of its adherents. African Americans have a distinct religious tradition deeply rooted in the African American past, yielding rituals and practices that are markedly African American. The majority of African Americans in the United States are generally associated with Christianity. African American churches have evolved in such a manner that the black church has influenced communication patterns and styles that mark African

American communication processes including argumentation strategies and ceremonial discourses. African American discourses are laden with Biblical tokens and warrants.

In addition to the characteristic biblical feature of African American discourses, the emergence of the Black Muslims in the 1930s added yet another religious component in the overall context of African American discourse. The Black Muslim religion was founded by an African American by the name of Fard Muhammad (Essien-Udom, 1962). The religion has already gone through a major schism, culminating in the death of Malcolm X, one of its major ministers, and the establishment of the Nation of Islam. African Americans, more so than the rest of the co-cultural groups in the United States, are associated with the Nation of Islam, providing another direct combination between religion and ethnicity.

In terms of the white population and the various ethnic groups contained in it, there are clear manifestations also of the combination of ethnicity and religion. The Irish are strongly associated with Catholicism. The white Anglo-Saxon Protestants carry a badge manifesting clearly the combination of ethnicity and religion—Anglo-Saxon and Protestant. Serbians are by and large associated with the Orthodox Church, as are the Greeks. Italians are generally recognized as Catholics.

RACE AND RELIGION

When we regard the importance attached to the combination of race and religion on the one hand and ethnicity and religion on the other, the impact on interracial and interethnic communication is obvious. Through religious teachings and warrants, the perceptions of "others" by believers become tainted. Black Muslims, for example, are taught through the precepts articulated by Elijah Muhammad that the white race is "the devil." It is a message with a powerful warrant that serves to justify acts of resistance. In terms of intercultural communication, it sets the stage for negative intercultural encounters, because the interaction is guided by race factors that are negatively portrayed. One does not normally do business with the "devil." In fact the "devil" is usually abhorred. It represents, therefore, a powerful warrant used by some followers of the Black Muslim faith. In this regard, religious warrants couched in the teachings of several faiths serve, on occasions, to foster strained interracial and interethnic communication. This is among the more negative aspects of religion as a factor in intercultural communication. Conflicting religious warrants augment the possibility for a breakdown of communication within a pluralistic setting.

In concluding this section, we must stress that ethnicity, race, and religion by themselves are strong factors in dealing with human behavior. The issue of which one is more important than the other does not negate their impact on intercultural communication. Essentially, therefore, in intercultural communication settings, we should be as cognizant of the impact of religion as we are of ethnicity. Caution has to be exercised, however, in arriving at judgments on an individual or group *solely* on the basis of their religious affiliation. That would be tantamount to stereotyping, which, when improperly used, represents a major stumbling block in intercultural communication (Barna, 1997). Recognizing the factors, and understanding their impact, could facilitate intercultural encounters and help reduce significantly the potential for breakdown in communication interactions.

CIVIL RELIGION

A final dimension of religion and culture as they pertain to intercultural communication within the diversity context is the manner in which the United States has successfully managed the evolution of "civil religion." Schaefer (1984), in addressing the issue of civil religion, reviewed research carried out between 1967 and 1976 (Bellah, 1967, 1970; Marty, 1976, cited in Shaefer, 1984), pointing out that civil religion "refers to that religious dimension in American life that merges the state with religious belief" (p. 157). He goes on to state that "civil religion exists along side established religious faiths and embodies a belief system incorporating all religions but not associated with any single one. It is the type of faith that presidents refer to in inaugural speeches . . ." (p. 158). Civil religion in this sense commits the state to recognize the "sanctity" espoused by various religions without preferential treatment to any, which would contradict the fundamental separation of state and religion. In so doing, civil religion recognizes also the locus of religious warrants regardless of faith or denomination, without compromising the first amendment of the Constitution. The implication for intercultural communication is simple: "Religion" in some form or another is a fundamental element in the belief systems of all cultures, hence having an impact in communication interactions. Its presence and influence add to the complex process of intercultural communication.

RELIGION AND COMMUNICATION IN A PLURALISTIC CONTEXT

The 1944 Democratic convention was a major event in the history of race, religion, and intercultural communication in the United States. The Democratic Party platform sought to promote religious tolerance and racial equality. The platform revealed a basic anomaly: calling for and promoting religious tolerance in a country that has a constitution that guarantees freedom of association and worship. It did not only highlight the apparent conflict and prejudice within the Christian faith and its denominations, it also alluded to interreligious concerns that were at the heart of the right of all Americans to be part and parcel of the political process. Jews were largely underrepresented in major political offices. African Americans did not even figure in the equation of power politics. A Catholic had never been elected president. It was only in 1960, sixteen years after the Democratic Party's platform that addressed the issue of race and religion in American politics, that a Catholic was elected president. Religion and politics, therefore, remain critical factors in influencing political behavior in the United States.

In addition to the political environment, the negative aspects of religion in facilitating communication are discernible in the confrontation between the government and certain cults. Perhaps the most memorable event in the history of religion and the breakdown of communication in the United States is the attack on David Koresh and his "religious" community in 1992, leading to the death of Koresh and several of his followers. Koresh, through his cult, was creating a counterculture based on his fundamentalist interpretation of the Bible. Concerned about the protection of his cult, he amassed weapons in large quantities. He had an arsenal of significant strength. Witkin (1994) reported that the Ranch Apocalypse's arsenal was comprised of "59 handguns, 12 shotguns, 94 rifles and 45 machine guns; 1.8 million rounds of ammunition, more than a dozen silencers, a variety of hand grenade parts and a hefty supply of other weapons components" (p. 42). Other categories of weapons were reported by Witkin in the same article.

Koresh and the Branch Davidians represented the difficulties involved in achieving effective intercultural communication: (1) the background of strong cultist/religious convictions, and (2) the existence of a deadly arsenal. The situation became disastrous when conflicts arose between the cult and the government and communication broke down. Koresh stood firm by grounding his position on the Bible. Negotiations required both parties to attempt to understand why each adopted the stances they took. Negotiations collapsed and Koresh and the authorities clashed, resulting in a fire that killed him and several of his followers.

In another incident prior to the Koresh debacle, Jim Jones and his Peoples' Temple in Georgetown, Barbados, had a confrontation with the authorities. Jones opted for mass suicide, resulting in the death of 913 followers including himself (Harrary, 1994). Excessive identification with the cult's worldview and religious tenets in both cases, as well as the strategies utilized by the authorities, created an intractable situation leading to the death of hundreds of followers.

Harper and LeBeau (1994) provide an illuminating discussion on "marginal religious movements" and social adaptation. They point out that "while social adaptation can be understood as a structural relationship between a movement [cult] and its social environment at a given time, across time *social adaptation is an emergent and dynamic social interaction process"* (p. 117). It is precisely because of the importance attached to "process" that people with interest in intercultural communication must be sensitive to the influence religion has on groups of people at a given time, and across time. People in the cults mentioned above preferred to die for their religion than face what they perceived to be a "defeat," as was evident in the cases of Koresh's Branch Davidians and Jim Jones' Peoples Temple incidents.

CHRISTIANITY AND ISLAM: INTERNATIONAL DIMENSIONS

In this section we examine the central role of religion within an international context. When groups from different countries meet and communicate, they are guided by their beliefs, values, perceptions, and other cultural factors. We are concerned here with intercultural contacts that are motivated by the spreading of religious beliefs from one region of the world to another. Christianity and Islam, much more so than Judaism or Buddhism, exert their religious beliefs in many parts of the world. The proselytization of Christianity and Islam was not carried out by what we would consider today effective intercultural communication in the twentieth century. The history of missionary work in Africa, for example, is one that attracted attention even during the nineteenth century. Blyden (1980) argued that Christian missionaries abroad carried out their work in such a manner that denigrated African belief and value systems and exalted European (Christian) beliefs and values (see also Calloway-Thomas, 1992).

In order to justify slavery, protagonists used the most significant religious warrant in Christendom—the Bible. Genesis, which, according to the Judeo-Christian heritage, informs us about "the beginning," was used by pro-slavery forces to justify the institution of slavery. The specific section in Genesis (9:27–29) purportedly explains why one of the descendants of Ham, Canaan was relegated to a position of a servant "unto his brethren." Biblical scholars argue over the veracity of the interpretation of the so-called curse on Canaan and the extent to which Europeans could justify slavery of the basis of the account given in Genesis (Wilmore, 1973). The result of the experience of slavery in the United States continues to have impact on the perceptions of African Americans and whites about each other that sometimes erupts into ugly racial confrontations.

Religion remains a powerful aspect in the lives of millions of people worldwide. At the international level, co-cultural groups in the same country belonging to the same religion but affiliated with different denominations engage in religious conflicts resulting in death and despair. The spread of Islam also had its toll on those that resisted the jihads that were fought in efforts to conquer and impose Islam on the vanquished. When religion is considered as a significant factor in intercultural communication, it is not to be taken lightly given the history of conflict among races and nations, ethnic conflicts, and the ostracization of groups and individuals who are perceived as "deviants" breaking the laws of religion. As individuals become more informed about the dangers of prejudice based on religious beliefs, the prospects for a better intercultural communication among co-cultural groups will be enhanced.

The lesson to be derived from this section is the following: When it comes to intercultural contacts and communication, it is important to have an understanding of the *historical* relations between groups and how such relations shape perceptions. The more we become aware of historical contexts, the better prepared we are for promoting effective intercultural communication. Furthermore, when we show respect for other cultures, we improve the chances of achieving effective intercultural communication devoid of ugly encounters and coercion. Let us turn our attention now to some other regions in the world whose intercultural conflicts are based on a complex mix of religious and social tensions.

NORTHERN IRELAND

In May 1998 Catholics and Protestants in Northern Ireland and the predominantly Catholic Republic of Ireland voted in favor of a peace accord that will bring about the end of a protracted sectarian war. Even though the vote signals a probable end to the conflict, there are lessons that can be learned from Northern Ireland that are pertinent for our understanding of religion and intercultural communication.

Religion is the most visible element in the crisis in Northern Ireland. The conflict in the region has resulted in the deaths of thousands. It is partly a denominational conflict. Basically, Catholics and Protestants adopt opposing views on the relationship and political ties that should exist between Northern Ireland and the Republic of Ireland on the one hand, and on the other, between Northern Ireland and the United Kingdom. The rift is deep, and the historical and religious dimensions are central. Protestants position themselves as "Unionists" supporting ties with the United Kingdom, and Catholics oppose any such union, preferring ties with Catholic Southern Ireland. The history of the crisis in Northern Ireland is long and could not be treated in a text of this nature. What we intend to present here is an example of how religion and intercultural communication feature in a crisis that has led to the creation of military forces such as the Irish Republican Army, which is the military wing of Sinn Fein, the Catholic political party in Northern Ireland. The Unionists argue strongly against breaking away from Britain because such a breakaway would subsequently result in "Catholic authoritarianism." For many Catholics, continued relationship with any degree of power by the Unionists over Northern Ireland would mean "Catholic enslavement" (Coogan, 1970).

It is important to bear in mind the combination of ethnicity and religion referred to earlier. The crisis in Northern Ireland could easily be misunderstood to be solely one defined by religion. The roots of the crisis lay in the tensions that developed following the settlement of English planters in Ulster, *long before Ireland was converted to Catholicism.* The English in Ulster, mainly Protestant, occupied positions of power because they established plantations and wielded economic power. The indigenous Irish population was seen as "savage," "unclean," "uncivil," and "barbarous." (O'Sullivan See, 1986). Present-day Northern Ireland, therefore, manifests tensions and conflicts that are grounded both in cultural/ethnic and religious differences. The emphasis on the religious aspect of the Northern Ireland crisis overshadows the contribution of ethnic rivalry between settlers and indegenes that have been at play for the past 400 years (O'Sullivan See, 1986).

BOSNIA-HERCEGOVINA

The conflict in Bosnia-Hercegovina, part of former Yugoslavia, is another example of how easy it is to misunderstand conflicts of intercultural relations. At the height of the bloodshed in Sarajevo in 1994, someone at a cafeteria at a university campus in the Midwest got quite annoyed with the reports he was listening to on television. He was a Muslim who had recently migrated to the United States. He exclaimed in disgust: "Those wretched Serbs! They shall never defeat Muslims!" People around the area in which he sat looked at him strangely. Some did not understand, others expressed feelings of anger at the "rude" behavior of the man.

Just listening to the expression by the Muslim man against the background of the image of Muslims in the United States at that time—fundamentalists who carry out terrorists acts against the West—could lead to a simplistic conclusion that the war in Bosnia-Hercegovina could be seen as Muslims versus the Orthodox (Christian) Serbs. Religion indeed is an important factor in the crisis. Ethnicity, however, is as central to the crisis as religion. Bosnia-Hercegovina is one of several entities that constituted the former Yugoslavia. Together with Slovenia, Croatia, Serbia, Montenegro, they constituted what was one nation under one ruler.

Before the fall of the Berlin Wall and the subsequent collapse of Communism in Eastern and Central Europe, the interethnic tensions and disputes did not receive media attention in the way they do today. Yugoslavia was one nation. Today, there are several nations in the "former" country, among which is Bosnia-Hercegovina where 40 percent of the population is Muslim. It is a unique country among the former republics that constituted Yugoslavia because of its ethnic and religious makeup. In addition to the 40 percent Muslim population, there are 33 percent Serbians, 18 percent Croatian, and 9 percent "other" (Bowman, 1994). Serbians, largely Orthodox, occupy a significant percentage of the land.

This dispute provides another example of the powerful combination of religion and ethnicity that has contributed to the misery of thousands in Bosnia with casualties on all sides of the war—Muslims, Serbs, and Croats. The roots of the crisis between the Moslems and Serbs, in particular, date back to the fourteenth century when Serbia was invaded by the Turks. The deep-seated hatred between the two groups, seemingly quelled under Communist rule in former Yugoslavia, became explosive after the fall of Communism.

Politicians exploited religious and ethnic prejudices in efforts to entrench their positions. Bowman observes, for example, that "Milosevic [the president of Serbia] fuelled his ascent to power in Serbia by stirring up popular animosity . . . promulgating the belief that 'Muslims' were, as they had in the fourteenth century, threatening to drive Serbs from their historic homeland of Kosovo" (p. 152). Not just the politicians but the official Serbian press also "began to run stories telling of instances in Kosovo of Albanian 'Muslims' raping Serbian women and desecrating Orthodox monasteries" (p. 153). Such statements fuel religious and ethnic combinations that trigger intercultural conflicts. The manipulation of emotional appeals aimed at existing religious and ethnic passions is clearly discernible in the Bosnian crisis. Such strategies impede effective intercultural communication because they stress prejudices. This results in nondiscursive means of settling disputes rather than *discursive* (discussion and negotiation) means of solving problems between ethnic and/or religious groups.

Some lessons we can learn from the disputes we have examined are that intercultural communication succeeds best when people from different cultural backgrounds are willing to engage in discussion and debate in efforts to solve problems, rather than use coercion and violent strategies (*nondiscursive* means). In addition, in order to discuss well within intercultural contexts that are potentially explosive because of past historical relations, people should try as hard as possible to get rid of their prejudices and stereotypes, find out accurate information about the other group they wish to communicate with, and approach the context with *mutual respect*. Without the above, chances of intercultural communication breakdowns leading to violence are exacerbated. Unfortunately, the examples above point towards the negative role of religion in the disputes mentioned.

But is there a role for "religion" in serving as a facilitator in the promotion of healthy and nonviolent intercultural, interracial, and interethnic communication? The next section provides a brief description of attempts to achieve such a role.

RELIGION AS GALVANIZER

Up to this point in the chapter, we have focused on the negative role of religion in various multicultural communication contexts. This section of the chapter focuses briefly on the views and perceptions on religion and communication as articulated by scholars on Christianity, Islam, and Judaism. The purpose of presenting these perspectives is to point out that religions are based on philosophies and warrants that promote cohesion rather than friction. In order to focus sharply on the issue of religion as galvanizer, the concept of pacifism is used.

Pacifism

Pacifism is defined in Merriam Webster's *Collegiate Dictionary* as "opposition to war or violence as a means of settling disputes, refusal to bear arms on moral or religious grounds. . . ." Our focus here is on "religious" grounds. In the 1960s, Muhammad Ali caused a stir in the nation when he refused to fight for the United States against the Vietnamese on the grounds of his religious beliefs. He had adopted the Black Muslim faith and argued that his faith served as justification for his resistance. He was called unpatriotic, stripped of his title, and his license to box was withdrawn. The Supreme Court eventually vindicated him and restored his license.

The Ali example is introduced to demonstrate that even though we discussed the concept of the jihad in Islam, Muslims such as Ali believed in using peaceful means for settling disputes. Intercultural communication ties in here by advocating communication between the United States and Vietnam with radically different cultures, worldviews, and ideologies.

Religion as a means of promoting social cohesion was also a strong concern of the late Reverend Dr. Martin Luther King, the celebrated civil rights leader and Nobel Laureate. In addition to his strong religious convictions, Martin Luther King was influenced philosophically on the issue of nonviolence by Mahatma Ghandi, usually considered the founding father of the independent nation of India. Ghandi employed nonviolent communication strategies as he successfully led his movement for independence from Britain. Hence with a strong pacifist stance grounded in religion and philosophy, Dr. Martin Luther King believed in the positive and galvanizing role religion could play within the context of a multiracial and multiethnic society. He always maintained that values emanating in religious texts serve as a better means of resolving disputes. If properly adhered to, religious values help promote social cohesion, which subsequently leads to the reduction of racial and ethnic tensions (see also Calloway-Thomas & Lucaites, 1993).

Pacifism in Major Religious Doctrines

Scholars on the three major faiths in the United States—Christianity, Judaism, and Islam—convened in July 1993 to address the issue of perspectives on pacifism from the point of view of each of the religious groups mentioned above. Smock (1995) presented a summary of the perspectives of a diverse group of scholars on religion who agreed on some issues that are central for our understanding of the galvanizing role of religion. He presented the following key points:

• The pacifist tradition is stronger in Christianity than in the other two faiths, but there are Jewish and Muslim pacifists as well. Moreover, even the nonpacifists in the three faiths generally agree that force should be avoided whenever possible. Peace and the resolution of violent conflict are highly valued by all three faiths.

• All three faiths face similar dilemmas with regard to violence, in that they understand God to be asking humanity both to eschew violence and to promote justice, which many believe cannot always be achieved nonviolently.

• Although all three faiths have honored traditions of quietistic withdrawal and even submission under special circumstances, nonviolence should not be equated with passive acquiescence but seen as an active means of legitimate intervention to promote justice and reconciliation.

• Pacifists and those who advocate use of force as a last resort disagreed regarding the legitimacy of violent measure in international peacemaking, but all agreed that more can be done in the following areas:

> Promoting reconciliation and conflict resolution skills
> Using teams of nonviolent peacemakers, either alone or as adjuncts to armed peacekeepers
> Advancing peace in areas of conflict through work with religious bodies and communities (p. viii)

The four major positions and subtopics articulated above represent, in succinct terms, the idea of religion as galvanizer, with pacifism as the primary philosophy. This image of religion is quite opposite to our earlier discussion that demonstrated the use of religion for purposes that promoted prejudice and enforced religious doctrines by use of force as was the case with the Christian Crusades and the Islamic jihads.

Besides the theological perspectives articulated by the three faiths contained in Smock's work, there have been open attempts by the Christian churches in the Southern hemisphere of the world, notably Africa, to use the church as galvanizer on issues of social and national concerns. The churches in Kenya and South Africa rallied support from all concerned to decry the deteriorating conditions of citizens in their countries on the issue of human rights and democracy. Catholic priests, bishops, and archbishops in Latin America and the Philippines are well known for their active work in rallying the poor and disfavored in society to fight for their rights as human beings using nonviolent means. The church becomes the rallying point and the ultimate galvanizer. The galvanizing function in such instances could be understood within the context of the church's role in protecting human rights and rallying support for that cause.

LESSONS DERIVED

So what are the lessons to be learned on the role of religion in intercultural communication? First of all, religion is a factor that cannot be ignored, because it is the source and ultimate warrant for ethical codes on issues surrounding good and evil, morality and immorality, and fundamental human relations. Even though there are several factual events such as the Crusades and the jihads, the essential doctrines of the main religions of the world place emphasis on the importance of values and ethics in human relations.

Second, religion, combined with ethnocentric tendencies, provides a vehicle by which racial and ethnic repression is carried out by dominant groups in society who use religion to justify their actions against other ethnic and racial groups. It is precisely the combination of religion and ethnocentricism that has led to the destruction of several areas in the world—Bosnia, Somalia, Lebanon, Egypt, Philippines, and others.

Third, religion shapes our perception of our place in the community of humankind. Through religion, some groups make distinctions: Jews and gentiles; the faithful and infidels; Christians and pagans/heathens. The dichotomies set the stage for potential interfaith disputes at the national, interpersonal, and group levels. Extreme adherence to such dichotomies produces essential stumbling blocks for intercultural communication and relations. Adherence to the dichotomies results at times in disruptions of marriage plans that involve partners from different faiths.

Fourth, religious warrants sometimes engage our minds to the extent that our judgment is blurred, enhancing further dichotomies that impede crosscultural communication and interactions. Of significance are warrants that tend to provide a feeling of superiority over differing religious warrants. As discussed earlier, warrants justify our claims and postulations about a phenomenon, event, cause, and action. Such a powerful device has a hold on the human psyche from which it is difficult to disengage.

CONCLUSION

Recognizing all of the above and *acting upon them* makes us better communicators within intercultural contexts. Besides questionable actions by cults, organizations like the KKK, whose members pride themselves as being Christians, contribute to the negative image of the faith. The same could be said for extremist Jewish militant organizations and radical Islamic fundamentalists.

To become interculturally competent in understanding the central place of religion in human affairs, one must learn to respect all faiths and try as hard as possible not to allow the dichotomies—Jew/Gentile, faithful/infidel, and Christian/pagan to blur our perceptions and influence our judgment on individuals, groups, and entire nations.

Furthermore, the importance attached to intercultural competency as a needed skill is now clearly manifested through the overt attempt by global bodies such as the World Council of Churches to provide a forum whereby all faiths and denominations could meet to celebrate their similarities and work on their differences. Ecumenism, which is the active promotion of collaboration among faiths to achieve improved communication across faiths and cultures, is a promising strategy that would help relax intercultural, interethnic, interracial, and international tensions that result from the abuse of religion.

QUESTIONS

1. Religion has a firm influence on people who adhere to the precepts of their given faith. Select a major religious conflict and explain the role of religion in escalating tensions between the groups involved in the conflict of your choice.
2. Discuss in detail an example of how religion has been used as justification for prejudice and discrimination in the world. What would you recommend to promote harmony rather than conflict in your example?
3. What do we mean by pacifism? Explain the key perspectives on which Christians, Jews, and Muslims agree in terms of regarding religion as a galvanizer in intercultural communication.

ACTIVITY

Select at least three major religious faiths and form groups of three or more, with each group assigned to a given faith. Each group should develop a profile of their faith and present the strong elements in their faith that could promote effective intercultural communication and those elements that tend to hinder successful intercultural encounters. Spend at least a week researching your given faith. Meet as a group to agree on your profile. Select a presenter to report on your assignment to the class. Each group should use 15 to 20 minutes for a presentation followed by questions. After all presentations have been made, make a list of the composite set of positive and negative elements. Discuss, as a class, ways and means by which negative elements could be reduced in efforts to achieve harmony within intercultural communication contexts.

REFERENCES

Barna, L. (1997). Stumbling blocks in intercultural communication. In L. Samovar & R. Porter, (Eds.), *Intercultural communication: A reader*. Belmont, CA: Wadsworth.

Bedell, K. (1995). *Yearbook of American and Canadian churches*. Nashville, TN: Abington Press.

Bellah, R. (1967). Civil religion in America. *Daedalus* (Winter), 1–21.

Blake, C. (1997, December). *Adopting traditional institutional communication processes in conflict resolution*. Presented at the CODISAL national conference on peace, stability and democratization in Sierra Leone. Bowie State University, Bowie, MD.

Blyden, E. (1980). The Koran in Africa. *The African Repository, LXVL* (4), October, 101–106.

Bowman, G. (1994). Xenophobia, fantasy and the nation: The logic of ethnic violence in former Yugoslavia. In V. Goddard, R. Lobera, & C. Shore (Eds.), *The anthropology of Europe*. Oxford: Berg.

Byrd, M. (1993). *The intracultural communication book*. New York: McGraw-Hill.

Calloway-Thomas, C. (1992). The rhetoric of providence and pan-Africanism: A case study. In M. S. Cummings, L. A. Niles, & O. Taylor (Eds.), *Handbook on communications and development in Africa and the African Diaspora* (pp. 25–33). Needham Heights, MA: Ginn.

Calloway-Thomas, C., & Lucaites, J. L. (Eds.). (1993). *Martin Luther King, Jr. and the sermonic power of public discourse*. Tuscaloosa: The University of Alabama Press.

Cleveland, H. (1995). The limits to cultural diversity. *The Futurist*, March-April, 23–26.

Coogan, T. (1970). *The I.R.A.* New York: Praeger.

Essien-Udom, E. (1962). *Black nationalism in America*. Chicago: The University of Chicago Press.

Jain, N.(1991). World view and cultural patterns of India. In L. Samovar & R. Porter (Eds.), *Intercultural communication: A reader* (6th ed.). Belmont, CA: Wadsworth.

Harper, C., & LeBeau, F. (1994). The social adaptation of marginal religious movements in America. In R. Long (Ed.), *Religious cults in America*. New York: H.W. Wilson.

Harrary, K. (1994). The truth about Jonestown. In R. Long (Ed.), *Religious cults in America*. New York: H. W. Wilson.

Marty, M. (1976). *A nation of believers*. Chicago: University of Chicago Press.

O'Sullivan See, K. (1986). *First world nationalisms: Class and ethnic politics in Northern Ireland and Quebec*. Chicago: The University of Chicago Press.

Random House Dictionary (2nd ed.). New York: Random House, p. 1628.

Schaefer, R. (1984). *Racial and ethnic groups* (2nd ed.). Boston: Little Brown.

8

LANGUAGE AND CULTURAL ROOTS

Objectives

After reading this chapter and completing the activities, you should be able to:

1. Explain the relationship of the triangle of meaning to intercultural communication.
2. Explain the concept of general semantics and its relationship to intercultural communication.
3. Define speech acts and give an example.
4. Using the Sapir-Whorf hypothesis, constructionism, and the Bernstein hypothesis, explain how language relates to culture.
5. Explain how differences in verbal style can lead to misunderstanding.
6. Define linguistic prejudice.

In the book *The Phantom Tollboth* (Juster, 1961) the young hero Milo finds himself in jail in the land of Dictionopolis. While there he meets a witch:

> *"Don't be frightened," she laughed. "I'm a witch."*
> *"Oh," said Milo, because he couldn't think of anything else to say.*
> *"I'm Faintly Macabre, the not-so-wicked Which," she continued,*
> *"and I'm certainly not going to harm you."*
> *"What's a Which?" asked Milo, releasing Tock and stepping a little closer.*
> *"Well," said the old lady, just as a rat scurried across her foot, "I am the king's great aunt. For years and years I was in charge of choosing which words were to be used for all occasions, which ones to say and*

which ones not to say, which ones to write and which ones not to write. As you can well imagine, with all the thousands to choose from, it was a most important and responsible job. I was given the title of 'Offical Which,' which made me very proud and happy.

"At first I did my best to make sure that only the most proper and fitting words were used. Everything was said clearly and simply and no words were wasted. I had signs posted all over the palace and market place which said:

Brevity Is the Soul of Wit.

But power corrupts, and soon I grew miserly and chose fewer and fewer words, trying to keep as many as possible for myself. I had new signs posted which said:

An Ill-Chosen Word Is the Fool's Messenger.

Soon sales began to fall off in the market. The people were afraid to buy as many words as before, and hard times came to the kingdom, but still I grew more and more miserly. Soon there were so few words chosen that hardly anything could be said, and even casual conversation became diffi-cult. Again I had new signs posted, which said:

Speak Fitly or Be Silent Wisely.

And finally I had even these replaced by ones which read simply:

Silence Is Golden.

All talk stopped. No words were sold, the marketplace closed down, and the people grew poor and disconsolate. When the king saw what had hap-pened, he became furious and had me cast into his dungeon where you see me now, an older and wiser woman. That was all many years ago," she continued; "but they never appointed a new Which, and that explains why today people use as many words as they can and think themselves wise for doing so. For always remember that while it is wrong to use too few, it is often far worse to use too many."

When she finished, she sighed deeply, patted Milo gently on the shoul-der, and began knitting once again.

This episode suggests the difficulty of using language effectively. One of the roots of our culture is our language. We learn the syntax, semantics, and pragmatics of our language. As long as we remain in our own culture, our ability to use language to communicate is fairly high. However, when we enter a culture with a language different from our own "roots language," our communication ability lessens. In this chapter we will suggest some reasons why this is so.

WHAT IS LANGUAGE?

Language is a code. In other words, meaning is conveyed symbolically. Symbols are units of meaning that are conventional (based on social agreement) and arbitrary. Words are symbols. As such their meaning is arbitrary and conventional. For example, consider the word "cat." The word is a symbol that refers to or "stands for" the actual furry, four-footed animal we have as a pet. We could have agreed (convention) to call this animal tac or anything else. In other words, the word cat is arbitrary. This symbolic, arbitrary nature of language can be diagrammed as in Figure 8-1.

This is called the triangle of meaning (Ogden & Richards, 1927). The word you speak (cat) is the symbol, the thought is the image in your mind of a cat, and the referent is the actual, live cat. Notice that the line connecting the

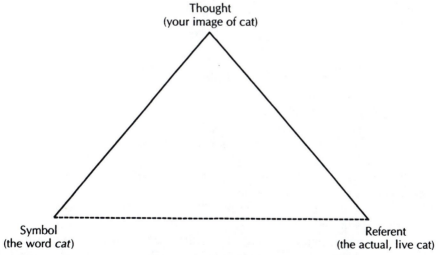

Thought
(your image of cat)

Symbol
(the word *cat*)

Referent
(the actual, live cat)

FIGURE 8-1   Triangle of meaning. (From: C. K. Ogden and I. A. Richards, *The Meaning of Meaning: A Study of the Influence of Language upon Thought and the Science of Symbolism*, 1927, p. 11. New York: Harcourt Brace. Used with permission.)

symbol and the referent is broken. This indicates that the symbol and the referent have no connection except that which you make in your mind—in your thoughts. This causes particular problems when the referent is not concrete, but abstract—such as freedom, family, and beauty.

This symbolic arbitrary nature of language suggests that words don't mean, people do. Put another way, meanings are in people, not in words. What I think of when I hear the word cat may not be what you think of. Our attributions, expectancies, and feelings about the referent may differ. Thus, our meanings differ.

Imagine the difficulty this idea of "meanings are in people" has as we move from our own language to those of another culture. For example, as Lewis (1996) suggests:

> *As the globalisation of business brings executives more frequently together, there is a growing realization that if we examine concepts and values, we can take almost nothing for granted. The word "contract" translates easily from language to language, but nationally it has many interpretations. To a Swiss, German, Scandinavian, American or British person it is something that has been signed in order to be adhered to. Signatures give it a sense of finality. But a Japanese regards a contract as a starting document to be rewritten and modified as circumstances require. A South American sees it as an ideal which is unlikely to be achieved, but which is signed to avoid argument.* (p. 11)

THE STRUCTURE OF LANGUAGE

Although symbols are arbitrary, language is rule-governed. These rules are the syntax and grammar of a language. These rules have to do with what letters can be combined with others to form words and what words can be combined, and in what order, to form sentences. For example, the sentence, "Communication is the process of creating meaning," makes sense to English speakers. However, "Creating meaning communication the process is of" does not because the word order makes no sense to English speakers.

Sentence order can differ across cultures. In Japanese the verb comes at the end of the sentence, making it difficult for English speakers to understand what is being said until the entire sentence has been uttered. Americans say, "How are you?" Chinese say, "Nie hau ma?" (ma at the end of a declarative sentence changes that sentence to an interrogative), meaning "You good?" Germans say, "Wie geht es Ihnen?" meaning "How goes it with you?" In Vietnamese the verb is followed by the subject of the sentence—the reverse of the English language.

Some languages are tonal and the meaning differs depending on the tone. Chinese, for example, is a tonal language, and different tones or intonations distinguish words that are otherwise pronounced identically. For example, ma with a high level tone means mother; in a low rising tone, horse; in a high rising tone, hemp; and in a high falling to low tone, to curse. To confuse matters even worse, each tone usually offers a large number of homonyms. For example, yi in a high level tone can mean, among other things, one, clothes, doctor, and to cure.

Plurals differ in the way they are formed in various languages. In America we generally form the plural of a word by adding "s" to the end of the word. In the Indonesian language plurals are formed by repeating the word, for example, angan means fantasy, angan-angan means fantasies. In Korean "the distinction between singular and plural is made by the context of the sentence" (Honig, 1992, p. 66).

Languages "look" different. The English alphabet consists of 26 letters; the Italian, 21. Some languages, like Russian, Chinese, Persian, Hebrew, Gaelic, and Thai, have alphabets that do not look like the letters of the English alphabet. Although a Thai alphabet may look "strange" to English speakers, remember that the English alphabet looks "strange" to a Thai speaker!

Finally, language structure affects what speakers focus on in their communication. In Asian languages, the language forces the speaker to focus primarily on human relationships. In Western languages the focus is on objects or referents and their logical relationships. For example, for Japanese, communication is meant to promote and maintain harmony. Thus, the way something is said is as important as how something is said. Threatening tones are avoided and the emphasis is on politeness and respect. The information that surrounds the words—the voice tone, gestures, even the words that aren't said—are extremely important. For Asians, communication is a tool for getting things done. Thus, it should be as clear and precise as possible. Americans tend to ask a lot of questions so that they have as much information as possible before making a decision. They generally pay less attention to factors such as voice tone and gestures than Japanese. Wallach and Metcalf (1995) provide the following business transaction, which clarifies these differences.

MR. PHILLIPS: "How long will you need to finish the project report you are working on?"

(PHILLIPS THINKS: I need to get this information for planning purposes.)

(WANG THINKS: Why is he asking me this?)

MR. WANG: "I do not know. When do you want it?"

(PHILLIPS THINKS: Why doesn't he know? He's in the best position to know.)

(*WANG THINKS*: He's the boss. He should tell me when he wants it.)

MR. PHILLIPS: "I need it as soon as possible. Can you get it to me in two weeks?"

(*PHILLIPS THINKS*: I need to press him on this project or else it will never get done.)

(*WANG THINKS*: I am working as hard as I can. I'm not sure when it will be done. It will depend on what other projects and demands come my way.)

MR. WANG: "Yes. I will finish it in two weeks."

(*PHILLIPS THINKS*: Great! I will finish it in two weeks. I don't have to worry about this any more.)

(*WANG THINKS*: He wanted a date so I agreed. I don't want him to get upset. I will try my best to meet it.)

In fact, the project report objectively required three weeks of work to be completed. Mr. Wang worked overtime to get the job done, but by the end of the second week he was still two days short of completing the report.

MR. PHILLIPS: "Where is the project report? You agreed it would be ready today."

(*PHILLIPS THINKS*: I must make sure he complies with his commitment. I can't trust Wang to do what he says he will do.)

(*WANG THINKS*: Can't he see I've almost killed myself trying to meet his timeline, which was unrealistic in the first place? This is an impossible man to work for! [(p. 179–180])

SEMANTICS

It is not enough to know the structure of a language. To communicate effectively, one needs to understand the meaning of words. Semantics is the study of meaning. At the simplest level, a meaning is denotative or connotative. The denotative meaning is the conventional meaning—the meaning that was agreed upon when the language code was constructed. In other words, we can find the denotative meaning of a word in the dictionary.

The connotative meaning is private and often emotionally charged. Connotative meaning becomes attached to words through our experiences and associations. For example, in our previous example of the word cat, the denotative meaning is a small furry domesticated animal often kept as a pet. My personal definition depends on my experience with cats. If I have had positive experiences, my emotional attachment to the word cat will be positive and a positive emotion will result. I will be happy. However, if my experience has been negative, a negative emotion will result. I may fear cats.

General semanticists (people interested in how humans use their language and how language relates to behavior) suggest that words are at various levels of abstraction. We organize and order our world by using language to classify things into general categories, thus helping make our world more predictable. For example, we classify some people into the category of foreigner. We abstract from each of these people the characteristics they have in common. This abstraction notes the similarities and overlooks the differences among foreigners. Based on this abstraction of *foreigners*, we make predictions about what foreigners will say and do.

However, abstractions can cause problems in intercultural communication. We often overlook the differences in people and things simply because they fall into the same category. If we respond to the stereotypes or the abstraction rather than to the person with whom we are trying to communicate, we will not be effective communicators.

General semanticists provide devices to aid us in avoiding the dangers inherent in abstraction. The first device is called dating. People, objects, events—everything is in constant flux. Thus, you in 1998 is not the same as you in 1970 or 2001. If you mentally attach a data to such statements as "That foreigner is rude" (by saying "that foreigner is rude now," you'll keep from assuming that the particular foreigner is always rude). You'll refrain from communicating as if people and events are static. Remember that one thing is different at two different times.

Indexing is closely related to dating. Indexing helps us to account for individual differences. People, as well as objects and events, differ from one another. Thus, foreigner 1 is not foreigner 2. If we index, we keep from making such generalizations as, "All foreigners are rude." If you've seen one, you haven't seen them all!

Both indexing and dating point to the fact that the verb *is* should be used with caution. When we say *is*, we imply a static, unchanging phenomenon. This negates the concept that communication is a dynamic, continuous, and ever-changing process. There's a difference between saying, "That foreigner is rude" and "That foreigner appears to be rude." When we say, "That foreigner is rude," we leave ourselves open for misevaluation.

Finally, the use of mental quotation marks reminds us that meanings are in people, not in words. When you say, "That foreigner is rude," you may mean that the person did not say "Excuse me," when bumping into you. Your friend might consider "rude" to mean that the foreigner fails to speak English. If you use mental quotation marks—"rude"—you'll be reminded that the term has different meanings to different people.

Whenever we leave the culture of our roots, it's important to remember that these principles of general semantics can help us be more competent communicators. As we travel the routes of other cultures, we need to remember that words are abstract and, as such, can limit our understanding in numerous ways.

As one student writes:

> *If I had known about general semantics when I went to study in France, I think my communication would have been more effective. I think it would have helped me avoid as much stereotyping as I did.*

PRAGMATICS

Knowing the rules of a language and possessing a large vocabulary will not guarantee effective communication. We have to know how to use the language in actual conversation. As anyone who has taken a foreign language knows, using a language in its native country with native speakers is very different from using it in a classroom! Pragmatics examine language as it is used in actual, everyday interactions.

When we use language, we use it to reach specific goals. These goals are called *speech acts*. Examples of speech acts are threats, jokes, questions, requests, and praise. Assume you are taking an art class. You've finished an abstract painting and you show it to your friend. Your friend looks at the painting, pauses, and says, "That's very unusual." What does your friend mean? Does your friend like your painting? Thinking about the syntax and the semantics of the sentence your friend uttered won't be much help. In order to understand what your friend actually means, you have to know what your friend was trying to do—compliment you, criticize you, or remain neutral.

How do we know how to interpret a speech art? A theory called the *coordinated management of meaning* (CMM) helps answer this question (Cronen, Pearce, & Harns, 1982). This theory suggests that we know how to use language because we follow rules that tell us how to understand and produce speech acts. Constitutive rules tell us how to recognize speech acts. Regulative rules identify, in a given context, the speech acts that are appropriate or inappropriate for the context. In other words, communication only makes sense in the context in which it occurs.

To interpret a speaker's intended speech act, you have to consult constitutive rules. Because words have different meanings in different contexts, to choose the right rule, you need to examine the context. If a professor says "You're in serious trouble," you will no doubt decide to interpret the words as a warning. If, on the other hand, these same words are uttered by a parent in an episode of "joking around," you'll interpret the meaning as a move in a game of teasing.

To respond to the speech act, you have to consider regulative rules. Remember that these rules tell us what speech acts are appropriate given your goals and understanding of the context. In the case of the professor, your regulative rules for this academic episode might be, "Given that I want to pass this course, the proper speech act for me to perform is a polite request for further information."

LANGUAGE AND CULTURE

Does the language we speak influence how we perceive the world? In 1921 Edward Sapir suggested that it did. He, along with his student, Benjamin Whorf, suggests that language did affect a culture's behavior and habits of thinking. As Sapir indicates (quoted in Whorf, 1956):

> *Human beings do not live in the objective world alone, nor alone in the world of social activity as ordinarily understood, but are very much at the mercy of the particular language which has become the medium of expression for their society. . . The fact is that the "real world" is to a large extent unconsciously built up on the language habits of the group. . . We see and hear and otherwise experience the world very much as we do because the language habits of our community predispose certain choices of interpretation.* (p. 134)

The Sapir-Whorf hypothesis has two versions: linguistic determinism and linguistic relativity. Linguistic determinism suggests that our language determines the way we interpret the world. Linguistic relativity suggests that since language affects thought, speakers of different languages will perceive the world differently. Most students of language today adhere to the linguistic relativity version.

Richard Lewis (1996) tells the story of how linguistic relativity "works." He was interested in why the Zulu language has 39 words for "green," while English has only one. So he asked a Zulu chief. The Zulu chief explained that prior to national highways the Zulu had to make long treks across the Savannah grasslands. Because there were no signposts or maps, the lengthy journeys had to be described by those who had traveled the road before. The language changed to accommodate the need for "finely wrought, beautiful logical descriptions of nature, causation, repetition, duration and results" (p. 16). Lewis describes the conversation:

*"But give me some examples of different green-words," I persisted.
My friend picked up a leaf. "What color is this?" he asked.
"Green," I replied.
The sun was shining. He waited until a cloud intervened. "What color
is the leaf now?" he asked.
"Green," I answered, already sensing my inadequacy.
"It isn't the same green, is it?'
"No, it isn't."
"We have a different word in Zulu." He dipped the leaf in water and
held it out again. "Has the color changed?"
"Yes."
"In Zulu we have a word for 'green shining wet.' "
The sun came out again and I needed another word (leaf-green-wet-but-
with-sunshine-on-it!)
My friend retreated 20 meters and showed me the leaf. "Has the color
changed again?"
"Yes," I screamed.
"We have another word," he said with a smile.
He went on to indicate how different Zulu greens would deal with tree
leaves, bush leaves, leaves vibrating in the wind, river greens, pool greens,
tree trunk greens, crocodile greens. . . he got to 39 without even raising a
sweat. (p. 16)*

Our language can tell us how to talk to others based on intimacy and
rank. The German language has formal and informal pronouns. If you know
someone quite well, you would use the *du* form of you. If you did not know
that person well or you wanted to show respect, you would use the *sie* form
of you. In Mandarin Chinese there are terms for younger sister (meimei),
older sister (jiejie), younger brother (didi), older brother (gege), paternal
grandfather (yeye), paternal grandmother (nainai), maternal grandfather
(laoye), maternal grandmother (laolao), your son's son (sunzi), your daughter's son (waisun) and so forth. Similarly, the Thai language uses different
pronouns, nouns, and verbs to represent rank and intimacy.

Not only does our language tell us how to talk to one another, it also tells
us what we talk about. The Navaho language contains five terms to designate
color. Hoijer (1994) explains:

*The Navaho color vocabulary includes, among others, five terms: ligai, dilxl,
lizin, lici?, and dokiz, to be taken as one way of categorizing certain color impressions. Ligai is roughly equivalent to English white, dilxl and lizin to
English black, lici? to English red, and dokiz to English blue or green.
Clearly then, the Navaho five-point system is not the same as English white-*

black-red-blue-green, which also has five categories. English black *is divided into two categories in Navaho (dilxl and Iizin), while Navaho has but one category (do-kiz) for the English* blue *and* green.

All this is not to say that English speakers cannot perceive the difference between the two "blacks" of the Navaho or that Navaho speakers cannot differentiate "blue" and "green." It is to say that it will be harder. If we don't have words for something, it takes longer to distinguish that thing from others. So, once again, our language roots can affect our communication as we move along the routes of other cultures.

In sum, the Sapir-Whorf hypothesis suggests that the way one culture sees the world may not be the same as the way another culture sees the world. What you believe to be true is based on the language you speak. Thus, when you come into contact with a speaker of a different language, you are entering a different view of the world.

SOCIAL CONSTRUCTIONISM

In contrast to the Sapir-Whorf hypothesis view of the relationship of language and culture is the view of social constructionism.

The basic premise of the social constructionists is that our meanings and understandings arise from our communication with others. Philosopher Alfred Schutz (1970) explains the social constructivist's view of reality:

> *The world of my daily life is by no means my private world, but is from the outset an intersubjective one, shared with my fellow men, experienced and interpreted by others: in brief, it is a world common to all of us. The unique biographical situation in which I find myself within the world at any moment of my existence is only to a very small extent of my own making.* (p. 163)

In other words, we can understand any one thing in several ways. Our language gives us words to describe and distinguish between things in our world. How we "lump" things together depends on the use of a particular social reality. In turn, how we react towards these things depends on the social reality we have. Although various theorists concerned with social constructionism vary in their thinking, several common assumptions are apparent (Littlejohn, 1996):

Communicative interaction is voluntary. *Most social constructionists view communicators as choice-making beings. The social environment* *does constrain what can and is done, but in most situations, some choice is available.*

Knowledge is a social product. *Knowledge is derived from interaction with social groups. Language constitutes reality and meanings determine our knowledge.*

Knowledge is contextural. *Our meanings for events are a product of interaction in a particular time and place, with particular people. Our understanding of events change as time changes.* (p. 180)

Thus, from a social constructionism point of view, communication creates our social world, can only be understood within a given context, occurs in many different forms, and is always in process, ongoing and changing. As Shotter (1984) suggests, communication determines how reality is experienced and the experience of reality affects communication.

People are constantly assigning meaning to and making sense of their experiences. The meanings assigned are closely tied to the language used among participants. For example, Eskimos view themselves in relationship to others. They may have private feelings, but these feelings are generally considered unimportant. Important matters related to self issues are usually defined in terms of relationships to others. Westerners would say, "I hear him." The Eskimo would say, "He is making a sound with reference to me" (Harre, 1979, p. 11).

Hence, once again we see that our language roots differ from those of others. If we are not careful, our language roots can limit our ability to find new meanings across time and place and with people different from ourselves. We need to understand that every person has language roots, and that these affect and are affected by communication with others, which in turn, affects subsequent communication. Only then can we begin to understand what communication choices are possible and appropriate along our journey into other cultures, our routes.

THE BERNSTEIN HYPOTHESIS

Another view of how language is related to culture is that of Basil Bernstein's (1971) concept of elaborated and restricted codes. Bernstein discusses how the structure of language in everyday communication shapes and reflects the assumptions of a social group. Bernstein's basic assumption is that the relationship established in a social group affect the type of speech used by that group. In addition, the structure of speech used by the group makes different things significant. In short, people learn their place in the world through the language codes they use.

The elaborated code provides a wide range of different ways to say something. This code is used by a group in which common perspectives are not shared. Thus, people have to explain in detail what they mean.

Restricted codes have fewer ways to say things. These codes don't allow speakers to expand on (elaborate) what they mean. The restricted code appears in groups that have a strongly shared set of assumptions and little need to elaborate on what is meant. They are oriented toward social categories— categories for which everyone has the same meaning.

In general, middle class speakers use an elaborated code and lower class speakers use a restricted code. Table 8-1 outlines the differences between two codes.

These two codes differ in their degree of openness. According to Bernstein (1971) an open system has roles that are not categorized and simple. These roles are individualized and negotiated—they can change. Therefore, a person's role or identity is not understood by everyone in the group and an elaborated code is necessary for effective communication to take place.

A closed role system is one in which roles are set and people are viewed or identified in those roles. An understanding of a person's role and identity is understood by everyone. Thus, an elaborated code is not necessary.

How do these codes develop in a group? Two factors appear important: the nature of the socializing agencies (family, friends, school, work) within the system and the values of the system. When the structure of the socializing

TABLE 8-1   Characteristics of Bernstein's Elaborated versus Restricted Code

Elaborative Code	Restricted Code
Direct messages	Indirect messages
Verbal elaboration	No verbal elaboration
Focus on verbal aspects of the communication message	Focus on nonverbal aspects of the communication message
No reliance on shared meanings between communicators	Reliance on shared meanings between communicators
Not taking others' intentions for granted	Taking others' intentions for granted
Orientation towards individual persons	Orientation towards the group
Planning messages	Little planning of messages

agencies is well-defined in terms of fixed roles, a restricted code develops. If the structure is less well-defined and the roles are fluid, an elaborated code is likely to develop.

In terms of values, a pluralistic society that values individuality promotes an elaborated code, while a less pluralistic society promotes restricted codes.

In a study in which young men from the working class and middle class in England discussed capital punishment, Bernstein found that middle class speakers used "I think" significantly more than working class speakers. They also had longer, more complex verb phrases, more uncommon adverbs and adjectives, more passive verbs and used the personal pronoun "I" more often. Working class speakers used short phrases at the end of sentences ("Isn't it?" "You know" and "Wouldn't he?") to confirm the other person's understanding more than did middle class speakers.

Of all the socializing agencies, the family seems to be of special importance. It is from within the context of the family that our cultural roots derive. It is these roots that accompany us on our routes—whether within the subcultures of our own culture or cross culturally. Bernstein defined two types of families—position-centered families and person-centered families.

As the term implies, position-centered families have a clear and formally determined role structure. They have a closed role system and use a restricted code. They define people in terms of their position in the family.

People-centered families determine roles on the basis of an individual's personal orientation rather than on formally defined divisions. These families use elaborated codes. Roles and regulations tend towards instability and are constantly being negotiated.

Families regulate behavior, but do so in different ways, depending on the type of family. Some families use the imperative mode. This mode is based on command and authority. If Dad says, "Take out the trash," you do it because he is in the authoritative role. This kind of control or regulation of behavior is in the restricted role.

Other families use positional appeals that are based on role-related norms. Control is exerted by relying on commonly understood norms associated with each role. "Girls don't play with trucks" is an example of this type of appeal. The code employed can be restricted or elaborated, depending on the degree of differentiation in the family.

Personal appeals are another way to regulate behavior. These are based on individualized rules and characteristics. These appeals consist of giving reasons for why a person should or should not do some thing. This type of appeal can be expressed with restricted or elaborated codes, depending on the degree of shared understanding in the family.

According to Bernstein, the elaborated code enables speakers to adapt to a wide variety of people. Yet, elaborated codes can be limiting because they "separate feeling from thought, self from other, private belief from role obligation" (p. 186).

Bernstein notes that those in power often devalue the restricted code, which perpetuates class systems. However, he suggests that the restricted code has its own advantages:

> Let it be said immediately that a restricted code gives access to a vast potential of meanings, of delicacy, subtlety and diversity of cultural forms. . . (p. 186)

In sum, the Sapir-Whorf hypothesis suggests that language precedes interaction and that our interaction patterns are a result of language structure. The social constructionists argue that language is an outcome of interaction and that reality is constructed through communication. Bernstein suggests that interaction shapes language and that language, in turn, shapes interaction. The type of interaction in socializing agencies, particularly the family, determines the sort of language learned, and language, in turn, reinforces the interaction patterns.

VERBAL COMMUNICATION STYLES

In their analysis of verbal and nonverbal communication styles across cultures, Gudykunst and Ting-Toomey (1988) present four verbal communication styles. Style is "a meta message that contextualizes how individuals should accept and interpret a verbal message" (p. 100). As you read this section, think about the style of your cultural roots, and how you might need to adapt this style as you venture along other routes.

Direct versus Indirect Style

This style refers to the extent that speakers reveal their intentions through explicit verbal communication. The primary function of language in a direct style is to express feeling, ideas, and thought as clearly and logically as possible. In other words, all the information is in the explicit coded message. Such a style occurs in low context cultures, primarily Western nations. In these nations speakers value specificity, clarity, and precision. Members talk more, find verbal people more attractive, and are relatively insensitive to nonverbal cues (to the context surrounding the verbal message).

In contrast, an indirect style occurs in high context cultures in which the message is highly dependent on the context or internalized with the people who are communicating and less on the actual words that are spoken. Thus, the meaning of message lies in when and where it is said as well as who says it and to whom.

People in high context cultures who use an indirect style often find people in low context cultures loud and insensitive. On the other hand, people in low context cultures, who use a direct style, can't understand why high context speakers don't say what they mean.

The following example from Okabe (1983) clarifies the ideas presented above:

> *Reflecting the cultural value of precision, [North] Americans' tendency to use explicit words is the most noteworthy characteristic of their communicative style. They prefer to employ such categorical words as "absolutely," "certainly," and "positively.". . . The English syntax dictates that the absolute "I" be placed at the beginning of a sentence in most cases, and that the subject-predicate relation be constructed in an ordinary sentence. . . By contrast, the cultural assumptions of interdependence and harmony require that Japanese speakers limit themselves to implicit and even ambiguous use of words. In order to avoid leaving an assertive impression, they like to depend more frequently on qualifiers such as "maybe," "perhaps," "probably," and "somewhat." Since Japanese syntax does not require the use of subject in a sentence, the qualifier-predicate is a predominant form of sentence construction. (p. 36)*

Elaborate versus Succinct Style

This dimension concerns the quantity of talk that is valued in different cultures. An elaborate style is the use of rich, expressive language in everyday conversation. On the other end of the continuum is the succinct style. This style includes the use of understatement, silences, and pauses in everyday conversation. In the middle of the continuum is the exacting style—one should give neither more nor less information than is required.

Arab speakers use an elaborate style. Their conversations are filled with exaggerations, assertion, proverbs, cultural idioms, and metaphors. Similarly, Mexican speakers delight in verbal play. They use double entendres, turn of phrases, and old quotations expressed at just the right moment in everyday conversation.

In contrast, the Japanese have a succinct style. Silence, or *ma*, is prevalent in Japanese communication. The Japanese believe that it is the silence between words that is significant to conveying meaning. In addition, they use circumlocution and indirectness. This is true in many Asian countries. For example, rather than telling you directly, "I don't agree with you" (as someone using an exacting style would do), a Korean speaker will be less direct, saying something like, "I agree with you in principle." Exacting style is characteristic of many Northern European cultures and the U.S. culture. People from these cultures tend to "say what they mean."

Personal versus Contextual Style

Verbal personal style is individual-centered language while verbal contextual style is role-centered language. In a verbal personal style, linguistic devices are used to emphasize the "I" identity. Meanings are expressed for the purpose of emphasizing "personhood." In a verbal contextual style, linguistic devices are used to emphasize the "role" identity. Meanings are expressed for the purpose of emphasizing prescribed role relationships.

English speakers tend to stress informality and power relationships while Chinese, using a contextual style language, stress formality and asymmetrical power relationships. Americans shun formal codes of conduct, titles, and honorifics in interaction with others. They prefer a first-name basis and direct address. Chinese, on the other hand, believe formality is essential to their human relationships. Similarly, Koreans use Confucian ethical rules of hierarchical human relationships. They have separate vocabularies for different sexes, different degrees of intimacy, different formal occasions, and different degrees of social status.

Instrumental versus Affective Style

The instrumental verbal style is sender-oriented, goal-oriented, and relies heavily on the digital code to accomplish goals. The affective verbal style is receiver-oriented, process-oriented, and relies heavily on the analogic code to negotiate relational definition and approval.

Western cultures, such as that of the United States, use an instrumental style. Most Arab, Asian, and Latin American cultures use an affective style. Note that the former are low context cultures; the latter, high, high context cultures.

Comparing North Americans to Koreans, Park (1979) suggests:

> In an instrumental communication pattern, like that of the [North] Americans, people assert themselves or make themselves understood by talking. . . whereas in a situation communication style like that of Koreans or Japanese, people try to defend themselves either by vague expressions or by not talking. [North] Americans try to persuade their listeners in the step-by-step process [regardless of] whether their listeners accept them totally. But a Korean or a Japanese tends to refuse to talk any further in the course of a conversation with someone once he [or she] decides that he [or she] cannot accept the other's attitude, his [or her] way of thinking and feeling in totality. (pp. 92–93)

LINGUISTIC PREJUDICE

Prejudice involves making a prejudgment based on membership in a social category. In general, we tend to think of prejudice as negative—an unfair or biased attitude toward another person or group.

One form of prejudice is linguistic prejudice. The language others use and that is used to describe them can affect our perception of them. According to Spender (1985), our language is prejudiced against women. Men have controlled the language, provided themselves with more positive words to describe themselves and given themselves more opportunities to use those words. For example, there is no feminine generic, that is, feminine words used to represent both the feminine and the masculine form of a word (Smith, 1985). According to Ayim (1993), the term *woman* is not even generic for all females, since it usually focuses on white women, excluding black women, Native American women, and other women of color.

Linguistic prejudice derives from our stereotypes. Stereotypes are rigid preconceptions that are applied to all members of a group or to an individual over a period of time, regardless of individual variations. Stereotypes are oversimplified, overgeneralized, and/or exaggerated.

Stereotypes can be based on ethnicity. Ethnic groups share a sense of heritage and history, and origin from an area outside of or preceding the creation of their present nation-state of residence (Banks, 1984). In most cases, ethnic groups share racial characteristics and may have a history of or experienced discrimination.

A major way that we make boundaries between our ethnic group and others is by the language we speak. Often we use the language styles of ethnic groups to support our stereotypes about them. For example, Kochman (1981) observes that African American speakers favor forceful outputs (e.g., volume of voice) during conflicts while white speakers prefer subdued outputs. Whites perceive African Americans' response in bad taste while African Americans view whites' responses as lifeless.

Another source of stereotypes is the media. In her book, *Don't Believe the Hype: Fighting Cultural Misinformation About African Americans,* Farad Chideya (1995) suggests that language can become "conventional wisdom." She indicates that words like "gana" are consistently used to describe groups of young black men—even when they have absolutely no gang affiliation. She also indicates that on television African Americans are relegated to the "sitcom ghetto." Nearly all of the portrayals of African Americans on television are comic.

Gudykunst (1994) describes stereotypes used in the media:

Anyone who watches Saturday morning cartoons, for example, knows that villains are non-Europeans. With respect to aging, the "dirty old man" is used frequently in the media, and aging is depicted as involving evil, fail-ure, and unhappiness on television dramas. Similarly, disabled people often are presented as bitter, self-pitying, and maladjusted. . . . Virtually all stereo-types of the old, disabled, and non-Europeans presented in the media are negative and inaccurate. (p. 91)

One final note before we leave the idea of linguistic prejudice. We need to be aware of the fact that we may engage in prejudiced talk ourselves. Often when we are going to say something negative about a group, we preface it by saying, "I'm not prejudiced, but . ." and then we go on to engage in preju-diced talk. Van Dijk (1984, p. 70) clusters prejudiced talk into four categories: (1) "they are different" (in culture, mentality), (2) "they do not adapt them-selves," (3) "they threaten our (social, economic) interests," (4) "they are in-volved in negative acts (nuisances, crime)."

Being aware of our communication can help us eliminate prejudiced talk from our communication. In addition, when we hear others using prejudiced talk, we can indicate to them that this form of communication is not accept-able to us.

CONCLUSION

Like Milo in the land of Dictionopolis we may often be confused when the language of our roots comes into contact with the language of our routes. When we communicate with people from cultures different from our own, our confusion as well as frustration mounts. Being attuned to the language differences we've discussed in this chapter may lessen that confusion and frustration. Knowing differences exist and knowing what form these differ-ences may take can help prepare you for using language in another culture.

QUESTIONS

1. Describe a situation in which language differences caused an intercul-tural communication misunderstanding. How did you handle the situa-tion? Was your way effective? Why or why not?
2. Think about the Sapir-Whorf hypothesis in terms of your own native lan-guage. Can you think of examples in your language that support this hy-potheses? Refute it?
3. To get a sense of the variety of languages in the world, read the book *Lan-guages of the World* by Katzner (New York: Routledge, 1995).

4. When traveling to another country do you consider it important to learn the language of the people of that country? If so, how much? If not, why not? How do you feel about foreigners who come to your country and don't know your language?

ACTIVITIES

1. Choose an abstract term such as "family," "marriage," "education," or "beauty." Ask a person from another culture to define this word for you. Compare her or his definition to your own. How might differences in your meanings create intercultural communication problems? How might similarities enhance your communication?
2. Every culture has proverbs that speak to a culture values. Bring a proverb from your culture to class. What value does it express? If you communicate with someone whose culture does not share that value, how might intercultural communication be affected? Ask a person from another culture to share one of his or her culture's proverbs with you and explain its meaning.
3. Bring to class examples from newspapers of intercultural communication problems that result from language differences. In small groups discuss the causes of misunderstanding and possible ways of alleviating the misunderstanding.

REFERENCES

Ayim, M. (1993). Issues in language and gender: An annotated bibliography. *Resources for Feminist Research*, 22 (1/2), 1–35.

Banks, J. (1984). *Teaching strategies for ethnic studies* (3rd ed). Boston: Allyn and Bacon.

Bernstein, B. (1971). *Class, codes and control: Theoretical studies toward a sociology of language*. London: Routledge & Kegan Paul.

Chideya, F. (1995). *Don't believe the hype: Fighting cultural misinformation about African Americans*. New York: Penguin.

Cronen, V., Pearce, B., & Harris, L. (1982) The coordinated management of meaning: A theory of communication. In F. E. X. Dance (Ed.), *Communication theory: Comparative essays* (pp. 61–89). New York: Harper & Row.

Dodd, C. (1998). *Dynamics of intercultural communication* (5th ed). Boston: McGraw-Hill.

Gudykunst, W. (1994). *Bridging differences* (2nd ed.). Thousand Oaks, CA: Sage.

Gudykunst, W., & Kim, Y. Y. (1997). *Communicating with strangers: An approach to intercultural communication* (3rd ed). New York: McGraw-Hill.

Gudykunst, W., & Ting-Toomey, S. (1988). *Culture and interpersonal communication.* Newbury Park, CA: Sage.

Harre, R. (1979). *Social being: A theory for social psychology.* Totowa, NJ: Rowan and Littlefield.

Hoijer, J. (1994). The Sapir-Whorf hypothesis. In L. Samovar & R. Porter (Eds.), *Intercultural communication: A reader* (pp. 194–200). Belmont, CA: Wadsworth.

Honig, B. (1992). *Handbook for teaching Korean-American students.* California Department of Education.

Infante, D. A., & Rancer, A.S. (1982). A conceptualization and measure of argumentativeness, *Journal of Personality Assessment, 46,* 19–170.

Juster, N. (1961). *The phantom tollbooth.* New York: Random House.

Katzner, K. (1995). *The languages of the world.* New York: Routledge.

Kochman, T. (1981). *Black and white: Styles in conflict.* Chicago: University of Chicago Press.

Lewis, R. (1996). *When cultures collide: Managing successfully across cultures.* London: Nicholas Brealey.

Littlejohn, S. (1996). *Theories of human communication* (5th ed.). Belmont, CA: Wadsworth.

Lustig, M., & Koester, J. (1996). *Intercultural competence: Interpersonal communication across cultures* (2nd ed). New York: Harper Collins.

Martin, J., & Nakayma (1997). *Intercultural communication in context.* Mountain View, CA: Mayfield.

Ogden, C.K., & Richards, I.A. (1927). *The meaning of meaning.* New York: Harcourt Brace.

Okabe, R. (1983). Cultural assumptions of east and west: Japan and the United States. In W. M. Gudykunst (Ed.), *Intercultural communication theory.* Beverly Hills, CA: Sage.

Park, M. (1979). *Communication styles in two different cultures: Korean and American.* Seoul, Korea: Han Shin Publishing Company.

Philipsen, G. (1992). *Speaking culturally.* Albany: State University of New York Press.

Samovar, L., Porter, R., & Stefani, L. (1998). *Communicating between cultures* (3rd ed.). Belmont, CA: Wadsworth.

Schutz, A. (1970). *On phenomenology and social relations.* Chicago: University of Chicago Press.

Shotter, J. (1984). *Social accountability and selfhood.* Oxford, England: Blackwell.

Smith, P. (1985). *Language, the sexes and society.* Oxford, England: Basil Blackwell.

Spender, D. (1985). *Man made language* (2nd ed.). London: Routledge and Kegan Paul.

Trenholm, S., & Jensen, A. (1992). *Interpersonal communication.* Belmont, CA: Wadsworth.

Van Dijk, T. (1984). *Prejudice in discourse.* Amsterdam: Benjamins.

Wallach, J., & Metcalf, G. (1995). *Working with Americans: A practical guide for Asians on how to succeed with U.S. managers.* New York: McGraw-Hill.

Whorf, B. (1956). *Language, thought and reality.* New York: John Wiley & Sons.

Zajonic, R.B. (1980). Feeling and thinking: Preferences need no inferences. *American Psychologist, 35,* 152–55.

9

ORIGIN AND NATURE OF NONVERBAL COMMUNICATION

Objectives

After reading this chapter and completing the activities, you should be able to:

1. Define the importance of nonverbal communication in the overall communication process.
2. Explain the relationship of verbal and nonverbal communication.
3. Provide an intercultural difference for each of the dimensions of nonverbal communication presented in this chapter.
4. List five universal characteristics of nonverbal communication.
5. Discuss three cultural variations in nonverbal communication.

> *I am convinced that much of our difficulty with people in other countries stems from the fact that so little is known about cross-communication. . . Formal training in the language, history, government, and customs of another nation is only the first step in a comprehensive program. Of equal importance is an introduction to the nonverbal language which exists in every country of the world and among the various groups within each country.*
>
> (Hall, 1959, p. 10).

Nonverbal communication (all communication except that which is coded through words) is, as Hall suggests, an extremely important variable in the intercultural communication process. Yet it is difficult to understand because it is usually performed spontaneously and often subconsciously.

Mehrabian (1982) estimates that only 7 percent of the meaning of any message is carried through the verbal message—through words. Ninety-three percent of the meaning is carried through the nonverbal communication channels, 38 percent through the voice, and 55 percent through the face. Birdwhistell (1970) presents a more conservative estimate, suggesting 65 percent of the message's meaning is conveyed through nonverbal channels.

Nonverbal communication reveals our attitudes, personalities, emotions, and relationships with others. By understanding how nonverbal communication influences us and others, we can understand other cultures better, as well as understand our own ethnocentrism.

Although we humans are a species with universal facial expressions for most of our basic emotions (sadness, happiness, anger, distrust, surprise, and fear), when, where, and to whom we display these emotions are culturally bound. They are learned within the culture to which we were born and in which we were raised (Ekman & Friesen, 1971). In addition, the rules regarding these are not taught verbally. Rather, we learn them through observation and personal experience in our culture. Thus, an examination of nonverbal communication in various cultures can help us understand another culture better. For example, Americans tend to see nonverbal communication as ancillary to verbal communication, while elsewhere in the world, for example, Japan, the nonverbal code may be used to convey the major message. In either case, nonverbal behavior is representative of deep cultural values. Stewart and Bennett (1991) provide the following example, which makes this point clear.

An American visitor to Mexico was describing his family to a Mexican. To describe his young children, the American tried to convey their ages by indicating their height. He held up his right hand, the palm open and facing down horizontally at the height of his child from the ground. At first the American did not notice the look of dismay on the face of the Mexican in response to the hand gesture. It was only later that the visitor found out what had gone wrong with the conversation. The gesture he had used is similar to the movement of the hand in petting a dog or some other animal on the head. Mexicans accept that hand gesture as the height of a dog, pig, or some other animal, but human beings are measured with the palm open and held vertical to the ground at the appropriate height.

The Mexican and American attitudes toward the two kind of hand gestures can be associated with the views of reality of members of the two societies. Americans accept an objective reality where people and animals are both biological elements in the world. The boundary separating man from the animals wavers in the Darwinian climate of the United States. But Mexicans are not ardent Darwinians, and they insist on an interpersonal reality restricted to human beings, which excludes privileged status for pets and other animals. Both verbal and nonverbal codes and the thinking patterns they represent act to construct meaning. Since American nonverbal communication is secondary to verbal, Americans are poorly prepared to cope with the strength of nonverbal communication in societies such as the Thai or Mexican. While systems of verbal and nonverbal representation of experience are powerful in themselves, they only compose the surface levels of deep structures and dynamics of reality. Underlying these verbal and nonverbal patterns, influencing them and also driving the higher levels, are cultural values and assumptions. (p. 59)

In addition to understanding another culture better, we can also understand our own enthocentrism through the study of nonverbal communication in interculture settings. Hindus greet one another by placing their palms together in front of them while bowing their heads slightly. This greeting behavior reflects the Hindu belief that the deity exists in everyone. Patting the top of a child's head in Thailand or Malaysia is not done, since the head is considered sacred and the center of a person's spiritual as well as intellectual powers. Understanding that our way of greeting or appropriate touching behavior is ours, and differs across cultures, can help us understand that there are other ways of doing things as well as our own.

RELATIONSHIP OF VERBAL AND NONVERBAL COMMUNICATION

Nonverbal communication can be used independently or in conjunction with verbal communication. Knapp and Hall (1997) suggest six primary relationships of nonverbal and verbal communication. The nonverbal cue may simply *repeat* the verbal—waving goodbye while saying "goodbye." Nonverbal cues may *contradict* the verbal—a friend has a sad expression but says, "No, I don't feel sad." If the verbal and nonverbal are contradictory, we adults most often believe the nonverbal because we consider nonverbal communication as more spontaneous and less likely to be contrived than verbal communication. Nonverbal cues can *substitute* for the verbal—waving goodbye with no accompanying verbal communication. Nonverbal cues can *complement* verbal cues—saying "I love you," while hugging the other person. Nonverbal cues can *accent* the verbal message—a child yells, "I hate you!" while stomping his or her feet. Finally, nonverbal cues can *regulate* the verbal communication—nodding our head in agreement, thereby signaling our communication partner to continue talking.

Regardless of how nonverbal communication is used, it, like verbal communication, uses a culturally agreed upon set of symbols. As Ramsey (1979) suggests:

According to culturally prescribed codes, we use eye movement and contact to manage conversations and to regulate interactions; we follow rigid rules governing intra- and interpersonal touch, our bodies synchronously join in the rhythm of others in a group, and gestures modulate our speech. We must internalize all of this in order to become and remain fully functioning and socially appropriate members of our culture. (p. 111)

DIMENSIONS OF NONVERBAL COMMUNICATION

As indicated previously, nonverbal communication is multichanneled. In other words, several dimensions of nonverbal behavior can be generated by a single person at any given time. For example, we observe the person's dress, gestures, and voice tone and make some assumptions about the person using these nonverbal cues.

There are numerous categories of nonverbal behavior. In this section we will examine five that are particularly important in intercultural communication: time, proxemics, kinesics, touch, and paralanguage.

Time

Hall (1983) distinguishes two types of time that govern different cultures: Monochronic Time (M-Time) and Polychronic Time (P-Time). People who use M-Time usually engage in one activity at a time, compartmentalize time, and separate task-oriented time from socioemotional time. In general, monochronic cultures value punctuality, completing tasks, and keeping on a schedule. Time is linear and is viewed as something that can be saved or wasted. People who use P-Time usually engage in several tasks at once, hold a more fluid attitude toward time, and integrate task-time and socioemotional time. Appointments can be broken easily, schedules ignored, and deadlines broken. If a family member or friend requires attention, this relationship is more important than any schedule.

Members of individualistic cultures such as Northern European, German, and North American are representative of M-Time. Collectivist cultures such as Latin American, Middle Eastern, Asian, and French cultures are representative of P-Time.

Table 9-1 summarizes the basic differences between these two time perspectives in terms of behavior.

These differences in time orientation can cause problems in intercultural communication. Perhaps the most obvious is in terms of punctuality. Hall (1959) also suggests five time intervals for arriving late for appointments:

TABLE 9-1   Comparison of Monochronic and Polychronic People

Monochronic People	Polychronic People
Do one things at a time.	Do many things at once.
Concentrate on the job.	Are easily distracted and subject to interruptions.
Take time commitments (deadlines, schedules) seriously.	Consider time commitments an objective to be achieved, if possible.
Are low context and need information.	Are high context and already have information.
Are committed to the job.	Are committed to people and human relationships.
Adhere to plans.	Change plans often and easily.
Are concerned about not disturbing others; follow rules of privacy.	Are more concerned with those close to them (family, friends, close business associates) than with privacy.
Emphasize promptness.	Base promptness on the relationship.
Are accustomed to short-term relationships.	Have strong tendency to build lifetime relationships.

Source: Adapted from Edward T. Hall & Mildred Reed Hall, *Understanding Cultural Differences: German, French and American* (Yarmouth, ME: Intercultural Press, 1990), p. 15.

(1) mumble something time, (2) slight apology time, (3) mildly insulting time, (4) rude time, and (5) downright insulting time. People on M-Time do not like to be late. If they are even a few minutes late, they engage in mumble something time. People on P-Time may be as late as an hour and not even "mumble something."

Time can also be viewed from a past, present, and future perspective. Individualistic cultures view time from a linear perspective—past, present, future. Those cultures that are past oriented emphasize tradition and the wisdom passed down from generation to generation. Present-oriented cultures emphasize experiencing each moment fully and spontaneity and immediacy. Future-oriented cultures emphasize the importance of present activity to future outcomes. As indicated by Gonzalez and Zimbardo (1985) differences in time orientations can cause difficulties in intercultural communication. A person from a future-oriented perspective might perceive a person from a present-orientation as hedonistic, self-centered, foolish, and inefficient. On the other hand, a present-oriented person might perceive a past-oriented person as too tied to tradition and a future-oriented person as materialistic.

Proxemics

Proxemics is our use of space. It includes territoriality and personal space. Territoriality is fixed space as furniture arrangement. Personal space has been compared to a bubble surrounding us that we carry with us wherever we go and expand or contract depending on the situation.

How culture uses space is linked to its value system. For example, people from individualistic cultures require more space because they value privacy. Collectivist cultures are interdependent. Thus, people work, play, and live in close proximity to one another. These cultures require less space. For example, in collectivist cultures the middle class home environment is integrated with a central plaza, a community center or a neighborhood dwelling. In individualistic cultures the middle class home environment is often separated from the community at large by a fence or through the use of frontyards or backyards (Gudykunst, Ting-Toomey, Sudweeks, & Steward, 1996).

Every culture has its rules for the use of space. In the Netherlands you might find yourself giving a sales pitch from a chair that seems uncomfortably far away. To move your chair closer would be an insult. Privacy is very important to Germans, both at work and home. Doors are kept closed and one must knock before entering. In Japan the person with the most authority sits at the head of the table, the lowest person in the hierarchy is nearest the door at the opposite end of the table from the person with the most authority (McDaniel, 1997). Chinese prefer side-by-side seating rather than arrangements that facilitate direct eye contact.

In terms of personal space, Hall (1959) analyzed Americans' use of personal space. In general, Hall found that Americans use personal space at varying distances for varying purposes. For example, the closer the space between people, the more intimate the communication. Very close (3 inches to 6 inches) is for intimate communication such as comforting, protecting, and lovemaking. Most dyadic encounters occur from 12" to 20". Social gatherings and business transactions take place between 4½ feet and 5 feet, while the largest distance between persons (20 feet or more) occurs in public speaking situations.

We may, because of our ethnocentrism, believe that all cultures use personal space in the same way we do. However, as Stewart and Bennett (1991) indicate:

Standing close in conversation may signal fight or flight from Americans while representing the appropriate distance for conversational interaction prescribed by another person's culture. Both spacing and touching are rather precisely coded with social and sexual meaning for Americans. Thus, the norms of Arabs, and to a lesser degree, of Latinos, may suggest to Americans that these people are socially aggressive and sexually promiscuous. (p. 58)

What happens when our personal space is violated? Bond and Iwata (1976) indicate that members of individualistic cultures take an active, aggressive stance when their space is violated. Members of collectivist cultures assume a passive, withdrawal stance when their space is "invaded" by another person. While living in an Asian culture, one of the authors had great difficulty with this issue of space. The pushing and shoving while in public places seemed "rude" from her Western perspective. She wanted to push back! However, the Chinese people simply kept walking. They did not see this closeness as invasive, but as normal.

Kinesics

Kinesics, the study of body language, includes such cues as gestures, head movements, facial expressions, and eye contact. As was the case with proxemics, each culture has its own interpretation of various kinesic behaviors.

In general, Americans tend to be moderately expressive in their kinesic behavior. In contrast to many Asian cultures, Americans use gestures freely. But compared to those in Mediterranean, Latin, or Arab cultures, Americans seem quite restrained.

A smile in Western culture generally means happiness. In Chinese society a smile can disguise embarrassment, mask bereavement, or conceal rage. In general, the Chinese don't show their emotions because displaying emotions violates face-saving norms by disrupting harmony and causing conflict (Wenzhong & Grove, 1991).

Gestures signify different meanings in different cultures. The simple gesture of nodding "yes" differs across cultures. A Westerner's head nod for "yes" signifies "no" in Thailand. In Turkey, this same movement means, "I don't understand." The Korean "come" is similar to the Western "goodbye." When a Westerner waves to a Korean from a distance, the Korean may think he is being asked to "come here." Koreans wave goodbye by waving their arm from side to side. Winston Churchill's famous victory sign is considered an obscene gesture in South America. Showing the bottoms of your feet is considered an insult in Egyptian culture. Harper, Wiens, and Matarazzo (1991) indicate that "making a circle with one's thumb and index finger while extending the others is emblematic of the word 'OK'; in Japan (and Korea) it signifies 'money' (okane); and among Arabs this gesture is usually accompanied by a baring of teeth, and together they signify extreme hostility" (p. 164). Standing with your hands on your hips is interpreted as an aggressive posture in the Philippines as well as in Mexico and Malaysia. Any gesture that displays an extended thumb, including the "thumbs up" gesture or a hitchhiker's gesture, is offensive throughout the Middle East. Yet, the hitchhiker's gesture in Indonesia means "You go first." The left hand is considered unclean in the Arab world so one should always eat with the right hand.

While Americans expect others to "look them in the eye" while communicating, and in fact may distrust someone who does not, Chinese and Indonesians lower their eyes as a sign of respect. Prolonged eye contact is considered rude in Japan and the Philippines, but expected in Arab cultures as a sign of interest in what the other person is saying. In France, eye contact among people is frequent and intense and sometimes intimidating to Americans.

Touch

Different cultures view touching behavior in different ways. In Southeast Asia people engage in very little touching behavior. As Kim (1992) observes, "Southeastern Asians do not ordinarily touch during a conversation, especially one between opposite sexes, because many Asian cultures adhere to norms that forbid public displays of affection and intimacy" (p. 322).

In general, cultures that believe in emotional restraint and rigid status distinctions (such as the German, Scandinavian, and English) touch less than cultures that stress collectivism and outward signs of affection (such as Middle Eastern, Latin American, and Eastern Europe). What happens to intercultural communication as a result of these differences? As Lustig and Koester (1996) suggest:

> *Germans, Scandinavians, and Japanese, for example may be perceived as cold and aloof by Brazilians and Italians, who in turn may be regarded as aggressive, pushy and overly familiar by northern Europeans.* (p. 204)

Gudykunst and Ting-Toomey (1988) review research that suggests that Japanese tend to engage in same-sex touch behavior more than North Americans, and North Americans tend to engage in opposite-sex touch behavior more often than do the Japanese. Japanese females tend to touch more than do Japanese males. In Mediterranean cultures male-male touch behaviors are more common than is female-female touch behavior. People in the Near East are less touch-avoidant to opposite-sex touching than both Mediterranean and Far eastern groups. The Far Eastern group is the most touch-avoidant cultural group in opposite-sex touch behavior among the four groups. These findings suggest that Far Eastern cultures are low-contact cultures, the North American culture is a moderate-contact culture, and the Arab and Mediterranean cultures are high nonverbal contact cultures.

Cultures vary in terms of their rules as to who touches whom, as well as the settings or occasions in which touch is acceptable. For example, in Thailand, the rules of touch that are important to know are:

1. Don't touch anyone's head for any reason. The head is the most important part of the body. It is the seat of the soul.
2. Do not touch a female on any part of her body.
3. The feet are considered the "dirtiest" part of the body. They are used only for walking. Thus, it is an insult to rest your feet on someone else's backrest, such as in the cinema or on a train.
4. Women must never touch a monk or his robe. Even in a bus or train, women cannot sit next to a monk.
5. Always accept things with your right hand. The left hand is used to wash the posterior and is therefore unclean.

As is the case with all nonverbal variables, it is extremely important for us to understand that the culture of our roots teaches us the appropriate form of touch for our culture. However, as we move along other routes, touching behaviors will differ, and we need to adapt to them.

Paralanguage

Paralanguage consists of how something is said, not what is said. It includes vocal qualifiers (volume, pitch, rhythm, tone), vocal segregates ("uh," "um," "shh"), and vocal characteristics (sobbing, laughing, whispering).

Cultural differences exist in each of these. For example, in terms of volume, Arabs tend to speak loudly since this suggests strength and sincerity. Thai and Japanese people speak softly since this is a sign of good manners and education. As Hoskin (1992) suggests:

> In Thailand, the voice should always be soft and calm. Those who had witnessed a car accident would have noted that even in such a grave situation, there was none of the shouting, accusing, finger-pointing, wild gestures, name-calling and everything else that is so common in the supposedly more advanced West. Don't raise your voice anywhere or anytime even when you feel cheated and you need to demand an explanation. To do so is to "lower yourself" and be seen as uncultured; perhaps a barbarian as one would say? (p. 118)

The high-pitched voice of the French should not be mistaken for anger. It generally means a great interest in the subject. The rate of speech also differs across cultures. Arabs, Jews, and Italians tend to speak faster than Americans.

In China, people use "hai" ("yes") as a vocal segregate. In fact, they often use it continually, even while the other person is speaking. Americans view this as rude because they view it as a violation of turn-taking cues. Vocal characteristics and their meaning also differ across cultures. The Japanese use laughter not only for joy, but also to mask anger, sorrow, or displeasure.

Appearance

Each culture determines what is appropriate attire and what is attractive. In Arab cultures, women might wear the *Hijab,* a long raincoat-like garment with a scarf placed on the head to cover the hair completely. This form of dress evolved because women in Islam are supposed to be covered completely except for their faces, hands, and feet. In Kuwait, women dress very modestly. To respect that culture, female visitors should do the same—the neckline should be high and the sleeves come to at least the elbows. Hemlines should be well below the knee. The entire effect should be one of concealment—a full-length outfit that is tight and revealing is not acceptable (Morrison, Conway, & Borden, 1994).

In Malaysia both sexes receive many tattoos, both for protection and decoration. Many tribes place long weights or simple wooden plugs in the ears of children in order to stretch the earlobe. However, only women wear the heaviest ones so that their ear lobes eventually stretch down to their chests. Long lobes are considered a sign of great beauty in Malaysia.

In Bali it is essential for every Balinese to have his or her teeth filed, so much so that in the event of the death of a youth, the teeth are filed before cremation. The purpose of teeth filing is to reduce the power of greed, jealousy, anger, lust, drunkenness, and "confusion"—emotions more suitable to animals than to humans. Thus, the two upper canine teeth and the four incisors between them are filed down.

NONVERBAL CROSSROADS: ROOTS VERSUS ROUTES

Some researchers suggest that there are universal nonverbal behaviors across cultures, that there are universal roots. For example, Ekman and Frieser (1971) and Fridlund, Ekman, and Oster (1987) report research indicating that the ability to produce emotional displays such as anger and happiness is consistent across cultures. Thus, there is probably a genetic or biological basis that allows these emotions to be produced by all humans. In addition territoriality, another nonverbal variable, also appears to be universal (Ardrey 1966). In other words, all humans mark and claim some territory as their own.

Michael Argyle (1975) outlines five characteristics of nonverbal communication that are universal across cultures: (1) the same body parts are used for nonverbal expressions, (2) nonverbal channels are used to convey similar information, emotions, norms, values, and self-disclosures, (3) nonverbal messages accompany verbal communication and are used in ritual and art, (4) the motives for using the nonverbal channels (such as when speech is impossible) are similar across cultures, and (5) nonverbal messages are used to coordinate and control a range of contexts and relationships that are similar across cultures (p. 95).

Although research suggests that there are nonverbal universals, how these are manifested across cultures differ. In other words, these may "look" different as we travel along the routes of other cultures. Lustig and Koester (1996) outline three cultural variations in nonverbal communication. First, cultures differ in their specific repertoire of behaviors. Movements, gestures, and spatial requirements are specific to a particular culture. Second, all cultures have display rules. These "indicate such things as how far apart people should stand while talking, whom to touch and where, the speed and timing of movements and gestures, when to look directly at others in a conversation and when to look away, whether loud talking and expansive gestures or quietness and controlled movements should be used, when to smile and when to frown, and the overall pacing of communication" (p. 191). Thus, display rules govern when and in what situations various nonverbal expressions are required, permitted, preferred or prohibited, and they differ across cultures. Third, as the examples in this chapter indicate, the meanings that are attributed to particular nonverbal behaviors differ across cultures.

Before we leave this discussion of nonverbal categories, it is important to note that we don't have to travel to another country to see differences. For example, within the American culture, American women tend to use smaller and fewer gestures than American men as well as more facial expressions and initiate hugs and embraces more than males (see research reviewed in Stewart, Cooper, Stewart, & Friedley, 1996). African Americans are more emotional and dynamic in their use of voice than most white Americans (Hecht, Collier, & Ribeau, 1993). In addition, African Americans often use BPT (Black People's Time) in which what is happening in the present takes priority (Horton, 1976).

CONCLUSION

Interpreting the meaning of nonverbal communication across cultures is "tricky." The rules of nonverbal communication are rarely verbally discussed. One must observe closely in order to "pick up" the appropriate roles and behaviors.

We'll close this chapter with an example of the problems a lack of understanding of nonverbal communication can cause (Storti, 1990). It is an apocryphal story of the American couple invited to a Moroccan family's home for dinner:

Having pressed their host to fix a time, they arrive half an hour late and shown into the guest room. After a decent interval, they ask after the host wife, who has yet to appear, and are told that she is busy in the kitchen. At one point their host's little son wanders in, and the couple remark on his good looks. Just before the meal is served, the guests ask to be shown to the toilet so they may wash their hands. The main course is served in and eaten from a large, common platter, and the couple choose morsels of food from wherever they can reach, trying to keep up polite conversation throughout the meal. Soon after tea and cookies they take their leave.

What did they do wrong? Almost everything. They confused their ho by asking him to fix the hour, for in the Moslem world an invitation to a me is really an invitation to come and spend time with your friends, during th course of which time, God willing, a meal may very well appear. To ask wh time you should come is tantamount to asking your host how long he war you around and implies, as well, that you are more interested in the me than in his company.

One should be careful about asking after a Moslem man's wife; she frequently does not eat with foreign guests, even if female spouse are present, nor would she necessarily even be introduced. In any case, she belongs in the kitchen guaranteeing the meal is as good as she can produce, thereby showing respect for her guests and bringing honor on her and her husband's house. Nor should one praise the intelligence or good looks of small children, for this will alert evil spirits to the presence of a prized object in the home, and they may come and cause harm. It was not appropriate to ask to be shown the toilet either, for a decorative basin would have been offered for the washing of hands (and the nicer it is the more honor it conveys upon the family). Nor should one talk during the meal; it interferes with the enjoyment of the food to have to keep up a conversation and may even be interpreted as a slight against the cooking. And one should only take food from the part of the platter directly in front, not from anywhere within reach.

Not only is it rude to reach, but doing so deprives the host of one of his chief duties and pleasures: finding the best pieces of chicken or lamb and ostentatiously placing them before the guest. (pp. 24–25)

QUESTIONS

1. Choose one nonverbal communication variable such as kinesics, the co cept of time, or spatial relationships. How will the concept you chose fluence communication with a person from a culture different from y own?

2. Review the percentages presented at the beginning of this chapter. Does your own personal experience support or refute the percentages? Give an example.
3. Describe an intercultural communication episode you have encountered in which nonverbal communication differences caused misunderstanding.

ACTIVITIES

1. With a classmate, view a foreign film. After viewing the film, discuss the differences you observed between the culture in the film and your own culture.
2. Visit an ethnic area in your city. Observe nonverbal variables such as greeting behavior, speech volume, spatial relationships, and gestures. How do these differ from your own culture? What do these differences tell you about being an effective communicator in that culture versus your own culture?
3. Interview a person from a culture different from your own about nonverbal rules in her or his culture. Share with him or her how these rules are different from or similar to your culture.

REFERENCES

Ardrey, R. (1966). *The territorial imperative: A personal inquiry into the animal origins of property and nations.* New York: Atheneum.

Argyle, M. (1975). *Bodily communication.* New York: International Universities Press.

Birdwhistell, R. (1970). *Kinesics and context.* Philadelphia: University of Pennsylvania Press.

Bond, M., & Iwata, Y. (1976). Proxemics and observation anxiety in Japan: Nonverbal and cognitive responses. *Psychologia, 19,* 110–126.

Ekman, P., & Friesen, W. (1971). Constants across cultures in the face and emotion. *Journal of Personality and Social Psychology, 17,* 124–129.

Ekman, P., Sorenson, R., & Friesen, W. (1969). Pan-cultural elements in facial displays of emotion. *Science, 64,* 86–88.

Fridlund, A., Ekman, P., & Oster, H. (1987). Facial expression of emotion: Review of literature, 1970–1983. In A. Siegman & S. Feldstein (Eds.), *Nonverbal behavior and communication* (2nd ed., pp. 143–224). Hillsdale, NJ: Erlbaum.

Gonzalez, A., & Zimbardo, P. (1985). Time in perspective. *Psychology Today, 19,* 20–26.

Gudykunst, W., & Ting-Toomey, S. (1988). *Culture and interpersonal communication.* Newbury Park, CA: Sage

Gudykunst, W.B., Ting-Toomey, S., Sudweeks, S., & Steward, L.P. (1996). *Building bridges: Interpersonal skills for a changing world.* Boston: Houghton Mifflin.

Hall, E.T. (1959) *The silent language.* New York: Fawcett.

Hall, E.T. (1983) *The dance of life.* New York: Doubleday.

Hall, E.T., & Hall, M.R. (1990). *Understanding cultural differences: German, French and American.* Yarmouth, ME: Intercultural Press.

Harper, R., Wiens, A., & Matarazzo, J. (1991). *Nonverbal communication: The state of the art.* New York: Wiley.

Hecht, M.L., Collier, M.J., & Ribeau, S.A. (1993). *African American communication: Ethnic identity and cultural interpretation.* Newbury Park, CA: Sage.

Horton, J. (1976) Time and the cool people. In L. Samovan & R. Porter (Eds.), *Intercultural communication: A reader* (2nd ed., pp. 274–284). Belmont, CA: Wadsworth.

Hoskin, J. (1992). *Introduction to Thailand.* Hong Kong: Odyssey Guide.

Kim, M-S. (1992). A comparative analysis of nonverbal expression as portrayed by Korean and American print-media advertising. *Howard Journal of communication, 3,* 320–324.

Knapp, M., & Hall, J. (1997). *Nonverbal communication in human interaction* (4th ed.). Philadelphia: Harcourt, Brace, Jovanovich.

Lustig, M., & Koester, J. (1996). *Intercultural competence: Interpersonal communication across cultures* (2nd ed.). New York: Harper Collins.

McDaniel, E. (1997). Nonverbal communication: A reflection of cultural themes. In L Samovar & R. Porter (Eds.), *Intercultural communication: A reader* (3rd ed., pp 256–265). Belmont, CA: Wadsworth.

Mehrabian, A. (1982). *Silent messages: Implicit communication of emotion and attitudes* (2nd ed.). Belmont, CA: Wadsworth.

Morrison, T., Conway, W., & Borden, G. (1994). *Kiss now or shake hands: How to do business in sixty countries.* Holbrook, MA: Adams Media Corporation.

Ramsey, S. (1979). Nonverbal behavior: An intercultural perspective. In M. Asante, E Newmark, & C. Blake (Eds.), *Handbook of intercultural communication.* Beverly Hills, CA: Sage.

Stewart, E., & Bennett, M. (1991). *American cultural patterns: A cross-cultural perspective* Yarmouth, ME: Intercultural Press.

Stewart, L., Cooper, P., Stewart, A., & Friedley, S. (1996). *Communication and gender* (3rd ed.). Scottsdale, AZ: Gorsuch Scarisbrick.

Storti, C. (1990). *The art of crossing cultures.* Yarmouth, ME: Intercultural Press.

Wenzhong, H., & Grove, C. (1991). *Encountering the Chinese.* Yarmouth, ME: Intercultural Press.

10

ECONOMICS AND CULTURE

Objectives

After reading this chapter and completing the activities, you should be able to:

1. Explain the relationship between economics and culture.
2. Explain how tensions between old and new settlers create misunderstandings.
3. Describe some basic cultural characteristics that are related to the workplace.
4. Explain how changes in the global economic community influence intercultural dynamics.
5. Define the difference between in-group and out-group.
6. Define uncertainty reduction.
7. Describe in writing how economic arrangements help to explain intercultural communication.

In *The Axemaker's Gift*, James Burke and Robert Ornstein (1995) write, "If a late Stone Age baby were to be transported to the present day, dressed appropriately, he or she would pass without notice and would be able, in time, to learn all modern skills" (p. 307).

Our Stone Age baby also would learn quickly that complex and wide-ranging changes are occurring worldwide. One of these changes is the economic global transformation that is affecting how we live and work. He or she would soon witness sophisticated computers, robotics, dislocations, replacement of machines for human laborers, reengineering, and corporate downsizing. Our Stone Age baby would also observe immigrants arriving in countries of their destination, bringing with them their old habits and attitudes about how to manage their lives.

Worldwide, we are being forced to rethink our economic role in human culture. In this chapter we focus on the relationship between economics and culture and the fact that cultural tensions are created by economic transformations.

ECONOMIC GLOBAL TRANSFORMATIONS

Global transformations refer to the worldwide economic and technological changes that influence how people relate to one another. For example, the global economy links people in desert and rural isolation in Mongolia via Worldwide Internet with those in urban areas of Minnesota (Ohmae, 1995, p. l). People in nearly every part of the world can buy blue jeans! East Indian movies are viewed throughout Southeast Asia and Africa. In 1991, while visiting a remote, pristine area of the Gambia, one of the authors was struck by sweet, musical sounds coming from a transistor radio, as a village elder vigorously pounded yams using a centuries-old pestle!

In each instance, these changes are occurring because of information and communications technologies and global market forces. Without knowledge of these changes, it is unlikely that we will understand the attitudes and behaviors that accompany such dramatic economic and cultural shifts. Consequently, we will not know how to respond to new and different cultural situations.

Alvin Toffler (1980) has identified several characteristics of global transformations that influence our ability to communicate competently with people from other cultures: (1) the ground rules of social life are changing; (2) the restructuring of time is intensifying loneliness and social isolation; (3) we are becoming an information society; (4) human tensions are being spawned by technological changes; (5) old values are clashing with technology; and (6) our role models of reality are changing from the teacher, the priest, and the family to multiple outside channels, such as mass media including television, newspapers, radio, and magazines.

Paul Kennedy's (1993) research on increased immigration and what happens when money and jobs cross borders also demonstrates the challenges and opportunities facing individuals of different backgrounds who live and work together. Kennedy believes that our social attitudes, religious beliefs, and culture are probably the most important influences on how quickly we respond to change. For example, it is believed that people who worship their ancestors, or have deeply rooted beliefs in extended families, will have a more difficult time adjusting to global and technological changes.

Another concern is what happens interpersonally when cultural products are transported across boundaries. A recent controversy in France over the Walt Disney Company's dress code illustrates these effects. The Walt Disney

Company insisted that its French workers shave their beards in keeping with Disney's image. The French saw this requirement as insensitive to their cultural norms. As we can see, even though global transformations have made it possible for companies to relocate in outside countries with greater ease, such arrangements threaten existing habits and ways of life. In the case of the Disney example, a basic dress requirement became an assault on French social and cultural standards ("A Disney dress code," *New York Times*, 1991, p. 1).

Tensions between Old and New Settlers

Settlers in a new country bring with them underlying cultural differences concerning job skills, thriftiness, work habits, lifestyles, and attitudes and behaviors, which are revealed in how they interact with others, whether they settle in China, Germany, Brazil, Australia, or the United States.

Consider, for instance, a West Indian woman's behavior in a Korean American grocery store in New York. The woman, attracted to the store's luscious-looking grapes, decided to taste some of them. She was stunned when the Korean grocer accused her of stealing. In the Caribbean culture from which she came, with its wide-open, colorful outdoor markets, it is appropriate for shoppers to sample food. In New York, however, food is displayed primarily for selling, and shoppers are supposed to pay for what they eat! As a result of the incident, race relations in the neighborhood became unsettled, creating serious tensions between African Americans and Korean Americans, which in many similar neighborhoods persist today. Thus, a very important concept for understanding intercultural communication is that changes in economic environments require knowledge of the *rules of conduct* that apply in specific transactions. The Caribbean woman used the rules of her native culture concerning the interaction between buyer and seller, the Korean grocer used his culture's rules. This is a good example of what happens when different cultural and historical experiences clash in an economic context.

There are several reasons why cultural tensions occur in economic exchanges. First, immigrants carry with them their own particular set of skills, knowledge, and behavior. Adrian Furnham (1992) sees an interplay between tension and expectation: "the relationship between a sojourner's expectations (social, academic, economic) for sojourn and the fulfillment (or lack of fulfillment) is a crucial factor in determining adjustment" (p. 341). Skills, values, and expectations follow immigrants and sojourners to other countries and become a source of conflict when they clash with the people and institutions around them. For example, the Japanese believe in group harmony and indirectness. Young Yun Kim and Sheryl Paulk (1994) found that much misunderstanding occurs between Japanese-owned car companies in the United States because of the Japanese preference for indirectness and the North American preference for directness (pp. 117–140).

Second, cultural tensions occur in an economic context because of fear of unemployment. It is easy enough to understand how immigrants from other countries might create unease among established community members in competition for jobs. One factor in this unease is that new immigrants often bring with them a set of work skills different from those of the native cultures. In the seventeenth century, for instance, the Chinese were expelled from Manila because the Filipinos believed that the Chinese, who were investors, retailers, bankers, middlemen, and investors, were responsible for rising prices and shortages of basic necessities and for impoverishing the indigenous population (Sowell, 1983, p. 25). A general feeling of uncertainty about the future potentially creates animosity between immigrants and nonimmigrants. Tensions between immigrants and nonimmigrants are also intensified by a general fear of job replacement. Worldwide, especially in industrialized countries, human labor is being replaced by machines. For example, in the United States between 1989 and 1993, 1.8 million workers lost their jobs in the manufacturing sector, many of them victims of automation. Of the 1.8 million only one-third were able to find new jobs in the public sector (Rifkin, 1995, p. 167).

Jeremy Rifkin (1995) believes that blue collar workers will disappear by the mid-decades of this coming century and that whole categories of workers will dwindle. Thus, men and women who used to count on a decent paying job with Ford, Chrysler, or General Motors following high school, now fear that they might become economic casualties. Unemployed individuals are not only trapped by an increasingly technological society, but are also becoming economically marginalized, which impacts upon human perceptions and, in turn, alters the way we communicate with others.

Economic and technological jolts and jars are bound to affect how we communicate interculturally. The following is a list of some basic characteristics that are tied to the workplace:

1. **Rising levels of stress.** Research indicates that people are more prone to strike out against others in times of stress. As Young Yun Kim (1994) observes: "Stress . . . is part and parcel of strangers' adaptation and growth experiences over time" (p. 393). Feelings of stress are readily translated into outward behavior. This means that the secretary or promotions director who used to communicate easily with others might become noticeably more impatient. Psychologist Craig Brod cites the example of an office worker who "becomes impatient with phone callers who take too long to get to the point" (Rifkin, 1995, p. 187).

Other examples can be seen in Great Britain, France, and especially in Germany where neo-Nazis are exacerbating tensions between recent immigrants and nonimmigrants. Our point is that stress frames our interaction with others. An individual who was once calm, cool, and collected could turn into a proverbial monster if suddenly his or her livelihood is jeopardized! It is easier to understand the transgressions of a co-worker if we know that she not only holds down a twenty-hour job and attends university classes, but is also forced to compete for a smaller slice of the economic pie!

2. **Loss of hope.** Although cultures differ concerning their attitudes toward the future, hope is tied to anticipation about the future, that is, whether we can see positive benefits instead of negative ones, a mode of perception that we refer to as *congenial expectation*. In the United States, this general feeling is tied to the belief that the future will be better and brighter. Edward C. Stewart observes that "most Americans feel that through their efforts a better future can be brought about which will not compromise the welfare and progress of others" (Stewart, 1972, p. 64). An absence of hope can create a bitterness that presents challenges to communication across cultures.

3. **Feelings of redundancy.** All of the things that we have mentioned above can indeed be a bitter curse for those enduring them; however, when we add to these problems a feeling that our skills might become useless in the workplace, our way of life is doubly threatened!

4. **Expressions of virtue.** Finally, tensions occur because of the way groups express their virtues. While most people work hard, some groups assign more importance to certain virtues than do other groups. For example, Thomas Sowell (1983) notes that in the United States, as in Southeast Asia, the Chinese became objects of hatred because of their virtues of endurance and frugality. In the United States, anti-Chinese feelings were so strong that labor unions and political groups organized against Chinese companies, and in some instances ran these companies out of business.

NEW PEOPLE IN THE WORKPLACE

The complexion of the workplace is changing. People who are employed in corporations, universities, fast-food restaurants, and the government are coming from increasingly different cultural backgrounds. African Americans, Latinos, Japanese Americans, gays and lesbians, and the disabled, as well as newly arriving immigrants, are occupying positions as managers, corporate executives, computer analysts, scientists, writers, gardeners, factory stewards, and farm workers.

This growing diversity is exacerbating ethnic tensions, as between Mexican immigrants and other Americans because of the immigrants' willingness to accept lower wages and fewer benefits ("A manifesto for immigration," *Wall Street Journal*, 1996, p. A14). Ponterotto and Pedersen (1993) provide some examples of the conditions that produce or exacerbate tensions between groups. These conditions include that: (1) society is heterogeneous, (2) social change is occurring rapidly, (3) minority group is large or increasing, (4) upward mobility is allowed and valued and (5) increasing minority group represents direct competition and a realistic threat. These characteristics define economic changes that are currently happening in the United States.

As we interact with an increasingly multicultural workforce, we can improve our interpersonal competence if we follow a few general rules.

1. Learn acceptable verbal patterns of address. People from different cultures have different ways to greet and address other people. Some relationships between people, such as student-teacher, father-son, customer-waiter, and boss-clerk, are heavily power coded, while others are not. In Korea, before addressing someone, relative rank must be assessed. In Belgium, you don't address somebody you don't know in a jovial way (Pinxten, 1993). In Bantu, names are frequently avoided in an address in order to express deference and/or intimacy (Mufwene, 1993). However, because of North Americans' insistence on the "perception of equality," we value first names and even use nicknames, forms of address that members of other cultures may find rude, or even offensive.

2. Learn about other groups in the workplace. A good place to start is to learn other cultures' histories, because they provide important clues about how to behave, and what to say or not say. For example, a man hired a student to help him with some chores around his house. One day, before Father's Day, the man asked the worker what he had gotten for his father. "I am a Jehovah's Witness and we don't celebrate Father's Day!" replied the worker. The employer was embarrassed. Of course, it will not be possible to learn every aspect of a specific culture, but we should try to learn as much as possible.

3. Know how friendship rules apply. Styles of friendships differ and are culturally generated. North Americans, for instance, as Edmund C. Glenn (1966) notes, have friendships that originate "around work, children, or political opinion—around charities, games, various occasions for sharing food and alcohol, etc." (p. 50). In the United States, since divisions of friendship are kept separate, it is possible for a person to have different work-related and social-related friendships. Other groups, such as Russians, tend to embrace the whole person in their friendships, rather than relegating them to separate divisions.

4. Recognize that information-based cultures differ from agricultural, industrial, or post-industrial cultures. Economic structures help to explain many of the beliefs, values, and norms of a culture (Carr-Ruffino, 1996). For example, people migrating from agriculturally based economies will normally have the values, myths, concepts, and morals of an agricultural society, such as dependency on an extended family. Such a family structure also carries much clearer decision-making processes and lines of authority, whereas more decisions may be made outside of the family in our information-based cultures.

5. Place communication and meanings in context. In our discussion of Hall's conception of high and low context cultures, we noted that some groups are more "We" oriented while others are more "I" oriented. Because the setting in which communication occurs organizes meanings, and because more unspoken meaning is taken for granted in some cultures than in others, it is important to remember that ignoring this rule can create cultural mischief. For example, an administrative assistant of a faculty council at a Big Ten university, observing that the president pro tem was absent, took it upon herself to tell the African American secretary of the faculty council the smallest details about how to conduct business, including calling the roll! She was accustomed to following her culture's rules of spelling things out and taking very little for granted. As an associate professor, the secretary could easily have taken offense at what looked like racially based condescension. Instead of responding negatively, however, the secretary replied by simply saying, "Thank you."

When messages are made very explicit, if users of such language are not careful, they can be construed as talking in a condescending manner. Knowledge and understanding of the role of such contextual dynamics in the workplace can facilitate interpersonal effectiveness.

6. Observe "because of" and "in spite of" behavioral differences. We may distinguish between things that happen to us because of our race, ethnicity, age, sex, size, or occupation, and things that happen to us "in spite of" these and other factors. For example, if a Native American is next in line at the office xerox machine and a white American approaches the machine, becomes momentarily distracted, and then cuts in front of the Native American did this behavior occur "because of" ethnicity or "in spite of" ethnicity? We will discuss this question more fully in Chapter 13.

Tradition versus Modernity

Change is inevitable, and yet it often brings anguish, disruption, and a rearranging of our lives. All around us are instances of change in everything from how we talk to others, to the music that we listen to, to how we manage our time. Clashes between traditional and new ways of doing things can influence interpersonal relationships. For example, before the advent of television, most families in the United States shared meals together and sat around the kitchen table discussing the events and activities of the day. It was even possible for us to visit rural India and not hear CNN there! We will take a look at a few specific aspects of the clash between tradition and modernity to further highlight how economic changes threaten existing habits and shape how we communicate with others. We have selected several factors that we believe have profound consequences for understanding the interplay between economics, communication, and culture.

Changing Concept of Global Economic Community

To understand the changing dynamics of the current economic global community and its influence on intercultural behavior, it is essential to begin with the breakup of the former Soviet Union. Prior to 1991, the world was clearly ideologically divided and full of "isms." The West, which included the United States, Western Europe, and their allies was on one side, and the Soviet bloc countries of Eastern Europe, which included Poland, Yugoslavia, and Czechoslovakia, were on the other. These bipolar groups were held together by a unifying concept of the "enemy." The Soviet Union and its allies supported communism while the United States and its allies supported democracy and a capitalist economy.

What is important in terms of communication is the fact that the two differing forms of thought served as a powerful means of unifying those who supported the respective doctrines. In a sense the world was much simpler then; individuals could readily distinguish "friend" from "enemy" based upon the geographical area in which a person lived. Then the proverbial "enemy from without," was clearly noticeable and North Americans could and did rally around things that were anticommunist. In fact, it used to be acceptable to use terms such as "better dead than red," or to speak of the Soviet empire and its people disdainfully. And, of course, the opposite also was true: The Soviet Union and its supporters were equally disdainful of the United States and its citizens.

As we interact with others, increasingly, we must assume a *burden of complexity*, because it is no longer acceptable to place people in tight ideological boxes. The rejection of easy categorization encourages thinking about the many-sidedness of others. For example, when a Russian and North American student communicate today, it is likely that they will have more in common with one another than with their parents. Mass media, including television, have played a tremendous role in making this communication possible, as we will see later.

Uncertainty Reduction

Geert Hofstede (1992) suggests that individuals carry with them images of their past that are rooted in childhood. These unconscious orientations strongly affect behavior in work situations. For example, in determining the role of culture in work situations, Hofstede studied a large multinational corporation and the employees of its subsidiaries in 67 countries. He was careful to compare employees working in similar jobs so that any difference would not be due to occupation but to nationality.

Using thirty-two value statements, Hofstede's statistical analyses revealed four basic underlying dimensions around which cultures can be grouped: individualism-collectivism, power distance, masculinity-femininity, and uncertainty avoidance. We will discuss the first three dimensions later. For now we will focus on uncertainty avoidance, because it is a crucial element in determining how cultures cope with economic change.

According to Hofstede, uncertainty avoidance is "the extent to which the members of a society feel comfortable with uncertainty and ambiguity" (p. 91). Unpredictability about the future creates anxiety. For example, how will individuals react to the fact that there is a new global economic game with new rules? And to the foreboding fact that in the United States jobs that used to require only a high school degree are increasingly being held by people with college degrees? It is important to remember that the powerful economic forces that are occurring as a result of globalization are testing our deeply rooted beliefs about the future.

When tensions about the future are paramount, the "how" of our economic lives is questioned. For example, the congressional sponsors of a bill for restricting immigration used the argument that immigration destroys the quality of life in America. ("A manifesto for immigration," *The Wall Street Journal*, 1996, p. A14). People are likely to feel more threatened by other cultures during periods of economic uncertainty.

Reactions to Uncertainty in General

Another way to think about the impact of global economic changes on our future is to consider the very notion of change itself. Lester C. Thurow (1996), a professor of economics at Massachusetts Institute of Technology, argues that despite the conception that people like to change, in reality "all humans hate to change." The Chinese curse, "May you live in interesting times" (which is comparable in damning intent to the North American saying, "May you burn in hell"), is a more realistic representation of reaction to change, says Thurow (p. 232). The following basic elements that economic change demands should help us to understand why we resist change and how this resistance influences our interpersonal interactions with others:

1. **Old modes of behavior don't work; new ones are required.** Think of all the things that are affected by economic change: habits of dress, what we eat, rules of courtesy, how to talk to newcomers, competition for jobs, worker stress, how to interact with computers, and a shift from face-to-face communication to communication with machines. These are only a few of the things that require new rules in the face of economic change.

2. Cherished values are threatened. Links between economic values and the economic uncertainty of not knowing what lies ahead threaten cherished beliefs (Thurow, 1996). For example, in the United States, abortion doctors have been shot because they are viewed as tampering with virtues that are firmly rooted in Christian morality. Other examples of defense of cherished values include the war against obscene music lyrics led by Vice President Albert Gore's wife Tipper and the National Baptist Convention's 1996 promise to boycott Disney films because the company recognizes the civil rights of gays and lesbians.

3. Tendency to retreat into religious fundamentalism. Because people don't react well to threats to their economic way of life, some individuals retreat into religious fundamentalism as a source of stability. For example, during the Middle Ages, when the world seemed to hold fewer certainties, people sought solace in religious fundamentalism, where the rules were clearer (Bredero, 1986). Today, religious economic instability has also triggered a rise of fundamentalism among many groups, including Hindu, Muslim, Jewish, Christian, and Buddhist (Thurow, 1996).

The major lesson in this section is that economic forces are powerful factors in intercultural communication. What can you do to lessen the tension and the uncertainty that comes from changes in our economic condition?

- **Convince yourself that the world is changing and that you must change with it.** The world is complex and various but you can learn enough about change to adjust. Just think of when the Model T Ford was invented. Some people could not envision themselves without the horse and buggy; obviously, however, they soon adjusted.
- **Adjust your attitude.** Develop a perspective that invites an intellectual knowledge of other participants in the new world economics and objectify the concept of change. Think of how, for instance, changes in technology, economics, trading, and other aspects of the global economy are affecting all of our lives. An objectification of your attitude should give you a fresh perspective on dealing with change.
- **Avoid blaming others.** Because the rules for interacting in the new world order are still being made, it is counterproductive to look for scapegoats. Use your energy to focus on yourself instead, and find new ways of coping.
- **Look for comfort zones.** In times of stress, it is essential to find outlets for your energy. For instance, join intercultural nature and exercise clubs.
- **Demonstrate civil verbal and nonverbal behavior.** Chances are very good that competition over jobs, and the tension caused by a new economic game with new rules, will test our linguistic habits. Be especially tactful and appropriate in your language and behavior around people of different cul-

tures. For example, one of the authors and her friend were en route to a wilderness area in Indiana when they came to a four-way stop. The author signaled that she was legally supposed to go first, but the other driver signaled his own desire to go first. Instead of turning this incident into an uncivil nonverbal competition, however, the author simply smiled, and motioned for the other driver to proceed, a gesture that was met with appreciation by the other driver.

- **Observe and record.** Moments of intense anxiety especially require that the facts fit the situation. If you can establish why, when, how, and with what effect something happened to you, chances are that your attitude will accord with the facts of the situation. For example, misunderstandings sometimes occur over matters such as affirmative action and equal opportunity.

COMMUNICATION BETWEEN STATUS AND PLACE

Imagine a world in which status, our place in the proverbial hierarchy, is more important than our country of origin or location. That world, according to Jeremy Rifkin, is here! As Rifkin (1995) notes:

> The growing gap in wages and benefits between top management and the rest of the American workforce is creating a polarized America—a country populated by a small cosmopolitan elite of affluent Americans inside a larger country of increasingly impoverished workers and unemployed persons. The middle class, once the signature of American prosperity, is fast fading, with ominous consequences for the future political stability of the nation. (p. 173)

Our purpose in pointing out this economic shift is not to conjure up pictures of gloom and doom, but rather to indicate a change that is accompanying this shift. Futurists imagine a world in which there will be little or no attachment to place, especially among the so-called "new cosmopolitans," that is, individuals who transcend space and truly participate in a borderless world (Rifkin, 1995, p. 173).

Rifkin has termed this new mobile group a "high-tech nomadic tribe who have more in common with each other than with the citizens of whatever country they happen to be doing business in" (p. 176). Think of the implications of this statement for intercultural affairs. The collapse of the former Soviet Union, which we discussed earlier, for example, has been a key factor in forming new partnerships along economic and social lines, rather than national and political lines.

Affluent people who live in cities such as New York, London, Tokyo, Berlin, and Paris are also creating a strong division between the "haves" and the "have-nots" in every industrial nation. This growing division suggests that we will have to rethink our entire concept of nation-states and the attitudes and behaviors of those who occupy specific countries. It used to be routine to group cultures based on the common things that they shared within a specific border. For example, previously it was easily assumed that a Russian scientist, because of ideological differences, shared little in common with his North American colleague. Today, however, their similarities in occupation and social status are more likely to overrule their national and political differences so that they may have more in common with each other than with the lower classes of their respective countries.

Our point is that new rules will have to be created in order to manage a world so divided along such different lines. For example, it is estimated that by the year 2020, a high-tech, well-to-do group will monopolize more than 60 percent of the income earned in the United States. Think about the influence that this economic reality will have on intercultural relations. To what extent will increasing separation of the rich from the poor influence geopolitical issues and cultural factors worldwide?

USING ECONOMIC ARRANGEMENTS TO EXPLAIN INTERCULTURAL COMMUNICATION

Values and Lifestyle Patterns

"It feels great here. This is a friendly home," says the *feng shui* (pronounced fung shway) consultant William Spear, walking through the entrance of an apartment. "It's not a formal family when there are books in the hall. You're very open, and spreading." This conversation took place between Joanne Kaufman, a writer in New York, and her feng shui consultant. Feng shui, the 3000-year-old Asian art of the study of electromagnetic energy lines, is a popular lifestyle choice among wealthy Westerners ("Feng shui puts your furniture," *Wall Street Journal*, 1996, p. A12).

Lifestyle patterns help to explain what people value. These patterns are concerned with the role of economics and culture in influencing how we live. These days multicultural lifestyle choices related to how we spend our leisure time and the uses we make of our material existence can act as class markers. For example, because of changing lifestyle patterns, upscale, pricy fashionable fast-food establishments are thriving in cities like New York and Dallas, promoting foods such as salmon with mango salsa, Thai noodles and sushi ("Feng shui puts your furniture," *Wall Street Journal*, 1996, p. A12).

To improve interpersonal relationships, then, it is necessary to accept diverse lifestyle preferences and manage differences in perception and expectations. For example, people who read *Gourmet* and *Yachting* magazines differ at some level from those who read *MAD* and *Glamour*.

Information and Decision Making

Today's global economic revolution also is influencing the way people manage information and make decisions. For example, until recently the flow of information in most Western European and North American companies was from the top down. This meant that chief executives, professional managers, field staff, and production workers were arranged in a pyramid-like form, and that each person was assigned tasks and held accountable for specific jobs. There was a clear separation of physical from mental work. Since the 1980s, however, there has been a trend toward teamwork with more workers participating in decision making, from production workers to distribution workers, to problem solvers.

This new approach, called a *team-based model of work*, is rooted in the Japanese cultural conception that all workers should contribute to decision making. It's one of the many examples of changes in work styles that have been brought about by intercultural communication.

KNOWLEDGE WORKERS AND SERVICE WORKERS

The terms *knowledge workers* and *service workers* refer to the increasing division of the global economy into a two-tiered society, with those who have critical knowledge skills in the top tier and those with "service" jobs, such as people who wait tables, provide custodial service, and the like, in the lower tier (Tilly, 1990). Economists note that the increase in these divisions is caused in part by the replacement of humans with machines in many manufacturing jobs, which formerly provided a middle ground between the two tiers.

Class division, absence of attachment to country, an imbalanced knowledge base, and restrictions on access to material goods such as food, clothing, and shelter, all jeopardize intercultural relations across class and national boundaries. For example, workers who possess higher valued knowledge—whether they are in India or in the United States—include bankers, architects, professors, civil engineers, software analysts, biotechnologists, lawyers, psychologists, research scientists, editors, writers, marketing specialists, and film directors. These are the creators, distributors, and processors of knowledge.

According to Rifkin (1995), knowledge workers comprise 4 percent of American income workers. Note the importance of the knowledge class to the global economy, and then consider the declining significance of service workers. Is it likely that intercultural tensions will be exacerbated? What about the divisions between rich and poor countries? To what extent will loyalty to a specific country be modified? And what effect will this factor have on perceptions of interpersonal competence?

Below is a list of changes that are affecting how we interact interculturally in the new global markets.

1. The decision-making process is faster. Because organizations are assigning individuals into work teams, and because these new assignments are eliminating the need to shuffle paper reports and memoranda between departments and divisions, the decision-making process is faster. For example, at one time IBM used to process information through five different departments, which could take up to five days. With restructuring, IBM reduced the time to less than 90 minutes! (Rifkin, 1995) The introduction of computer-based technologies also allows information to be processed horizontally rather than vertically (Rifkin, 1995). By horizontally, we mean the social-solidarity dimension, and by vertically, we mean the status dimension; for example, our role as boss or supervisor.

As we consider decision making in relation to intercultural communication, we should remember that some cultures are in technological infancy and are not at the same informational level. Consider, though, how the introduction of technology will likely shape intercultural interactions. With the introduction of machines, the way we make decisions is bound to change how we interact with others. For example, as biotech farming eliminates more small family farms, the decision-making ties that used to bind parents and children together on farms worldwide will dissolve, requiring new structures of authority.

2. Communication breakdowns, conflicts, and failures are occurring in the workplace. People are becoming more aware of the perception of "unfairness" in the marketplace. As more African Americans, white women, Latinos, and Asians enter the workplace, competition for jobs increases the likelihood of conflict. For example, a National Opinion Research Center poll in 1990 found that over 70 percent of white male Americans believed that whites were being hurt by affirmative action for blacks ("Affirmative action, on the merit system," *New York Times*, 1995, p. A11).

3. There is need for reeducation. Economic challenges facing all cultures will require a vast reeducation campaign to help people understand *why* our economic world is changing and *how* we should adjust to such changes. Such a rapid change of pace could create problems as cultures traditionally less concerned about education are left behind (Kennedy, 1993). For example, the role of women in some countries, such as Somalia, will require new and innovative thinking as models of working women penetrate the country's boundaries.

4. The gap between the rich and the poor requires a new cultural commitment to community. As machines replace people, and as traditional jobs are lost, the gulf between the well-to-do and the poor will widen with huge consequences. For example, it will lead to East–West and North–South tensions, and even to environmental damage (Kennedy, 1993). Think about the differences between rich and poor countries. Can you list any specific ways that these differences affect how people communicate with one another? How does the fact that the United States has less than 5 percent of the earth's human population and yet consumes more than 30 percent of the world's remaining energy and raw materials shape perceptions between North Americans and the rest of the world? (Rifkin, 1995).

INTER-GROUP VERSUS OUT-GROUP ATTITUDES

When we consider all of the economic global changes that are occurring, it is clear that goods and services, along with factors of production and consumption, shape inter-group and out-group attitudes. If we fail to understand the connection between economic factors and change, conflict, and sometimes sustained hostility, is likely to result. For example, Sowell (1994) notes that there were no race riots between the Sinhalese majority and the Tamil minority in Sri Lanka during the first half of the twentieth century. Now, however, there is mob violence between the two groups largely because of the country's economic hardship. In the United States economic factors are intensifying the hostility between Korean Americans and African Americans. Here we consider a few factors that shape in-group and out-group economic and cultural attitudes.

Employment

Employment is an important factor in shaping in-group and out-group attitudes. Employment opportunities are based on skills, work patterns, and compatibility with coworkers. Whether certain groups of workers begin at the top of the employment ladder or rise from the bottom to the top also influences in-group and out-group behavior. For example, immigrants from China, Italy, and Japan have often begun at the bottom of the ladder, holding down menial jobs that are often disdained by members of the countries in which they reside. Once these groups have risen from humble beginnings to positions of influence, however, they sometimes continue to be discriminated against because of their economic origins.

Discrimination

By *discrimination*, we mean the extent to which individuals or certain groups are denied access to jobs because of the racial, ethnic, or other group membership to which they belong (Sowell, 1994). Discrimination, for example, may result in a Malay Chinese being paid more than a Malay Indian, although both are performing the same task with the same degree of efficiency. Whether discrimination is "real" (factually) or "perceived to be real," it can be costly to intergroup relations. In South Africa prior to the 1980s, for example, much hostility existed between blacks and whites because of individual and group job discrimination.

Extent to Which Groups Assimilate

When individuals migrate to other countries, they have an option of moving toward the larger society or away from it. This movement toward or away from others can influence intergroup behavior. Groups that move toward the larger society are perceived as being assimilable while those who resist such movement are in general considered to be "clannish." Henry Taijfel and John C. Turner (1992) note that "pressures to evaluate one's own group positively through in-group/out-group comparisons lead social groups to attempt to differentiate themselves from each other" (p. 117). Walter G. and Cookie White Stephan (1992) see still another reason for conflict between in-groups and out-groups. "In the absence of prior interaction," they say, "in-group members are apt to assume that out-group members are different from them" (p. 16).

The perception of "clannishness" increases when groups are socially isolated from one another. This perception can lead to hostility or provoke outright violence. For example, over the centuries, the Jews of Western Europe were forced to play the role of the "middleman" by performing economic functions such as advancing credit, which other groups did not perform. On many occasions Jews were ostracized, or even killed because they were perceive as materialistic and in economic control. Especially relevant in this example is the way in which economic factors can influence people's perceptions and behavior.

To what extent have you attributed "clannishness" to a group because you failed to understand the complex social and economic factors that shape their behavior?

CONCLUSION

The chapter began with discussions of the fundamental transformations occurring in the global economy that will reshape intercultural communication in the future. Specific factors, such as the changing concept of the global community, uncertainty reduction, information and decision making, and communication between status and place were noted. We suggested some ways that we might adjust to our current economic situation as we confront a more diverse and changing workplace.

Learning to interpret our perceptions of others correctly increasingly depends on our ability to understand those whose lives are being radically affected by economic changes.

QUESTIONS

1. In what ways do economic factors influence our relationship with others?
2. What steps would you take in order to prepare for "a new world order"?
3. What is meant by a burden of complexity?
4. Do you agree with the authors' suggestions on how to lessen tensions and uncertainties that grow out of changes in economic arrangements?
5. Can you cite specific examples of how clashes between cultures occur based on differences in ethnicity and behavior?

ACTIVITIES

1. Select a book such as J. C. Beaglehole's *The Journals of Captain Cook on his Voyages of Discovery*, Augustus Earle's *Narrative of a Nine Month's Residence in New Zealand*, or a book from your university library that tells a story of one group's first encounter with another group. Chart the journey that the writer took when he or she first came into contact with cultural diversity. Note in particular the author's encounters with artifacts and tools, such as jewelry, cowrie beads, and other symbols of economic power or wealth. Describe some of the strategies that both sides in the interpersonal exchange used to communicate with one another. To what extent do struggles over economic goods alter the course of intercultural events?
2. Hugh Duncan notes that there is a relationship between the goods and services that we surround ourselves with and our sense of who we are—our identity. How do consumer goods, such as Nike shoes, Calvin Klein

jeans, or Gucci bags reveal a sense of identity? Do such goods create divisions between classes and cultures, or do they serve as unifying symbols?

3. Make a list of the various economic and social contributions that ethnic groups have made to human culture. Then explain how the ecology of the area and geographic features—mountains, rivers, climate, soil, etc.—helped to shape the culture's contributions. For instance, the first examples of writings occurred in the Near East and grew out of a need for the people to mark quantity and ownership.

REFERENCES

Affirmative action, on the merit system. (1995, August 7). *The New York Times*, p. A11.

A Disney dress code chafes in the land of haute couture. (1991, December 25). *The New York Times*, p. l.

A manifesto for immigration. (1996, February 29). *The Wall Street Journal*, p. A14.

Bredero, A. (1986). *Christendom and christianity in the middle ages.* Grand Rapids, MI: William B. Eerdmans.

Burke, J., & Ornstein, R. (1995). *The axemaker's gift: A double-edged history of human culture.* New York: G.P. Putnam's Sons.

Carr-Ruffino, N. (1996). *Managing diversity: People skills for a multicultural workplace.* International Thomson Publishing.

Feng shui puts your furniture and your life in order. (1996, January 18). *Wall Street Journal*, p. A12.

Furnham, A. (1992). Strangers adaptation. In W. Gudykunst, & Y. Y. Kim (Eds.), *Readings on communicating with strangers: An approach to intercultural communication* (pp. 336–345). New York: McGraw-Hill.

Glenn, E.S. (1966). *Mind, culture, politics.* Mimeographed.

Hofstede, G. (1992). Cultural dimensions in management and planning. In W. Gudykunst & Y. Kim (Eds.), *Readings on communicating with strangers: An approach to intercultural communication* (pp. 89–109). New York: McGraw-Hill.

Kennedy, P. (1993). *Preparing for the twenty-first century.* New York: Vintage Books.

Kim, Y.Y., & Paulk, S. (1994). Interpersonal challenges and personal adjustments: A qualitative analysis of the experiences of American and Japanese coworkers. In R. Wiseman & R. Shuter, (Eds.), *Communicating in multinational organizations* (pp. 117–140). Thousand Oaks, CA: Sage.

Kim, Y.Y. (1994). Adapting to a new culture. In L. A. Samovar & R. Porter (Eds.), *Intercultural communication: A reader* (pp. 393–404). Belmont, CA: Wadsworth.

Mufwene, S (1993). Forms of address: How their social functions may vary. In P. Devita & J. Armstrong (Eds.), *America as a foreign culture* (pp. 60–65). Belmont, CA: Wadsworth.

Ohmae, K. (1995). *The end of the nation state: The rise of regional economics.* New York: Free Press.

Pinxten, R. (1993). America for Americans. In P. Devita & J. Armstrong (Eds.), *America as a foreign culture* (pp. 93–102). Belmont, CA: Wadsworth.

Ponterotto, J., & Pedersen, P. (1993). *Preventing prejudice.* Thousand Oaks, CA: Sage.

Rifkin, J. (1995). *The end of work: The decline of the global labor force and the dawn of the postmarket era.* New York: G.P. Putnam's Sons.

Sowell, T. (1983). *The economics and politics of race, An international perspective.* New York: William Morrow.

Sowell, T. (1994). *Race and culture: A world view.* New York: BasicBooks.

Stephan, W., & Stephan, C. (1992). Intergroup anxiety. In W. Gudykunst & Y. Kim (Eds.), *Readings on communicating with strangers: An approach to intercultural communication* (pp. 16–29). New York: McGraw-Hill.

Stewart, E. (1972). *American cultural patterns: A cross-cultural perspective.* Pittsburgh, PA: Intercultural Communications Network.

Tilly, C. (1990). *Short hours, short shrift: Causes and consequences of part-time work.* Washington, DC : Economic Policy Institute.

Taijfel, H., & Turner, J. (1992). The social identity theory of intergroup Behavior. In W. Gudykunst & Y. Kim (Eds.), *Readings on communicating with strangers: An approach to communicating with strangers* (pp. 112–119). New York: McGraw-Hill.

Toffler, A. (1980). *The third wave.* New York: Bantam Books.

Thurow, L. (1996). *The future of capitalism: How today's economic forces shape tomorrow's world.* New York: William Morrow.

11

CULTURE AND PEDAGOGY

Objectives

After reading this chapter and completing the activities, you should be able to:

1. Explain the functions of schools.
2. Identify the cultural dimensions that affect the classroom.
3. Define learning styles.
4. Describe the learning styles discussed in this chapter.
5. Explain how learning style and culture are related.
6. Outline ways to prepare to work with others from diverse backgrounds.

> *The familiar nursery school activity*
> *of having children mix flour and water*
> *to make paste fails completely when Native*
> *American children refuse to make the*
> *paste because flour is food*
> *and one does not play with food.*
>
> (Rivlin, 1977, p. 109)

As the above quote indicates, the educational environment is fraught with intercultural stumbling blocks. Yet most teachers are not trained to work in multicultural settings. In fact, as Condon (1986) argues, the classroom culture is, to a great extent, an extension of mainstream American culture. For example, the values of the American classroom are those of independence, individualism, and concern for relevance and application. As a result, students whose backgrounds are different from this dominant culture may have a difficult time adjusting to the classroom culture.

This is true because, as Bowman (1989) tells us, culture influences both behavior and psychological processes. It affects the way we perceive the world. Culture "forms a prism through which members of a group see the world and create shared meanings" (p. 118).

Education, both formal and informal, seeks to help form the prism of each culture. Thus, in every culture, schools serve a variety of functions. Samovar, Porter, and Stefani (1998) suggest three. According to these authors, schools

1. Help fashion the individual since it offers children a set of guidelines and values and makes them aware of what they need to know in order to become productive and successful members of their culture.
2. Are a primary means by which a culture's history and tradition are passed from one generation to the next.
3. Teach the informal knowledge of a culture such as the rules of correct conduct, hierarchy of cultural values, gender-role expectations, and how to treat others. (pp. 198–199)

Cultural background affects attitudes, beliefs, and values about education, ideas about how classes ought to be conducted, how students and teachers ought to interact, and what types of relationships are appropriate for students and teachers (Collier & Powell, 1990). As classrooms in the United States become more diverse culturally, it is important for both teachers and students to understand some of the cultural factors that affect learning. In a recent article in *Education Week* (April 10, 1986), Debra Viadero demonstrates this in the following example:

> *Ms. White, a teacher in an isolated rural community, is teaching her first graders how to tell time. She points to a clock, telling her students that it's ten o'clock because the big hand is on the twelve and the little hand is on the ten.*
>
> *"What time is it?" she asks the students. Many of the white children raise their hands, eager to answer. The black students sit silently. A few give her a puzzled look. Ms. White concludes that many of her black students do not know the answer, and she silently makes a note to herself to revisit the concept with them later. But researchers who study the role that culture plays in learning say that Ms. White may have the wrong take on what is going on with her students. What is really happening, they say, is that two distinct cultures are bumping up against one another, forming an invisible wall that stands in the way of learning and communication. Like their teacher, the white children in this community grew up in families where adults routinely quizzed children the way their teacher does. "What color is this?" a parent might say, pointing to a red ball. In the African American*

children's families, such questions were posed only when someone genuinely needed to know the answer. "What is she asking us for?" some of the black children might have wondered. "She just told us it was ten o'clock." (p. 39–40)

No doubt roadblocks such as this one will become increasingly common since statistics suggest that by the year 2000, 40 percent of the children in American classrooms will be non-white. However, teachers are primarily white and research suggests this will continue to be the case (Viadero, 1986). African American, Asian, Hispanic, and Native American teachers now make up just 10 percent of the teaching force (Viadero, 1986). In addition, 6.3 million children in the United States report speaking a non-English language at home (National Association of Bilingual Education, 1993).

The cultural differences in classrooms are important to understand for three major reasons: (1) cultural differences may result in differences in learning style, (2) cultural differences affect relationships in the educational environment, and (3) understanding cultural differences can help us communicate more effectively with our classmates. Before we explore each of these three areas it is useful to examine the cultural dimensions that affect classroom communication.

CULTURAL DIMENSIONS

In his work Hofstede (1991) suggests four cultural dimensions that affect what occurs in a classroom. The first of these is individualism/collectivism. Individualist cultures assume that any person looks primarily after his or her own interest and the interest of his or her immediate family (husband, wife, and children). Collectivist cultures assume that any person through birth and possible later events belongs to one or more tight "in-groups," from which he or she cannot detach him- or herself. The "in-group" (whether extended family, clan, or organization) protects the interest of its members, but in turn expects their permanent loyalty. A collectivist society is tightly integrated; an individualist society is loosely integrated.

In terms of classroom behavior, the dimensions suggest that in collectivist cultures students expect to learn how to do, speak up in class only when called upon personally to by the teacher, and see education as a way of gaining prestige within their social environment and of joining a higher status group. Formal harmony is important and neither a teacher nor any student should ever be made to lose face. On the other hand, in individualistic cultures, students expect to learn how to learn and will speak up in class in response to a general invitation by the teacher. Education is viewed as a way of improving one's economic worth and self-respect based on ability and competence. In addition, confrontation is not necessarily avoided; conflicts can be brought into the open; and face-consciousness is weak.

In a collectivist culture, harmony with nature, circularity, and the group is emphasized rather than the individual. That is why Native American children learn better in an environment that is noncompetitive, holistic, and cooperative (Lustig & Koester, 1996). Mexican children, because their culture emphasizes cooperation, allow others to share their homework or answers. This shows group solidarity, helpfulness, and generosity—important characteristics of their collectivist culture (Grossman, 1984).

Contrast this with the American educational system, which emphasizes competition and the individual. If an American student shares his or her homework, he or she is seen as dishonest, perhaps even a cheater!

A second dimension is power distance. Power distance as a characteristic of a culture defines the extent to which the less powerful persons in a society accept inequality in power and consider it normal. Inequality exists within any culture, but the degree of it that is tolerated varies between one culture and another.

If the power distance of a culture is small, appropriate behaviors are different than those of a culture that has a large power distance. In terms of classroom behavior, the power dimension suggests that in small power distance societies, the educational process is student centered. The students initiate communication, outline their own paths to learning, and can contradict the teacher.

In large power distance societies, the educational process is teacher centered. The teacher initiates all communication, outlines the paths of learning students should follow, and is never publicly criticized or contradicted. In large power distance societies, the emphasis is on the personal "wisdom" of the teacher, while in small power distance societies the emphasis is on impersonal "truth" that can be obtained by any competent person.

In Asian societies, the teacher is given much respect. There is a large power distance between teacher and student. A Chinese student would never consider arguing with a teacher. The role of the Asian student is to accept and respect the wisdom of the teacher. The teacher presents information and the student accepts it without question. Asking questions is seen as a challenge to the teacher's authority or as an admission of the student's ignorance. Neither is desirable (Wallach & Metcalf, 1995).

In the United States, where the power difference is small, students are encouraged to challenge the teacher and one another. The teacher encourages students to discuss and debate issues, learn how to solve problems, and create their own answers to the questions posed. Americans prefer to learn through personal discovery and problem solving rather than through memorizing facts presented to them by an authority figure.

Uncertainty avoidance is the third of Hofstede's dimensions. As a characteristic of a culture it defines the extent to which people within a culture are made nervous by situations that they perceive as unstructured, unclear, or unpredictable, situations that they therefore try to avoid by maintaining strict codes of behavior and a belief in absolute truths. Cultures with a strong uncertainty avoidance are active, aggressive, emotional, compulsive, security seeking, and intolerant; cultures with a weak uncertainty avoidance are contemplative, less aggressive, unemotional, relaxed, accept personal risks, and are relatively tolerant.

In a weak uncertainty avoidance society, students feel comfortable in unstructured learning situation (vague objectives, no timetables, broad assignments) and are rewarded for innovative approaches to problem solving. Teachers are allowed to say, "I don't know," interpret intellectual disagreement as stimulating, and seek parents' ideas.

In strong uncertainty societies, students feel comfortable in structured learning situations (precise objectives, strict timetable, detailed assignments) and are rewarded for accuracy in problem solving. Teachers are expected to have all the answers, interpret intellectual disagreement as personal disloyalty and consider themselves experts who do not need parents' ideas (and parents agree).

In a strong uncertainty avoidance culture, students prefer clear instructions, avoid conflict, and dislike competition. Examples of cultures with strong uncertainty avoidance are France, Chile, Spain, Portugal, Japan, Peru, and Argentina. The United States, Great Britain, Denmark, Ireland, and India are characterized by weak uncertainty avoidance. Students in these countries are competitive, need fewer instructions, and see conflict as stimulating.

The final dimension is masculinity/femininity. Masculinity as a characteristic of a culture opposes femininity. The two differ in the social roles attributed to men. The cultures labeled as masculine strive for maximal distinction between what men are expected to do and what women are expected to do. They expect men to be assertive, ambitious, and competitive, to strive for material success, and to respect whatever is big, strong, and fast. They expect women to serve and to care for the nonmaterial quality of life, for children, and for the weak. Feminine cultures, on the other hand, define relatively overlapping social roles for the sexes, in which, in particular, men need not be ambitious or competitive but may go for a different quality of life than material success; men may respect whatever is small, weak, and slow. In both masculine and feminine cultures, the dominant values within political and work organizations are those of men. So, in masculine cultures these politicalizational values stress material success and assertiveness; in feminine cultures they stress other types of quality of life, interpersonal relationships, and concern for the weak (Hofstede, 1991).

In terms of the classroom, we can again make some assumptions about behavior depending on whether a culture is feminine or masculine. In feminine societies, teachers avoid openly praising students because academic achievement is less important than successful interpersonal relationships, and cooperation among students is fostered. Teachers use average students as the "norm." In feminine societies a student's failure in school is a relatively minor event. The system rewards students' social adaptations.

In masculine societies, teachers openly praise good students because academic achievement is highly regarded and competition is fostered. Teachers use the best students as the "norm." Academic failure is a severe blow to the self-image. The system rewards academic performance.

A masculine culture values assertiveness and competitiveness. High masculinity countries include Japan, Mexico, Ireland, Austria, Venezuela, Switzerland, Great Britain, and Germany. High feminine countries include Chile, Portugal, Thailand, Sweden, Norway, the Netherlands, Denmark, and Finland. These countries place a high value on interpersonal relationships, compassion, and nurturing.

LEARNING STYLES

These cultural dimensions lead to differences in terms of how students learn. Researchers and teachers have, in recent years, been giving increased attention to the way people learn in intercultural settings (e.g., Cole & Means, 1981; Cooper, 1995; Cushner, 1990; Cushner, McClelland, & Safford, 1992). The underlying assumption of this increased attention is the idea that the way students in one culture learn may not be the way students of a different culture learn (Brislin & Yoshida, 1994; Taylor, 1994). For example, after lecturing to a class of Chinese students at the Chinese University of Hong Kong, one of the authors of this book asked students if they understood and all responded that they did. However, their subsequent actions made it clear that they did not. It became clear that students often said they understood, whether they did or not, out of respect for the professor, or their desire not to lose face.

Learning style refers to the way in which a learner learns and processes information. According to Dunn, Dunn, and Price (1979, p. 53), "learning style is the way in which responses are made because of individual psychological differences." Keefe defines learning style as "cognitive, affective, and psychological traits that serve as relatively stable indicators of how learners perceive, interact with and respond to the learning environment" (1982, p. 44). For example, Sinatra (1986) reviewed a large body of research that indicates that the learning style of the gifted and talented can be described as independent, internally controlled, self-motivated, persistent, perceptually strong, task committed, and nonconforming. These learners prefer learning through independent studies and projects rather than through lecture or discussion.

As Dunn, Beaudry, and Klavas (1989) indicate, no learning style is better or worse than another. In fact, all learning styles are found within all ethnic groups to a varying degree but with a dominant style for each ethnicity (Hollins, King, & Hayman, 1994). What is important, however, is the fact that the closer the match between a student's style and the teacher's, the higher the student's grade point average. When students are permitted to learn difficult academic information or skills through their identified learning style preferences, they tend to achieve statistically higher test and aptitude scores than when instruction is dissonant with their preferences.

COGNITIVE LEARNING STYLES

The first is a preference for groups versus individual learning. In Euro-American cultures, education typically emphasizes individual learning. Each student strives for his or her individual grade or praise. In many collectivist cultures, group learning is expected. For example, children of Hawaiian ancestry come under the guidance of their older siblings very early in life. Parents interact with their children as a group, not so much as individuals. As a result of this kind of upbringing, children learn best from siblings and peers in group situations, not from one adult, as is typical in Euro-American cultures as well as in the school setting (Cushner & Brislin, 1996).

In other words, some cultures emphasize cooperation while others emphasize competition. African Americans, Asian Americans, and Hispanic Americans raise their children cooperatively, and the educational system perpetuates this cooperativeness. Peers offer help to one another. In contrast, U.S. students are encouraged to work alone. Even when they work in groups, each student is expected to "carry his or her own weight."

A second difference in learning style is field dependent versus field independent. In a field-dependent learning style, people tend to "take elements or background variables from the environment into account. . . [and] to perceive the event holistically, including the emotionality and the feelings associated with the entire event" (Lieberman, 1994, p. 179). By contrast, field-independent learners are analytical and use strategies to isolate elements of the field (Brown, 1987). Field-dependent learners prefer to work with others, seek guidance from the teacher, and receive rewards based on their relationship with the group. In contrast, field-independent learners prefer to work alone, are task oriented, and prefer rewards based on individual competition (Lieberman, 1997). To put it simply, some people see the forest; some see the trees. Field-dependent style is prevalent in group-oriented, high context, collectivist societies. Field-independent styles predominate in low-context, highly competitive, highly industrialized societies (Lieberman, 1994).

Tolerance for ambiguity is related to learning style. Some cultures have more tolerance for ambiguity than others. Tolerance (or intolerance) of ambiguity is related to open-mindedness about differences and/or contradictions. Cultures with a low tolerance for ambiguity tend to emphasize bipolar languages. As Lieberman (1994) suggests, the English language emphasizes bipolarity. In a problem-solving situation, bipolar language might be: "This is either right or wrong, black or white, good or bad, yes or no, correct or incorrect" (p. 179). Thus, as Samovar and Porter (1995) state:

> *Therefore, tolerance for ambiguity is tied to the degree of bipolarity in the structure and meaning of a cultures language. In the scientifically oriented, competitive American culture, tolerance for ambiguity is not perceived positively in the average classroom. On the other hand, in cultures where bipolarity is deemphasized, there is much higher tolerance for ambiguity. Cultures such as that of India are high in tolerance of ambiguity, as exemplified by Nemi Jain who states: "One must know that one's judgments are true only partially and can be no means be regarded as true in absolute terms."* (p. 252)

Some students learn best in real-life settings. Some cultures emphasize this type of learning particularly those without long histories of written language. As Cushner and Brislin (1996) explain:

> *Hunting and gathering societies, in which young males accompany the adults on hunting expeditions from a relatively early age, offer an example of in-context learning. The child learns through active involvement and participation with the adult teacher in the hunting process, with his contributions being of some value to the task at hand, not by passively observing procedures and techniques for future application. He is immediately rewarded when he masters the required skills and completes a kill, not by internalizing the procedure and reproducing it in symbol form (either orally or in writing) upon command.* (p. 339)

Communication and Relational Styles

Not only do learners have cognitive preferences for how they learn, they also have preferences for their communication and relational styles of learning. For example, some cultures value reflectivity (a slow, deliberative seeking of answers) while others value impulsivity (quick guesses). In American society students are rewarded for risk taking and creativity, for trial and error methods of learning. Often, low context cultures value impulsivity. High conte cultures, such as China, value reflectivity. An individual is expected to consider multiple variables before making a decision since a problem resulting from a decision reached in haste can result in a loss of face (Grossman, 1995).

Topic-centered versus topic-associating, that is, how students study a problem, is influenced by culture. Euro-American children tend to be topic-centered. Their accounts of events focus on a single topic or closely related topics and are ordered in a linear fashion and lead to a resolution (Au, 1993). The topic-associating style, often used by African American children, presents "a series of episodes linked to some person or theme. These links are implicit in the account and are not stated" (Au, 1993, p. 96).

What happens when a teacher is topic-centered and a student is topic-associating? Stefani (1997) answers this question: When the instructor is not familiar with the topic-associating style, he or she may inadvertently mis-time questions or not allow the student to finish his or her thought because the instructor does not understand how each episode is connected to the other.

Culture influences how independent or dependent a learner is. Some cultures foster independent learning. The student doesn't rely upon the support or opinions of the teacher. Most European-American students are independent learners. Dependent learners, for example, Hispanic Americans, Asian Americans, and Native Americans, rarely "go off on their own." Rather, they ask their teacher for directions and feedback (Grossman, 1995).

Direct and indirect communication is affected by culture. American culture tends to be direct in its communication—blunt and frank. Yet, to cultures that value indirect communication, such as Asian cultures, such directness violates many of their cultural norms. Nguyen (1986) makes this clear: American straightforwardness is considered at best impolite if not brutal. In Indochina, one does not come directly to the point. To do so is, for an American, a mark of honesty and forthrightness while a person from Indochina sees it as a lack of intelligence or courtesy. (p. 6).

Some cultures have very informal styles of communication while others have more formal styles. These styles influence the classroom. For example, in Turkey, Egypt, and Iran, when the teacher enters the room, students stand. These cultures are quite formal. In contrast, American classrooms are very informal. Certainly students are not expected to stand when the teacher enters the room. In American college classrooms professors are often called by their first name. That would never happen in a more formal culture such as China or Japan.

We discussed nonverbal communication and culture in Chapter 9. In terms of the classroom, identify what the following behaviors mean:

- Wrinkling of the nose
- Raised eyebrows
- Snapping of the fingers

If you are in Puerto Rico, a wrinkled nose signals, "I don't understand."
In Alaskan native cultures it signals "no." Raised eyebrows in Alaska native
culture signifies "yes." Accompanied by a shrug, it may mean "I don't know"
in an American classroom. Snapping your fingers would be considered rude
in an American classroom, but in Jamaica it signals you know the answer to
the question the teacher asked. And so it goes. Nonverbal cues differ greatly
across cultures and affect the communication and relational styles of classrooms.

Differences as a Result of Learning Styles

It would be impossible to outline the cultural characteristics of every ethnic
group here. We must identify the groups present in our classrooms and learn
about the characteristics of each.

In terms of our focus, the communication variables that "are identifiable
as culturally determined, as constituting ethnic communication styles, and as
being influential in shaping interactions among members of different ethnic
groups" (Gay, 1978) are the following:

Attitudes

Social organizations (status of people within the structure)

Patterns of thought role prescription (how people are supposed to behave)

Language

Use and organization of space

Vocabulary

Time conceptualizations nonverbal expressions

Thus, the above list constitutes the categories of knowledge you will need
about a particular ethnic group in order to communicate effectively with that
group.

Anderson and Powell (1988), in their article on cultural influences on education processes, review research that highlights intercultural differences.
For example, there is virtually no classroom interaction in Vietnamese, Mexican, or Chinese classrooms. In contrast, in an Israeli kibbutz students talk
among themselves, address teachers by their first names, and criticize teachers when they feel teachers are wrong.

Cooper (1995) outlines research suggesting that in Italian classrooms,
children greet their teacher with a kiss on both cheeks, and students and
teachers touch one another frequently. Black children may use back channel-
ing—a vocal response that is meant to encourage or reinforce the speaker

("yeah," "go on," "right on," etc.). Often Anglo-American teachers view this interaction as an interruption rather than a reinforcer. Looking at the teacher is a sign of disrespect in Jamaican and black African cultures, but sign of respect in the United States.

While the Anglo-American culture values punctuality and a monochronic view of time, other cultures may not. This can cause problems in the educational process. For example, Hispanic students are not conditioned to use every moment in a productive, task-oriented way. American Indians have a polychronic view of time—things are done when the time is right, not by the time on a clock or a date on the calendar.

Thus, in the past decade, considerable research has focused on students' learning styles. In general, the research supports the conclusions that Hispanic American, American Indian, black, and female students respond better to teaching methods that emphasize holistic thinking, cooperative learning, a valuing of personal knowledge, a concrete orientation, the oral tradition, and a reliance on imagery and expressiveness. This learning style is quite different from that of most college instructors, Asian Americans, and male students, whose learning style is characterized by an abstract, independent, written, technical orientation.

Although general statements such as these can be made as a result of existing research, careful attention must be given to individual differences so that stereotyping can be avoided. Teachers need to identify their students' learning styles. There are numerous commercially published instruments that measure one or many aspects of learning style. However, Cornett (1983) suggests that even without formal instruments, it is possible to obtain assessment information from observations of students or discussing with students their own views by asking "How, when, where, and what do you learn best?" Another technique is to ask students to write or tell about a learning or study situation in which they were either productive or nonproductive and analyze the situation.

Kleinfield (1994) indicates that "the concept of learning styles is useful when it reminds teacher to create rich and interesting classrooms where children can learn in many different ways" (p. 156). She provides an example of how this might be done. In a remote Eskimo village a teacher tried to introduce the concepts of "calories" and "energy formation" through a lecture. But the expressions on the children's faces indicated that they were bored. So, the teacher later asked the children to attend a steambath, an important event in the village's culture. As they observed what happened to the water when it was gas, solid, and liquid, they asked questions such as, "What happens to the steam when it goes out the steambath when someone opens the door?" Kleinfeld points out that the teacher adapted the science lesson to the cultural setting and the learning styles of the children.

EFFECTIVE INTERCULTURAL COMMUNICATION
IN EDUCATION ENVIRONMENTS

Using the work of Condon (1986), Cooper (1995) suggests that in order to communicate effectively in an intercultural classroom, it is necessary to consider the following:

1. Our expectation for appropriate student behavior. We may, for example, expect students to use Standard English in both speaking and writing.
2. The student's actual behavior. The student may or may not use Standard English.
3. Our feeling about the student's behavior as well as the basis for this feeling ("I'm angry because the student refuses to learn Standard English").
4. Our explanations for the behavior ("The student isn't motivated to team"), remembering that these explanations reflect our cultural values.
5. Our response to the student's behavior. We may reprimand the student—either publicly or privately. Again, our response reflects our cultural values and norms.

When teachers are aware of the cultural differences in their classrooms, understand their attitudes concerning them, and understand the five steps outlined above, they can begin to structure their classroom so that they communicate effectively with all students. They can, for example, respect the ethnic background of their students and demonstrate that respect by reading stories with varied ethnic and racial content in literature class, have students study world events from different cultural perspectives in social studies class. However, multicultural education is not content alone: A teacher's attitude toward culturally diverse students and how she or he communicates that attitude is extremely important.

Gail Sorensen (1989) suggests that although there is much research in multicultural issues, little of it is helpful in guiding teachers. She shares an example of what she learned from public school teachers in Fresno, California:

First, never touch Hmong children on the top of the head. This is where the spirits reside and they become angry when touched. Second, allow children to wear strings around their wrists and ankles. Blue string keep the good spirits in, while red string keeps the evil spirits out. Third, watch for signs of a sore throat and subsequent distress. Many of the Asians treat sore throats by having their children eat sand. Fourth, contact the family if students are absent for prolonged periods. When a member of the family is believed to be dying, children may be kept home to protect the ailing person from evil spirits. Fifth, if homework is rarely completed, check on the living conditions at home. Many refugees come here in extended families. No mat-

ter what housing arrangements are made, they may be living with more than 10 people in a two-bedroom apartment. Additionally, it has been discovered that some refugees have brought in dirt and "grow lights" to raise their own food in one room of the apartment. The school children may have no place to do their work. (p. 52)

One of the authors of this text taught Chinese students at the Chinese University of Hong Kong. American teaching strategies can be problematic for the Chinese. For example, never ask Chinese students, "Are there any questions?" To ask a question would show one's ignorance, and a loss of face would result. However, if a teacher asks, "Have I explained this clearly?" students are free to ask question because it is the teacher's "fault" that they don't understand. If she had explained clearly, there would be no need for questions!

These examples tell us that teaching in a culturally diverse classroom is not an easy task. Teachers need special training. In preparing to work with a diverse group, Chism, Cano, and Pruitt (1989) suggest the following:

1. Understand nontraditional learning styles.
2. Learn about the history and culture of nontraditional groups.
3. Research the contributions of women and ethnic minorities.
4. Uncover your own biases.
5. Learn about bias in instructional materials.
6. Learn about your school's resources for nontraditional students.

Finally, teachers should use a variety of teaching methods—discussion, simulations, role-plays, lectures, active, hands-on experiences. In addition, teachers should provide opportunities for students to work cooperatively as well as individually; to stress cooperation as well as competition. Students should also be given choices in how to complete an assignment—a paper, an art project, an oral report.

CONCLUSION

In this chapter we have discussed how cultural differences affect educational environments. How simple it sometimes can be to avoid problems in the classroom if we simply understand that culture affects how students learn. Imagine if the teacher in the opening example of this chapter had considered the culture of the students!

If we hope to be effective communicators in the educational environment we need to understand that cultural differences may result in differences in learning style and affect the student/teacher relationship as well as the relationships among students in the educational environment. In addition, we need to remember that understanding cultural differences can help us to avoid problems such as that presented at the beginning of this chapter.

QUESTIONS

1. Describe your learning style. How might your learning style cause you difficulties in another culture?
2. Consider a classroom in which you are a member. Describe how the teacher does or does not take into account Hofstede's four cultural dimensions.
3. Using Gay's list (p. 202) analyze your own culture. What communication problems might occur in educational environments as a result of the differences between the two cultures?
4. Examine the textbooks used in the courses you are taking. What biases do you see? What effect might these have in the educational environment?

ACTIVITIES

To check your understanding of the principles discussed in this chapter, read the following critical incident (Cushner & Brislin, 1996, pp. 200–201) and decide what is the best course of action. Answers appear on page 207 (Cushner & Brislin, 1996, p. 222).

Critical Incident
The New ESL Teacher

After two years of travel throughout Asia and Europe and a year of study and preparation in a master's program in English as a Second Language (ESL), George felt quite confident. Although he had not had any real classroom experience, he had taught English informally to a Malaysian student he met while traveling, had studied all the latest approaches to teaching English, was keen to employ intercultural dimensions in his teaching, and was quite eager to get to know as many international students coming to the United States as he could. He was, not surprisingly, excited to be offered his first position at a nearby university to teach in a special ESL summer program for a group of visiting Japanese students. He eagerly prepared for his upcoming teaching assignment.

The first day of class arrived. George had found out earlier that the majority of his students would be business majors, because the importance of English for business purposes had become quite evident. From the very first day, even though he had learned a bit of Japanese during his earlier travels, George made sure to only use English in class to communicate and to teach his students. He tried to be as friendly as he could and to maintain interaction with his students. It puzzled him that when he approached a student with a question, the student inevitably looked down at his or her textbook and would not give an answer to the question he asked. This behavior continued down the line, with each student maintaining an embarrassed silence. The students were not the only ones embarrassed by the silence—George was also in a quandary. He did not know how to manage the situation. He decided to sit next to one of his students in order to communicate better. To his dismay, he noticed after he tried this that more and more students started sitting at the back of the classroom rather than filling the chairs up front.

Things finally flared up when George asked a particular student to summarize the points made in the previous class. What he had neglected to notice was that the student he chose had been absent the previous day. As a result, the student maintained a long and uncomfortable silence. George had had enough. He told the student to look at him directly and tell him if she knew the material. After this confrontation, most of the students stopped coming to class.

What insights might you offer George that would help him better understand what was going on?

1. Japanese students revere and respect elderly teachers. There was not enough of an age gap between George and his students.
2. In Japanese custom, in order to gain full respect, it is necessary to greet people in the Japanese language. Because George made a point of using only English, he never really gained the respect of his students.
3. George's style of teaching was in direct conflict with the manner in which Japanese students learn.
4. George was struggling because he was a new teacher. The situation would certainly improve as he gained experience and confidence.

Answers

1. It is true that Japanese students revere and respect elderly teachers, but Japanese students tend to revere and respect any and all teachers. The title *sansei*, given to teachers, is a sign of honor and respect. George would most probably have been afforded all the respect coming to any teacher by Japanese students—certainly far more respect than would be given by most American students. Please select an alternative explanation.
2. It is true that there may be certain customs for greeting that are important to the maintenance of interpersonal relationships. However, these students came to the United States with the express intention of learning English

in an American context. There is no indication in the story that George's use of English only was the problem. Please select an alternative explanation.

3. This explanation provides the most insight into this situation. In George's classroom there were many instances where instructional style and learning style seemed to be in conflict. George's attempts at friendliness and informality would have been rather uncomfortable for students accustomed to a more formal, structured between teacher and student. In addition, in Japan, where group conformity is strongly encouraged, a teacher would rarely single individual students out from the group. Students thus singled out would become quite uncomfortable, which would explain George's students' reluctance to return to class. On another level, this incident demonstrates how many people who are well-traveled believe they know how to be effective when working intimately with those from other cultures; George's problems clearly suggest that this is not always the case.

4. It is true that George was a new teacher and was probably learning to adapt all that he had in school to the real world of teaching. However, in this case, without attending to the cultural differences in learning and teaching style, it was unlikely things would change. There is a better explanation for the problems George experienced. Please choose again.

REFERENCES

Anderson, J., & Powell, R. (1988). Cultural influences on educational processes. In L. Samovar & L. Porter (Eds.), *Intercultural communication: A reader* (pp. 207–214). Belmont, CA: Wadsworth.

Au, K.H. (1993). *Literacy instruction in multicultural settings.* New York: Harcourt Brace

Bochner, S. (1994). Cross-cultural differences in the self-concept. A test of Hofstede's individualism-collectivism distinction. *Journal of Cross-Cultural Psychology, 25* 273–283.

Bowman, B. (1989). Educating language minority children: Challenges and opportunities. *Phi Delta Kappan, 1,* 18–120.

Brislin, R.W., & Yoshida, T. (Eds.). (1994). *Improving intercultural interactions: Modules for cross-cultural training programs.* Thousand Oaks, CA: Sage.

Brown, H.D. (1987). Principles of language learning and teaching (2nd ed.). Englewood Cliffs, NJ: Prentice-Hall.

Chism, N., Cano, J., & Pruitt, A. (1989). Teaching in a diverse environment: Knowledge and +j skills needed by TAs. In J. Nyquist, R. Abbott, & D. Wulff (Eds.) *Teaching assistant training in the 1990s: New directions for teaching and learning* (pp 23–35). San Francisco: Jossey-Bass.

Cole, M., & Means, B. (1981). *Comparative studies of how people think.* Cambridge, MA Harvard University Press.

Collier, M.J., & Powell, R. (1990). Ethnicity, instructional communication and classroom systems. *Communication Quarterly, 38,* 334–349.

Condon, J. (1986). The ethnocentric classroom. In J. Civikly (Ed.), *Communicating in college classrooms* (pp. 11–20). San Francisco: Jossey-Bass.

Cooper, P. (1995). *Communication for the classroom teacher* (5th ed.). Scottsdale, AZ: Gorsuch Scarisbrick.

Cornett, C. (1983). What you should know about teaching and learning styles. Bloomington, IN: *Phi Delta Kappa* Education Foundation.

Cushner, K. (1990). Cross-cultural psychology and the formal classroom. In R.W. Brislin (Ed.), *Applied cross-cultural psychology* (pp. 98–120). Newbury Park, CA: Sage.

Cushner, K., & Brislin, R. (1996). *Intercultural interactions: A practical guide* (2nd ed.). Thousand Oaks, CA: Sage.

Cushner, K., McClelland, A., & Safford, P. (1992). *Human diversity in education: An integrative approach.* New York: McGraw-Hill.

Dunn, R., Beaudry, J., & Klavas, A. (1989). A survey of research on learning styles. *Educational Leadership,* p. 50–58.

Dunn, R. Dunn, K., & Price, G. (1979). Identifying individual learning styles. In E. Kieman (Ed.), *Student learning styles: Diagnosing and prescribing programs* (pp. 51–60). Reston, VA: National Association of Secondary School Principals.

Frankel, C. (1965). *The neglected aspect of foreign affairs.* Washington, DC: Brookings Institute.

Gay, G. (1978). Viewing the pluralistic classroom as a cultural microcosm. *Educational Research Quarterly, 2,* 51–55.

Gibb, J. (1961). Defensive communication. *Journal of Communication, 2,* 141–148.

Grossman, H. (1984). *Educating Hispanic students: Cultural implications for instruction, classroom management, and assessment.* Springfield, IL: Charles C. Thomas.

Grossman, H. (1995). *Teaching in a diverse society.* Boston: Allyn & Bacon.

Hofstede, G. (1991). *Cultures and organizations: Software of the mind.* London: McGraw-Hill.

Hollins, E.R., King, J.E., & Hayman, W.C. (1994). *Teaching diverse populations: Formulating a knowledge base.* New York: State University of New York Press.

Keefe, J. (1982). *Student learning styles and brain behavior.* Reston, VA: National Association of Secondary School Principals.

Kleinfield, J. (1994). Learning styles and culture. In W.J. Lonner & R.S. Malpass (Eds.), *Psychology and culture* (pp. 151–156). Boston: Allyn and Bacon.

Lieberman, D. (1994). Ethnocognitivism, problem solving and hemisphericity. In L. Samovar & R. Porter (Eds.), *Intercultural communication: A reader* (7th ed., pp. 178–193). Belmont, CA: Wadsworth.

Lieberman, D. (1997). Culture, problem solving, and pedagogical style. In L. Samovar & R. Porter (Eds.), *Intercultural communication: A reader* (8th ed., pp. 191–207). Belmont, CA: Wadsworth.

Lustig, M., & Koester, J. (1996). *Interpersonal competence: Interpersonal communication across cultures* (2nd ed.). New York: Harper Collins.

Myers, L. (1981). The nature of pluralism and the African American case. *Theory Into Practice, 20,* 3–4.

National Association of Bilingual Education (1993). Census reports sharp increase in number of non-English speaking Americans. *NABE News, 16* (6), 1, 25.

Nguyen, L. (1986). Indochinese cross-cultural adjustment and communication. In M. Das & H. Grossman (Eds.), *Identifying, instructing, and rehabilitating Southeast Asian students with special needs and counseling their parents*. (ERIC Document Reproduction Service No. ED 273–068)

Pusch, M. (1979). *Multicultural education: A cross cultural training approach*. Yarmouth, ME: Intercultural Press.

Rivlin, H. (1977). Research and development in multicultural education. In F. Klassen & D. Golnick (Eds.), *Pluralism and the American teacher: Issues and case studies*. Washington, DC: American Association of Colleges for Teacher Education.

Samovar, L., & Porter, R. (1995). *Communication between cultures* (2nd ed.). Belmont, CA: Wadsworth.

Samovar, L., Porter, R., & Stefani, L. (1998). *Communication between cultures* (3rd ed.). Belmont, CA: Wadsworth.

Sinatra, R. (1986). *Visual literacy connections to thinking, reading and writing*. Springfield, IL: Charles C. Thomas.

Sorensen, G. (1989). Teaching teachers from east to west: A look at common myths. *Communication Education, 38*, 330–335.

Stefani, L. (1997). The influence of culture on classroom communication. In L. Samovar & R. Porter (Eds.), *Intercultural communication: A reader* (8th ed., pp. 349–364). Belmont, CA: Wadsworth.

Taylor, E. (1994). A learning model for becoming interculturally competent. *International Journal of Intercultural Relations, 18*, 389–408.

Viadero, D. (April 10, 1986). Culture class. *Education Week*, 39–42.

Wallach, J. & Metcalf, G. (1995). *Working with Americans: A practical guide for Asians on how to succeed with U.S. managers*. New York: McGraw-Hill.

12

MEDIA AND CULTURE

Objectives

After reading this chapter and completing the activities, you should be able to:

1. Define the role of the media in propagating cultural norms.
2. Explain how the media portray various co-cultural groups.
3. Explain how the media handle race, gender, and class issues in America.
4. Provide examples of cultural and gender issues in advertising.
5. Define and discuss international dimensions of media and culture, notably cultural domination.

We are bombarded by the media whether we attend to them or not. Even when we do not listen, we hear the voices of radio broadcasters and musicians in the form of songs and instrumentals from our neighbor's house or the car directly behind us. When we sit in public places, we invariably see evidence of the print media—discarded newspapers, magazines on the tables. The media are all-pervasive and ever-present.

Such a powerful presence of an institution has its effects on us. We smile at images we recall from television programs while waiting for the traffic light. We sing and sway our bodies to the music being played on the AM or FM radio station as we walk along with our walkman, earphones slapped over our ears or deeply lodged in them. We observe children playing games they had seen on cartoon shows and impersonating Daffy Duck, Bugs Bunny, the Jetsons, or the Flintstones.

In this chapter we will examine the major role of the media in the propagation and reaffirmation of cultural norms and value orientations in society. We do so by conducting an analysis of several contexts within which the media are central in providing their audiences with an image of the culture in which they function. Besides the examination of contexts such as popular criminal trials that are ethnically and racially charged and popular music and sitcoms on television, we examine also the role of advertising and the international dimensions of media and culture. At this juncture it is important to note that the emerging new technology called the world wide web functions as a mass medium. The implications for intercultural communication are discussed in the final chapter of the book. We start with media and ideology.

MEDIA AND IDEOLOGY

The media in various forms carry a variety of messages. Our perceptions on issues are influenced one way or the other by exposure to the media. Radio talk shows are dominating the airwaves with show hosts representing practically every train of thought in the political, social, economic, religious, scientific, technological, and other professional entertainment areas. Our worldview gets impacted upon and reshaped constantly as we receive information from the media. What do mean by ideology and how does it work?

Lull (1995) defines ideology as "organized thought—complements of values, orientation, and predispositions forming ideational perspectives expressed through technologically mediated and interpersonal communication" (p. 6). He states further that "ideology is a fit expression to describe values and public agenda for nations, religious groups, political candidates and movements, business organizations, schools, labor unions, even professional sporting teams and rock bands" (p. 7). MacDonald (1979) makes an interesting observation about broadcasters: They do not traditionally deviate from the general cultural norms of American society. Blake (1979) argues that the media in America "perform their function in keeping with the ideology of the nation" (p. 225). Ideology cuts across all aspects of our political, social, and economic well-being. Given this characteristic feature, the media are undeniably couriers of ideology through programming for electronic media and published reports, stories, cartoons, and so forth for the print media.

Being couriers of ideology, media influence and shape culture and cultural identities. They present to us through the manipulation of images how we are to see ourselves and others. For example, an African boy and hundreds of his compatriots used to stand in long lines for hours waiting just to purchase tickets to attend *Tarzan* movies. Edgar Rice Burroughs created this superman—Tarzan, a white man supposedly in the so-called "jungles" of Africa. Tarzan the super hero always conquered his detractors—Africans and renegade whites. Africans who attempted to challenge Tarzan in territory that was portrayed as theirs—the "jungle," did not just get defeated, they manifested fear and behaved in an inferior manner towards the white super

hero. Tarzan movies were quite popular and the African youth and his countrymen usually sided with the hero and laughed at the Africans who were
being defeated by one white man and forced to flee.

The youth traveled to America. Whites and some African Americans perceived him in the manner in which the Africans on the Tarzan movies were
portrayed—as someone from the "jungle," always defeated by Tarzan. Baf-
fled, he defended himself relentlessly by telling his hosts that he was not from
the jungle and did not realize that the movies actually denigrated Africans.
He did not have an image of himself as someone inferior and always afraid
in the presence of white people. In his culture, he had a worldview that had
shaped his perception of himself. He saw Tarzan movies as stories about acts
of heroism by a white man living in the forest instead of a "jungle." He did
not interpret the image of Tarzan as that of a white super hero, or the image
of the Africans as spineless and inferior. He got furious each time he was
asked about Tarzan in terms that denigrated Africans.

This anecdote demonstrates the double-edged nature of media as they
portray images deeply lodged in ideological roots. Super/inferior relationships between whites and Africans, whites and Native Americans, and
whites and Asians were, and to some extent still are, portrayed and reinforced through cinema and television programming. Western movies in
which whites always disgracefully defeat Native Americans form a significant folkloric culture of the United States. Likewise, African American characters in several movies during the 1940s and 1950s performed menial and
servile roles in keeping with a superstructure that glorified whites and denigrated non-Caucasians. Hence, the media, as represented at least by the cinema industry and television, have, for many years, fostered division among
the various racial and ethnic groups in a multiracial and multiethnic society
such as the United States. It is through the consistent repetition of negative
images of the denigrated and exalted images of the power structure that ideologies get inculcated.

Let us examine several aspects of the media's handling of race and ethnic relations in news reports, music, and other elements that depict the powerful and strategic location of the media in mediating messages to a racially,
ethnically, culturally, and linguistically diverse population such as the United
States. The main point of emphasis in the segment that follows is the *centrality of the media* in its portrayal of race and ethnic relations.

THE RACIAL DIVIDE?

The coverage of the O.J. Simpson verdict in the criminal case was a watershed
in understanding the inextricable relationship between American cultural heritage and the media. The television reports portrayed reactions to the "not

guilty" verdict by the jury in a manner that split America into two camps: black and white. African Americans were invariably portrayed as jubilant and basking in a celebration marking a victory for a "brother." Whites were portrayed as angry and dismayed over the verdict that went against two white families who had lost their loved ones—Nicole Brown Simpson and Ronald Goldman—by the hands of an African American. Throughout the trial, Ron Goldman's father was consistently featured in news reports, with tearful outbursts at times against the defense team led by an African American.

U.S. News and World Report carried reports on the O. J. verdict with pictures that showed jubilant African Americans and defiant whites. The cover of the October 16, 1995 issue of the weekly asked a rhetorical question that placed the debate within the grip of the media: "What Now? The Great Racial Divide." The interesting aspect of the media dynamics in covering the O.J. Simpson trial was the seemingly naive innocence of its folly—the escalation of racial tension through the manipulation of images, which provoked prejudices deeply rooted in a long American tradition.

Through the media coverage of the O.J. Simpson criminal trial, a culture of hatred and prejudice that seemed to dominate the workings of the Los Angeles Police department was uncovered. The department, though headed by an African American, seemed to be shrouded by prejudice against African Americans and other ethnic groups. Mark Fuhrman of the Los Angeles Police Department was pictured in magazines with the caption: "Racist Cop." The tapes of an interview with Fuhrman conducted by a media researcher brought out in clear terms the language of hate that provided ammunition for O.J. Simpson's defense team. The O.J. Simpson trial was a media and cultural phenomenon that revealed the extent to which people's perceptions about race and ethnic relations are shaped by the media, reinforced through news coverage and talk shows.

In addition to racially charged issues such as the O.J. Simpson trial, other media forms provide insights into the central locus of the media in mediating among various co-cultural groups. One such form that has gained popularity over the past ten years is rap music. Let us examine this form of communication and its implication for mass media and intercultural communication.

RAP, MEDIA, AND CULTURE

Rap music is increasingly being studied to gauge its impact and to decipher its messages (Henderson, 1996; Johnson & Adams, 1995). The media carry several interview programs that focus on various aspects of popular culture. During an interview on Black Entertainment Television (BET) after the tragic death of hip hop, gangsta rap artist Tupac Shakur in September 1996, Chuck

D, a popular rapper, observed that people are misunderstanding the overall thrust of gangsta rap or hip hop music. He argued that the genre presents the filler to a void created in the African American leadership structure on issues of civil rights. The civil rights culture, according to Chuck D, is in a state of demise, requiring rejuvenation.

Chuck D's line of reasoning was that images portrayed in rap lyrics and music put forth in vivid terms the problems of African Americans trapped in poverty and still struggling to protect their civil rights. Through rap songs, artists seek to energize a lame movement for the rights of the oppressed in the African American communities.

The interview of Chuck D was part of a panel discussion on BET. A member of the panel was openly uncomfortable with the questions that were being put to Chuck D about certain negative aspects of rap music and vehemently questioned the approach of the African American moderator. The participant said that the moderator was no better than white program moderators in the media in general, who consistently focused on the negative aspects of African American life and custom with limited discussion and portrayal of the positive. The participant had such a strong reaction to the moderator's approach that he withdrew from the discussion—walking out and insulting the moderator. The incident during the interview revealed several factors that are relevant to any discussion on media and culture.

First of all, the media today are the primary channels and means by which we share our perceptions and opinions about the cultural dynamics of a multiracial and multicultural society. Second, the program was representative of the manner in which non-majority populations that are disfavored in society perceive the role of the media in cultural denigration of non-white co-cultural groups in the United States. Third, the media, through film, newspaper and magazine reports, radio and television interviews, sitcoms, police stories, news broadcasts, talk shows, and entertainment channels such as cinema, videos, songs and drama shape cultural perceptions, reinforcing certain stereotypes of the dominant and non-white groups in American society.

If the media occupy such a strategic location in the cultural matrix of a nation, the owners of media invariably manifest a lot of power in shaping our perceptions of each other and influence the quality of intercultural communication among the various co-cultural groups. It is to this issue of media ownership and cultural perception that we now turn.

MEDIA OWNERSHIP AND CULTURAL PERCEPTION

During the interview with Chuck D, the popular artist made an observation that is of crucial importance in discussing media and culture. In clear terms,

Chuck D informed his audience that rappers and hip hop performers have no control over the lyrics of their songs—they write songs that the owners of the recording companies, mostly white, want. The violence that dominates gangsta rap is unavoidable, according to him. Violence sells. The industry believes that profits could be made mainly through the play of violence in the lyrics and video promotional tapes. Because the artists do not own the companies, they comply if they want to earn "a million" dollars—monies never imagined by several gangsta rap recording artists.

The same argument could be made for television ownership and the production of programs. The main networks and cable stations are white-owned. The program content is determined by the owners. The comfort zone for diversity on television programming is exhibited by mainly sitcoms that star comedian and non-white police officers in crime related programs. Non-white cultural heritage receives periodic treatment. The dominant culture remains the mainstream, through which "American values" and counter-values are portrayed, such as the challenges to family values manifested by the increasing number of gays and lesbian themes on TV and cinema.

The 1996 and 1997 fall TV programs revealed an interesting departure on the part of the networks, in particular, with few non-white led sitcoms. Ownership is an important element of control in a society in which the media are privately owned. The government cannot force owners to portray a more balanced cultural map of a multiracial and multiethnic society such as the United States. The government cannot legislate diversity in the media structure. If, however, the *ownership* of the media structures is more diverse, the composition of society will be reflected, portraying the multicultural makeup.

In sharp contrast to television ownership, print media ownership is more diversified. Popular magazines such as *Ebony, Essence,* and *Black Enterprise* are owned by African Americans and nationally circulated. The audience reach, however, cannot be compared with the audience reach of television or radio programs. The popular African American magazines are read mainly by African Americans. Other co-cultural groups do not benefit from whatever African American cultural content is carried by them. The power of the visual electronic media is overpowering and overshadows all other media forms. Diversification of ownership of the electronic media may enhance the chances of co-cultural groups to portray their culture in a manner that is consistent with their position in society.

There are African American and Latino/Chicano owners of radio stations. The program content, however, is largely limited to a format that is restricted to music. African American music reaches a much wider national audience than African American magazines. A music writer in an interview on BET in September 1996 informed the audience that more white youth buy African American music than blacks. It is not surprising. There are more white youths than black youths. What is instructive about his observation is that African American life and custom as portrayed on music played over and over on radio is absorbed by whites, contributing to their understanding or misunderstanding of African American culture.

Stemming from the above, one can conclude that the media play a significant role in articulating cultural norms in society. Let us examine this role and function of the media through an examination of a controversy surrounding "family values."

CULTURAL NORMS AND THE MEDIA

Former Vice President Dan Quayle made an observation about a popular sitcom, starting a national debate that attracted participation from the political, religious, and educational sectors. "Murphy Brown" is a highly successful sitcom aired by one of the major TV networks, featuring a hardworking, aggressive, single female with a gift of gab and uncanny wit. The star of the show—Murphy—had a boyfriend and became pregnant. She did not marry her lover throughout the gestation period. She gave birth as a single mother. The program created a stir in America, and Vice President Quayle led the attack on "Murphy Brown," condemning the idea of an unmarried woman getting pregnant and becoming a mother on prime-time television. Mr. Quayle regarded the event as an attack on family values. His position started a debate on the role of the media in dealing with values that are considered sacred and a very essential dominant cultural norm: Children should be born in wedlock. The media picked up the debate and politicians across the political spectrum made pronouncements on the issue. Family values remain a national issue, with organizations such as the Christian Coalition providing a forum for pro-family values spokespersons to articulate their concerns.

Television is a critical medium on the issue of family values. It was not even possible for a husband and wife to share the same bed in highly popular shows such as "The Lucy Show" in the 1960s. Sex was something that should not be an issue for public entertainment, particularly through the medium of television. The decades of the 1950s and 1960s witnessed the celebration of core values through the television medium. Things gradually changed in the 1970s and 1980s. In the 1990s traditional values about pregnancy and marriage are not demystified, but sexual orientation and preference issues occupy prime-time television as well. The battle over family values persist, and the medium continues to forge ahead, portraying alternative lifestyles together with some of the traditional values that are deemed sacred. In essence, the television medium in particular has contributed significantly in broadening the spectrum of values, reflecting traditional and non-traditional values.

So critical is the debate on the important role of television in the perceived destruction of traditional values that President Clinton proposed the introduction of "V chips" that would help parents block television programs that are considered out of the norm and potentially harmful to young viewers. The V chip gives parents the right to censor television programs, because their collective voices and those of groups like the Christian Coalition cannot deter the television industry from covering the broad spectrum of values and violence in their programming. Television programs now have a rating system like that used by the cinema industry.

It is clear that the media are powerful agents of cultural transmission, and thus, provide a forum for debate on the various tenets of culture. The Constitution of the United States guarantees freedom of speech. The economic philosophy promotes free enterprise and dissuades government control and undue interference in the private sector. Given such a national characteristic feature—freedom of choice and action—media entrepreneurs and program developers have a powerful grip on the transference of culture and the critique of its tenets. The problem that has emerged over the family values debate is an end product of a democratic tradition that prides itself on open discourse as a means of solving problems on issues such as values and other ethical considerations. Let us now turn our attention to the print media, notably tabloids.

TABLOIDS AND CULTURE

The presence of tabloids in supermarkets all over the United States and many foreign countries has given rise to yet another dimension of media and culture. Tabloids are notorious for carrying stories that are questionable and that usually have a sensational flavor. They are rife with gossip, innuendoes, or tales of inappropriate behavior of people in the limelight and scandals. The tabloids bring to our attention the crises among popular artists and their families, royalty such as Prince Charles and the late Princess Diana, political figures, and sports heroes.

They perform an interesting function in terms of the media and culture—they popularize the nontraditional aspects of fundamental cultural norms and for some of their readers provide entertainment as well. It would be wrong, however, to create the impression that tabloids never carry accurate stories. Some major tabloids have been the sources of "breaking news" that have resulted in the downfall of powerful figures in the political arena when they carry reports that clearly depict unethical practices unbecoming the people of such "breaking news." A senior adviser to President Clinton fell victim to the tabloids at the height of the 1996 presidential campaign. He resigned his position and did not challenge the paper.

Tabloids vigorously pursue their targets for reporting. A group of photographers popularly known as the *paparazzi* who sell their pictures to tabloids are notorious for stalking their targets. A serious controversy emerged from the death by car accident in Paris, France, of the late Princess Diana and her companion, Mr. Al Fayed, and the driver of the vehicle. It was widely reported that the paparazzi were chasing the Princess and her companion. The driver drove at high speed presumably to evade the paparazzi and ended up in a fatal accident. Even though test results later showed that the driver had alcohol content in his blood above the legal level and was also on medication, the chase by the paparazzi remained a major factor associated with the accident.

Notwithstanding the misgivings about the practices of tabloids, they are increasingly gaining grounds on the old, established traditional media as a source of information, mainly gossip. In order to keep pace, television in particular has adopted programming formats that present an electronic version of tabloid journalism. Examples are programs such as "Hard Copy," "Entertainment Tonight," "Access Hollywood," and "Extra."

Besides issues of location of the media and ownership, sensitive intercultural elements such as class and gender are also evident in the media. Let us review briefly a watershed period in the media industry and how they handled the delicate transition from programming that was predominantly white to one that sought to reflect the changing realities of race and cultural relations in the United States. The decades of the 1960s and 1970s are essential to understanding how sociopolitical trends found their way into media programming. Let us, therefore, discuss gender, class, race, and the media.

GENDER, CLASS, RACE, AND THE MEDIA

The media play an important role in shaping our perceptions on issues of gender, race, and class. We focus our attention on sitcoms to deal with the issue because of their popularity. The sitcoms examined here were originally aired from the 1960s to the present. As Douglas (1994) observes, there is a clear manifestation of a "proliferation" of these programs in the various networks in the form of reruns and a definite increase in radio stations that play "oldies" only. Some of the examples, therefore, cannot be viewed as untimely, even though they may not be well-known to young adult viewers of the 1990s.

For instance, the "I Love Lucy Show" in the 1960s depicted females as housewives—Lucy and her friend Ethel bask in gossip and are forever asking their husbands for money. Even though there were several episodes in which the two women outsmarted their husbands, the overall image of women was locked within the stereotype that casts women as solely dependent on men, occasionally smart, and unable to work on a sustained basis.

The gender theme, couched in a cultural package that reinforces the dominant white male figure is seen also in the "All in Family" series of the 1970s.

Edith Bunker is a humble housewife with a blue-collar working husband, Archie, who symbolizes white bigotry. She assumes a subordinate position when talking to Archie and obeys his every command. As the women's liberation movement gained momentum in the 1970s, challenging the fundamental pillars of gender culture, Edith Bunker's role increasingly reflected the emerging gender culture that challenged the taken-for-granted superiority of the white American male in the household.

"The Jeffersons" evolved out of Bunker's "All in the Family." An African American entrepreneur as bigoted as Bunker but wealthier, moved into Bunker's white neighborhood. Even though Jefferson is wealthier, he manifests what Engen (1995) in his analysis of George Foreman's newly found media popularity, calls the traditional stereotypes of the African American male. The black female gender stereotype is heavily featured in the "The Jeffersons." Louise Jefferson and Mother Jefferson are domineering black females. Louise and Mother Jefferson are the epitome of the black matriarchy that supposedly characterizes the African American household.

Gender and class tension is also present in this series. As mentioned earlier, the Jeffersons were entrepreneurs. They owned a cleaning business that eventually became a chain. The Bunkers, their neighbors at the initial stage of the cleaning business, were an ordinary, blue-collar working-class family. Furthermore, Jefferson eventually expanded his business and moved "on up" to a deluxe apartment in Manhattan, leaving the Bunkers behind.

The gender/class/race culture is a significant theme in the two sitcoms mentioned above and reflect the debate on cultural norms in post-civil rights America of the 1970s. Out of the civil rights movement blossomed a new media consciousness—the need to mirror the nation the way it is. African Americans like Jefferson do have businesses and do participate in the integration of neighborhoods. Integration as a cultural theme is pervasive in the episodes. The media, however, used caution in introducing new models and images of African Americans and Chicanos against the background of the gains made during the civil rights struggle. Even though Jefferson made it and moved on up, the integration of the neighborhood was not as easily accepted by the white working class. The media, however, achieved success in presenting images of the emerging culture that was hitherto not feasible in the 1950s and 1960s. "The Jeffersons" had in its cast an interracial couple and provided the African American character—George Jefferson—an opportunity to beat up on the white male to the extent of using pejorative names for whites openly.

In concluding this section, it is important to point out that the decade of the 1970s was a watershed for the media's role in disseminating and enacting "culture" as it pertained to race, class, and gender. The 1980s witnessed the emergence of the Huxtables in the "The Bill Cosby Show," portraying a highly professional African American husband, wife, and children. The gains of the Civil Rights movement were shown in a setting in which an African American family headed by a medical doctor husband and a lawyer wife is portrayed in a positive image and role model for all Americans regardless of race. Inniss and Feagin (1995) studied black middle-class reactions to the program and found out that although there was a certain degree of ambivalence on the part of the respondents, they were by and large concerned that the program may cause some people to minimize the larger problems of African Americans, while at the same time recognizing that with hard work, their conditions in life could improve.

Besides the Huxtables, "Roseanne" provided another vehicle for the "new" culture mediated by television. Roseanne, the main star, is a strong woman who talks to her husband, in particular, in ways that were unthinkable in the days of "All in the Family." Roseanne demystified the white male image that was all-powerful and all-knowing. In the 1990s, television introduces us to "Ellen," who "came out" during prime time to announce that she is a lesbian.

These changes are discussed by Evans (1996) who characterized the media debates on issues of abortion, sexual orientation, and preference for example, as "culture wars."

Through the evolution of liberal approaches to programming that continues the debate on family values, the media serve as the major route Americans use in experiencing the changing attitudes towards cultural norms that were deeply rooted in the American past.

The role of the media in facilitating such a journey from the bases of old cultural norms to new ways of viewing social phenomena demonstrates clearly that culture is not static. The dominant trends of the day are quickly captured by the media and performed over and over in the form of sitcoms, soap operas, documentaries, TV magazine shows, and news coverage and reporting. Because of the combination of sound and vision, television remains a very potent source of cultural transmission. Cinema also serves as a powerful medium but without the flexibility of television that has multiple approaches to packaging cultural content. The sound and visual aspects of the cinema, however, coupled with a wide distribution system nationally and internationally, make it a powerful medium for the transmission of cultural norms and the reinforcement of values.

MEDIA POWER AND CONTROL

Media and culture are complex issues that involve not only the debate on what is transmitted through the media but also on who controls what and to what extent. Ross Perot, the 1996 presidential candidate of the Reform Party, complained bitterly about being left out of the televised presidential debate.

The audience for the debate was put at 80 million viewers. The two major political parties arrived at a consensus that excluded Perot. Though wealthy and with some sign of support from voters judging from the 1992 presidential elections, Perot's inability to benefit from accessing 80 million viewers considerably weakened his campaign. The Perot situation during the 1996 campaign demonstrates clearly the position of television as the primary medium through which movers and shakers of society seek to send their messages and through which cultural norms are presented by entertainment or news programs.

In addition to the political dimension, the social dimension is even more controversial. The political leadership in the major parties in the United States take issue with Hollywood and the television industry for glamorizing sex, drugs, and violence. Sayre (1995–1996) provides an interesting analysis of the assault on Hollywood by politicians, who accuse the film industry of being anti-government and perverting mainstream American values. Television and Hollywood are the major channels through which culture and values are articulated. Moving away from our discussion on sitcoms, let us examine briefly the place of advertising, which is the life-stream of the private media. The sitcoms discussed above are made possible because of sponsors who use the television medium to advertise their products and services. Advertising plays a major role in the realm of media and culture.

ADVERTISING AND CULTURE

Advertising is indeed the life-stream of the media in America. Because the media are mainly privately owned, they depend on businesses and others interested in selling their products to buy spots on radio and television programs and space in the print media in order to survive. Whole programs are sponsored by major businesses that exert considerable influence on the media. Janus and Roncagliolo (1986) observe that advertising is a creation of the United States. Vivian (1997) states that advertising is "a keystone in a consumer economy, a democracy and the mass media" (p. 313). Their observations are critical in trying to understand why, in America, we are bombarded with advertising on a 24-hour basis.

Television and radio programs are punctuated at regular intervals by a series of advertisements ranging from automobiles to wrist watches. Janus and Roncagliolo point out the need to analyze advertising as an important phenomenon having the following characteristics: (1) Advertising is both a national and international business involving huge amounts of money. (2) Advertising is a purveyor of cultural content. In addition to cultural messages advertising carries political content nationally and internationally. (3) Advertising has made such an impact on the media that the media serve as the primary link between consumers and producers of commercial and industrial products.

Focusing our attention on the cultural aspects of advertising, a controversy developed in 1996 over the use of animals—frogs in this instance—for Budweiser advertisements. Those who opposed the use of animals usually seen in children's television programming argue that children identify with the animals and may recognize beer drinking as something positive for them to do, since the animals in the commercial appear to promote such behavior. Another major controversy emerged regarding the potential negative effect of advertising on children. A major clothes designer got into trouble by using young children to advertise a new line of blue jeans by having young people pose lewdly, with sexual connotations that were decried by opponents to the ad as negative and ran contrary to the value and cultural orientations.

Underlying the protests to the beer commercial and that of a leading designer is the fundamental concern for the preservation of cultural norms in a society that has been going through a transformation process that pits believers of traditional values against those espousing "new" attitudes towards traditional values. The advertising industry is caught in the middle of this debate. The designer, Calvin Klein was forced by voices opposed to his use of children in his commercials to withdraw the advertisements.

Interestingly, however, "sex" is a centerpiece of the advertising industry in terms of the images advertisers use to promote several products, among which is the ever-popular automobile. The issue of sex in advertising hits hard at the debate on gender and communication with specific reference to women's concern. Women have, by and large, been portrayed as sex symbols (Douglas, 1994). The use of women as sex symbols is under severe criticism from several women's groups who argue that it is not only a bias against their gender, but an abuse. Stewart and colleagues (1996) observe that two important factors need to be considered when looking at the possible negative effects of advertising: (1) "advertisements are repeated over and over, so exposure levels are higher than for any other medium, and (2) since advertisements are carefully crafted persuasive pieces designed to sell products and attitudes, so they may sell the images of men and women contained in them more powerfully than other media" (p. 192).

The gender culture in American society is enacted every second through advertisement in the various media. We have referred above to the portrayal of women as sex symbols. Men, on the other hand, are portrayed as macho figures, guardians and heads of households, and decision makers (Douglas, 1994). Because of the entertaining quality of messages contained in advertisements and the fact that they are repeated over and over gain, they represent a powerful cultural weapon that does not only entertain but also teaches

(Berger, 1995). Sensitive structuring and dissemination of advertising content are essential if advertising is to perform a positive role in intercultural communication with regard to race, gender, creed, national origin, and class.

INTERNATIONAL DIMENSIONS

This chapter would be incomplete in some aspects if the *international dimension* of the media and culture are not treated. The media are all-pervasive and represent a powerful industry with transnational importance. Hedges (1995), for example, examines the struggle among nations over the issue of proselytizing Western values and culture overseas and the fundamental issue of "cultural hegemony" through the dissemination of film, cable television, and electronic mail systems. The final segment of this chapter presents the international dimensions of media and culture.

For decades the cinema industry was the most powerful in the media industry structure in transmitting cultural and value orientations internationally. The example provided earlier, regarding the African youth and the "Tarzan of the Apes" string of movies, is a classic example of the global reach of the movie industry. Hollywood symbolized the roots of entertainment and glamour. The name "Hollywood" is known in most parts of the world and recognized as the source of American values seen and enacted on the screen.

Through Hollywood, the world views the American interpretation of its early roots—the battles with the indigenous populations of present-day America, which were invariably won by the whites, be they cavalry men or cowboys. Western movies as a genre became popular in every major continent in the world. It was revealing to observe a staunch Soviet Communist President Brezhnev hugging a big western character in the series "Rifleman" during one of his visits to the United States. Hollywood also dominated other movie production centers in places like Britain, Italy, and France.

In the Southern Hemisphere, India took the early lead in attempts to globalize its dissemination of movies originating from the Indian subcontinent. Because of the sprawling diaspora, the Indian movie audience-reach extends to Africa, Europe, the United States and several other areas in the world. Probably because of the "minority" status of Indians in diaspora, the movies did not attract very wide audiences in their host nations as did the Hollywood movies.

Beside the cinema halls, the invention and widespread dissemination of video machines and tapes make movies accessible to smaller units—families, social groups, and so forth—who can afford to purchase, loan, or exchange videos from the Western and Asian countries that have developed movie industries. The advantage of the video is that even when movies from the West are banned or censored by governments in various parts of the world, peo ple usually smuggle video cassettes into these countries for private viewing. The video remains a popular item for entertainment globally.

CULTURAL DOMINATION AND INTERNATIONAL FLOW OF INFORMATION

Amidst the proselytization of Western culture through video, film, and music there emerged a strong concern echoed by Western scholars initially. The concern is variously referred to as "cultural domination" or "cultural imperialism." The meaning of the two expressions is the same: the unadulterated and massive flow of Western values and orientations into countries of the Southern Hemisphere. Schiller (1969) is the most celebrated of the Western scholars who raised the alarm regarding the potential dangers of cultural domination from the West.

The rationale for the concern includes another dimension that is critical in the study of intercultural communication. The world is multicultural, with various regions having their peculiar roots, values, beliefs, and an overall normative structure that help to hold society in a cohesive manner that constitute the global community. This form of pluralism is what is potentially threatened if the flow of values and beliefs and norms of one country or region dominates all other countries in the world. The American media system is powerful, with wealthy entrepreneurs backing it.

Schudson and King (1995) critically examine what they call the "power of news," accounting for the historical and sociological bases of "news" as culture. If we approach "news" as culture, there are some examples of its manifestation that are not unfamiliar. Every night at 7 P.M. (EST), Christopher Glenn of the CBS radio network presents a news broadcast titled "The World Tonight." The bulk of the news is about America or American interests abroad. The sports segment of the media also portrays America as the "world." Hence, in baseball we have the "World Series." The winning team of the National Football League is the "World Champion." The National Basketball Association Champions are also "World Champions," despite the fact that Canada is the only other country represented in the National Baseball Association. The teams do not play against any foreign country beside Canada.

Besides the sporting arena, several countries in the world buy, at fairly cheap rates, American syndicated programs for their local television programming and viewing. There are numerous syndicated programs in Africa, Asia, Europe, and elsewhere featuring series such as "Dallas." "Baywatch" is shown in China. It is this dousing of American programs on foreign countries that has contributed to the discourse on cultural domination.

Boonyakatmala (1986) presents a thorough discussion on the influence of transnational media in Thailand, covering several aspects of the media: advertising, film (cinema), and television. He concludes that "In the whole area of international communication as it concerns Thailand, it is apparent that along with most developing nations in the world, the country suffers from all the crucial imbalances familiar to researchers in the field. The case study on film and television clearly reveals a pattern of dependency. Thailand has always been on the receiving end of the international information flow" (p. 260). There is an important observation in this conclusion—the situation in Thailand is symptomatic of the situation of other countries in the Southern Hemisphere.

Hamelink (1986) articulately presents a discussion on "Dependency and Cultural Choice," showing how cultural systems use media to inform people about themselves. In a sense, messages contained in media content are directly related to the "story" of the culture in which the media system is located. He cautioned that "Although the international communications flow tends to consist mainly of entertainment products, the role of international news in transferring values should not be underestimated" (p. 229).

What is instructive in Hamelink's work is the emphasis on the power of the media in transmitting cultural content, particularly since the dominant media outlets are located primarily in the West—the United States, Britain, and France. Given the centralization of information outlets in the West, the rest of the world develops a dependency syndrome that can result in unfavorable circumstances for the development of local media industries. Japan was dependent to a significant extent on foreign programming in particular until it made a conscious decision to develop local programming and to reduce its dependency on foreign programs.

The international aspect of media and culture is dominated by concern for the maintenance of a pluralistic world system in which various cultures should be in a position to tell their story in the best interest of their respective countries. Because of the apparent imbalance that exits in the area of media industrial capacity from region to region and country to country, dependency on strong media outlets in the West can have catastrophic consequences for non-Western consumers of such media content. This is all predicated on the idea that media content is primarily cultural in form and content.

Beside the concern for pluralism, another aspect of the concern expressed by scholars and researchers is the negative effect on the economic development of countries in the Southern Hemisphere because of the weakened media industry segment or its nonexistence due to heavy reliance on Western media outlets. The development of local media industries helps to demonstrate the pluralistic dimension of culture in the sense that everybody can exchange stories. Such a context will help resolve the debate of the 1980s that centered around the flow of international information resulting in the creation of what was called the New World Information and Communication Order (NWICO).

NWICO was the brainchild of Ahmadou Muctar M'Bow, former Director-General and Chief Executive Officer of the United Nations Education Social and Cultural Organization (UNESCO). The thrust of NWICO, as presented in the McBride Report (1980), was on the need to expand the flow of international information and culture that would reverse the one-way flow of information from the west to the rest of the world and to reflect a multiflow system in which countries in all parts of the world would be in a position to report about themselves and present programs rooted in their culture. The McBride Report thus sought to improve upon the routing system of the international flow of information and culture.

The crisis of one-way flow of culture via television programming is not a unique South-North or East-West problem. The Canadian position is interesting to observe. In a news report carried by a daily newspaper in the Midwest, *The Times*, the Canadian government recently expressed concern over the fact that "Canadian children know more about Los Angeles street life than their own culture" (p. 3). The report further stated that the government of Canada "is pledging $73 million to boost home grown television production and reduce the dominance of U.S. shows" (p. 3). The Heritage Minister of Canada went on to state that Canadians "watch an average of 23 hours of television weekly, mostly foreign-made shows." (Times Wire Services, 9/11/96).

It is clear from reports about cultural domination that it is not an issue that is restricted to the flow of culture through television from rich to poor countries. It is a fundamental issue on the extent to which sovereign states could sustain their cultural norms without strong and negative outside influences.

CONCLUSION

This chapter has focused mainly on the media and how they disseminate cultural norms and value orientations. Furthermore, we examined how the media depict race, gender, and class issues through television programming and the cinema industry. More attention was given to the electronic visual medium than to the print medium and radio because of the fantastic audience reach of television and film.

We also discussed the position of advertising as an aspect of media that contributes to the dissemination of cultural norms and value orientations. Advertising is an important activity within the overall media structure of the United States because the media are privately owned and depend on advertising for their revenues. Without the advertising business, media organizations could not succeed in the United States and several Western countries. With the spread of consumerism all over the world, advertising has taken center stage in sustaining the free-enterprise capitalist ideology.

Finally, we examined the intricacies involved with the international dimensions of media and culture by discussing the concept of cultural domination or cultural imperialism. We observed that the issue is not just the problem of potential cultural damage to the recipient nations but the suppression of local programming and the stifling of the growth and development of media/entertainment-related industries. The Canadian example on the question of cultural domination suggests clearly that it is not a North-South problem, but rather one that could threaten the cultural fabric of societies that fall victims to it. The determination of the Canadian government to provide millions of dollars to ensure that Canadian heritage and culture could be the focus of Canadian television programming demonstrates further the disadvantages of nations in the Southern Hemisphere that do not have such funds to combat cultural domination via the media.

The extent to which countries use their media to present a broad spectrum of cultures, particularly in multicultural and multiracial societies, could help determine the effectiveness of intercultural, interethnic and interracial communication, grounded in a better understanding of the cultural roots and bases of the various populations of the country. Within the American context, a commercial by a major corporation puts it most succinctly: People always try to identify the typical American family. It is impossible to do so because the families are so different, yet all are American.

QUESTIONS

1. What is the role of the media in propagating and reaffirming cultural norms and value orientations in society? Feel free to select examples from television programs you watch, movies you have seen, or magazines and newspapers to which you subscribe or read. You may want to begin your answer to this question by working from the standpoint of ideology.
2. How do the media use advertising to play on some of the cultural values in American society? Address issues of sex and gender in this question and also the vulnerable position of young children.
3. Is cultural domination a valid concept? Explain your position on this subject and how it relates to the media industry as a whole in countries of the Southern Hemisphere.

ACTIVITIES

1. Break up into groups of four. Identify and discuss at least two sitcoms that are familiar to the group. After selecting two sitcoms, assign one each to a subgroup of two people. Each subgroup should watch the programs over a 2-week period. Prepare notes on the programs as you watch on the most dominant cultural norms and value orientations that you observe; the treatment of gender, race, ethnic, class, and nontraditional values that are present. Convene a meeting of the group, with each member reporting to the group. Develop a report that presents a picture of the composite observation of the group. Each group in the class will make a 15-minute presentation to the class as a whole and be ready to answer questions arising from their reports.

2. Form two groups: Group one is from a country in the Southern Hemisphere, and group two represents a group of American media and entertainment business people. The main task of group one is to select a leader among you that will act as the most senior official in the information and entertainment department of a country in the Southern Hemisphere. You are interested in negotiating with the media industry in the United States to assist in developing the media and entertainment industry in your country. How would you go about handling the potential problem of cultural domination? The leader will assign each member a task in the form of questions that will be necessary to raise during your negotiations with the American companies. It may be useful to consider preparing a brief background information of your country of choice, containing the basic demographic data such as population, ethnicity, language, level of education, per capita income, etc. After developing the necessary background information, work together on a strategy to come up with proposals to the American media and entertainment people in group two and try to persuade them to work with you with the least interruption of your cultural values through media programming and entertainment. You may need at least a week to prepare for the final meeting with the business people. The meeting between the two groups should take up one class period, during which they will engage in negotiation and discussion.

REFERENCES

Blake, C. (1979). Communication research and African national development. *Journal of Black Studies, 10, 2,* 225

Berger, A. (1995). *Manufacturing desire: Media, popular culture, and everyday life.* New Brunswick, NJ: Transaction Publishers.

Boonyakatmala, B. (1986). Influence of the transnational media in Thailand. In U. Kivikuru & T. Varis (Eds.), *Approaches to international communication* (p. 260). Helsinki: Publications of the Finish National Commission for UNESCO.

Douglas, S. (1994). *Where the girls are: Growing up female with the mass media.* New York: Times Books.

Engen, D. (1995). The making of a people champion: An analysis of media representations of George Foreman. *Southern Communication Journal, 60,* 2 (winter), 141–151.

Evans, J. (1996) "Culture wars" or status group ideology as the basis of U.S. moral politics. *International Journal of Sociology and Social Policy, 16,* 1–2, 15–34.

Gray, H. (1995). *Watching race: Television and struggle for "blackness."* Minneapolis: University of Minnesota Press.

Hamelink, C. (1986). Dependency and cultural choice. In U. Kivikuru & T. Varis (Eds.), *Approaches to international communication* (p. 229). Helsinki: Publications of the Finnish National Commission for UNESCO.

Hedges, I. (1995). Transnational corporate culture and cultural resistance. *Socialism and Democracy, 9,* 1(18) (spring), 151–164.

Henderson, E. (1996). Black nationalism and rap music. *Journal of Black Studies, 26,* 3, 308–339.

Inniss, L., & Feagin, J. (1995). The Cosby show: The view from the Black middle class. *Journal of Black Studies, 25,* 6, July, 692–711.

Janus, N. & Roncagliolo, R. (1986). Advertising, mass media and dependency. In U. Kivikurn & T. Varis (Eds.), *Approaches to international communication* (pp. 95–112). Helsinki: Publications of the Finnish National Commission for UNESCO.

Johnson, J., & Adams, M. (1995). Differential gender effects of exposure to rap music on African America adolescents' acceptance of teen dating violence. *Sex Roles, 33,* 7–8, 597–605.

Lull, J. (1995). *Media, communication, and culture, a global approach* (pp. 6, 7). New York: Columbia University Press.

MacDonald, F. (1979). Government propaganda in commercial radio: The case of *Treasury Star Parade, 1942–43. Journal of Popular Culture,* 12 (2) 285–304.

McBride, S. et. al. (1980). *Many voices one world.* Paris: UNESCO.

Sayre, N. (1995-1996). Assaulting Hollywood. *World Policy Journal, 12,* 4, 51-60.

Schiller, H. (1969). *Mass communication and American empire.* Boston: Beacon Press.

Schudson, M., & King, E. (1995). *The power of news.* Cambridge, MA: Harvard University Press.

Stewart, L., Cooper, P., Stewart, A., & Friedley, S. (1996). *Communication and gender.* Scottsdale: Gorsuch Scarisbrick.

Times Wire Services, September 11, 1996.

U.S. News and World Report, October 16, 1995.

Vivian, J. (1997). *The media of mass communication* (4th ed.). Boston: Allyn & Bacon.

13

BECOMING A COMPETENT COMMUNICATOR

Objectives

After reading this chapter, you should be able to:

1. Explain the factors that shape intercultural encounters.
2. Describe in writing the components that influence intercultural competence.
3. Explain the ten basic rules of intercultural communication.

We began this book with a fascinating story about an experience that Appiah (1992) and his (white) English friend had while traveling in the Ghanaian city of Takoradi. Recall that all was well until the Englishman, who was at the wheel, stopped at a road junction behind a large timber truck that a Ghanaian driver was backing up. Despite the Englishman's sounding his horn to warn the Ghanaian of an impending accident, the driver of the truck went on backing up until he struck the Englishman's truck. Recall as well that although it was clear that the Ghanaian truck driver was at fault legally, none of the witnesses was willing to support the Englishman's version of what happened.

Real or imagined differences between groups are frequently highlighted, and they are the source of much intercultural difficulty worldwide. Communication problems are compounded when the people communicating are different or strange to each other. Throughout this book we have provided you with information about why and when diversity matters. All of our discussions have served one major purpose: to give you sufficient sense-making materials to help you better understand and respond to others' ideas, meanings, beliefs, experiences, and feelings. In this section we discuss more practical steps that you can take to become a more competent intercultural communicator.

Many models (Spitzberg & Cupach, 1984 a & b; Spitzberg, 1989) exist to explain the rules and practices that individuals should observe in their efforts to improve or adapt interculturally. For example, Kim (1991) believes that the different approaches should be integrated and that individuals differ in their capacity to adapt. Rather than argue for one approach over another, here we simply list the factors that shape an individual's ability to manage intercultural encounters.

The cognitive dimension. The cognitive dimension refers to an individual's ability to change his or her knowledge base, or as Kim (1991) observes, "the sense-making activities" for determining the meaning of nonverbal and verbal codes that one receives (p. 269), for example, how to make sense of the sentence, "All Chinese are farmers."

The affective dimension. The affective component focuses on the emotional aspects of an individual. It is associated with feelings such as fear, love, anger, dread, panic, hatred, and so on, for example, "Ya Ping adores people who eat with their fingers."

The behavioral dimension. The behavioral dimension refers to an individual's ability to adapt or change his or her actions based on skills acquired in the cognitive and affective realms. For example, if you believe that communicating interculturally is important, one would expect you to interact with people from different cultures should the opportunity arise.

Before we discuss specific strategies for improving your intercultural skills, we need to mention two things that are essential to changing your cognitive, affective, and behavioral dimensions: *an appreciative orientation* and *empathy.*

AN APPRECIATIVE ORIENTATION

"I am not blind to what the Greeks valued—their values may not be mine, but I can grasp what it would be like to live by their light. . . ," philosopher Isaiah Berlin (1991, p. 11) wrote. His statement expresses a guiding principle of this book: true intercultural interaction requires a *willingness* to engage with people unlike ourselves. Without a will to understand other people whose myths, music, and tales may be different, there are grave doubts that you will participate in a personal journey of intercultural discovery. So, as we come to the end of our cultural journey with you, ask whether you are truly committed to a path (passages) marked by beliefs and behaviors different from your own.

EMPATHY: A SUFFICIENT EFFORT
OF IMAGINATION

It is not enough, however, to be willing to communicate. You must also develop *empathy* or a *sufficient effort of imagination*. Sufficient effort of imagination refers to your ability to "grasp what the world" looks like "to creatures, remote in time or space. . ." (Berlin, 1991, p. 60). It is the capacity to participate imaginatively in another person's cognitive, affective, and behavioral world. The key term is *imaginative participation* because it assumes movement from your perspective to the perspective of a person unlike yourself. The Indian saying, "Walk a mile in my moccasins" expresses what we mean by *empathic communication*. Our emphasis on empathic communication is guided by a belief that there is enough common to all of us to warrant human understanding.

For example, to appreciate Shakespeare's tragic story of Romeo and Juliet or Pocohontas's role in helping Captain Smith during the establishment of the Virginia colony, you must attempt to understand and interpret how these characters felt and behaved. Your human connection bestows upon you the expectation that you can know what it is like for others to feel pity, to love, to pray, to fear, to dream, to fight, to care. A sufficient effort of imagination means that you can imagine what it would be like to roast your hotdog over a fire made from cow dung; win an Olympic gold medal as a Russian; live in Brazil; paint your body all over with ocher; lug firewood five miles daily; begin your arguments frequently with "Let me tell you a story. . ."; and touch your food with your left hand only at dinner.

Admittedly, trying to infer the feelings and thoughts of others is daunting. A number of observations should prove helpful.

FACTORS INFLUENCING INTERCULTURAL
COMPETENCE: A SYNTHESIS

Knowledge of Self

In his classic book, *The Principles of Psychology*, William James (1890) wrote, "*a man has as many social selves as there are individuals who recognize him* and carry an image of him in their mind. . . . (emphasis mine)" (p. 294). James's comment reminds us that we have multiple selves, such as student, parent, gardener, sorority sister, doctor, lawyer, plumber, and teacher. Despite our multiple selves, we must not only know who we are, but also how who we are affects our interaction with others, including the moral choices we make, our strengths and weaknesses, our sense of our own roots, our communication style, and our prejudices, as well as the emotions that guide our behavior.

For example, if you have a strong bias against people who wear fur coats, it might be difficult for you to communicate with them. Knowing that you are biased, however, should at least help you to decide what you could say to such people and how to say it. In suggesting that you know yourself, then, we are exhorting you to do two basic things.

First, know what kind of person you are, or your own cultural content; that is, *know what makes you tick*. We are not suggesting that you undergo some deep psychological analysis by consulting a psychic phone hotline or your local psychologist. Rather, we are suggesting that you know your roots and have a pretty good idea of what constitutes your thinking, feeling, and acting lines. By thinking, feeling, and acting lines we mean those major characteristics, practices, and values that influence the way people see the world. For example, the basic notion of whether the proverbial glass is considered to be half-full or half-empty conveys much about how individuals perceive the world. And how that also, in turn, helps to shape individuals' reactions to people who hold similar or dissimilar views. The following questions should guide your self-analysis: What are your likes and dislikes? What are your values? What moves you to action? What are your own qualities? What does it mean to be true to self? Which models should we live by? What is your place in society?

Once you have answered these questions, you should have a sense of how your self-regarding thoughts and behaviors potentially influence your other-regarding thoughts and behaviors. In other words, you should find a balance; as Selznick (1992) notes, "If we go too far in one direction we suffer loss of self; in the other direction we slight the claims of others" (p. 228). By claims of others Selznick means other individuals' notions of what and how the world is or ought to be.

It should be noted that our discussion of self has a Western bent. If we asked the Gahuku-Gama of New Guinea, "Who are you?" they would probably find the question curious because their conception of man/woman "does not allow for any clearly recognized distinction between the individual and the status which he occupies" (Shweder, 1991, p. 123). Buddhists also depart from the Western conception of self-regard. The cornerstone of their philosophy is "the assertion that there is no 'self' " (Selznick, 1992, p. 223). In analyzing your own self if you are a North American, you should acknowledge that the notion of human selves as understood in North American society is at odds with the notion of human selves in other cultures. Recognizing this bias, however, should not interfere with your efforts to become fully informed about your efforts to understanding your own self.

The second thing you should understand is your communication style. Communication style refers to "those communication characteristics that are part of your personality" (Samovar & Porter, 1991) and that "contextualize" how you "should accept and interpret a verbal message" (Gudykunst & Ting-Toomey, 1988, p. 100). In Chapter 8 we introduced you to this concept by noting that language is a powerful means of social communication and that it mirrors cultural beliefs and values. For example, a soft-spoken person can be valued highly by one individual and negatively by another.

Think of the last effective encounter that you had with an individual. Then consider the extent to which style affected the outcome. Here is a list of terms that should help you to gain insight into your communication style: direct, humorous, tough, superior, intuitive, affective, condescending, paternalistic, personal, indirect, aggressive, assertive, and so on. Once you identify your own communication style you are ready for the next step, which is to recognize that your style can be used as a prototype for judging others. Hudson's (1980) explanation of how people use information in terms of prototypes is helpful: "If characteristics A and B are typically ('prototypically') associated with each other, we assume the presence of B whenever we observe the presence of A and vice versa" (p. 202).

For our purposes, prototypical communication style thinking works this way: If person A (who uses directness as a preferred style) interacts with person B (who uses indirectness as a preferred style), directness and indirectness serve as clues to personality, values, and beliefs. The next step is for person A or B, or both, to assign a value judgment, such as good or bad. Needless to say, communicating with individuals whose styles differ from your own requires not only knowledge of how your own subjective orientations influence your perceptions, but also an open mind.

Sociocultural Roots

Rootedness is a primary determinant of our relationships with others. It can bind us firmly to a particular past, with little interest in people, places, and ideas beyond our own village or town, or it can give us freedom to participate in the folkways and practices of others, or it can render us neutral. But rarely are individuals neutral regarding others. Above all, though, as Tuan (1977), notes, "we are oriented, which is a fundamental source of confidence. We know where we are and we can find our way to the local drugstore. Striding down the path in complete confidence, we are shocked when we miss a step or when our body expects a step where none exists" (p. 199).

Communicating competently involves "finding our way" through the brambles and branches that make us who we are. A continuing theme of this book is that who we are influences, sustains, and shapes our world. In this section we focus on the most salient factors that we believe have the most potential to define or modify our basic (or commonsensical) approach to other cultures. It might be useful at this point to discuss some of the most important sociocultural factors that challenge our intercultural competence.

Family
The absolutely basic element of all societies is the family. Traditionally, in almost all human societies, this unit has consisted of a mother, a father, and children. Although, today, the conception of family, especially in Western societies, is in flux, we can say that however families are constituted, they bestow a kinship status. Kinship status, and the way we are oriented toward it, gives us a foundation with which to organize the content of our world. For example, among the Nayar in India, it is not unusual for a woman to go through a ritual marriage ceremony with a man who may well have no further role in her life (Murphy, 1986).

Families can be defined in a variety of ways. Among them are nuclear, extended, and mixed. *Nuclear families* consist of a husband-wife, mother-father duo. This type of family has relatives, but they do not play a key role in decision making, duties, and responsibilities. The *extended family* consists of larger kinship groups, including grandparents, cousins, sisters, brothers, and other individuals who are essential to the maintenance of the group. These individuals assume parental roles and responsibilities. For example, in Gambia, West Africa, families live in what are called compounds comprised of several family members.

The *mixed family style* is emerging and consists of gay partners and their children. *Matrifocal families*, or those headed by women, are also common in the United States. Different family styles reflect the core values of their members, including homely pleasures such as sentiment for the land, special foods, and family rituals, activities, and expectations. An orientation toward key values is reflected in Jeanne Kim's experience. Kim grew up partly in New York but her parents were born in Korea. In reflecting on the clash between family values and expectations in Korea and the United States, Kim observed that her parents' values prohibit boys and girls from touching each other. According to Kim, if a young woman is touched in Korea, the young woman is tainted. Because Kim's experience in the United States has been quite different, it has caused her some interpersonal concern.

In addition to kinship networks, a family's interactional style is also bound up in the nature and types of relationships we have with others. Condon and Yousef (1975) identify several general styles of home that subtly influence our feelings and intentions, including the Japanese home, the German home, and the Middle Eastern home. If it is the case that attachment to home is a profound common human emotion, then it is reasonable to assume that preferences for one mode of home over another can be problematic if we do not take these things into account. So, again, we expect styles to carry meaning.

Condon and Yousef note, for example, that in the Middle Eastern home, despite the fact that in most homes all rooms look alike, there are specific activities that take place in particular rooms. Because Middle Easterners are very concerned about *face, facade,* and *appearances,* they are careful to maintain guest-host, male-female interactional spaces. As an illustration, it is not unusual in the Middle East for two men to have known each other for a long period of time without either having met the female members of the household. Knowing this, you would not visit a Middle Eastern home and ask, "May I meet your wife?"

In Japanese-style homes, we can also see the potential for intercultural misunderstandings. For example, in traditional Japanese homes, the sense of privacy differs from the concept of privacy in the United States. In fact, some scholars note that there is no word for "privacy" in Japan. This suggests that Westerners' notions of a clear separation between a private room and a public room, and the ease with which they go into their own rooms and lock their own doors, differ significantly from the Japanese notions of separation. For example, in the United States, our bath and toilet areas generally are in the same room. In Japan, however, these two rooms are separate.

Inherent within this separation of the bath from the toilet area is also an idea of what constitutes cleanliness. Japanese see a distinction between a dirty place and a clean place. For example, Andrew Pollack (Pollack, 1995, p. A4) observes that at some laundromats in Japan, customers are permitted to wash out the machine quickly before inserting their dirty clothes, "to wash away any lingering effects from the last customer." It is crucial to note here how different cultural patterns can contribute to our knowledge and understanding. We could cite other examples, but for now, let us turn to another sociocultural factor that provides additional insights into ways of managing intercultural relations.

Economics
We have touched on this before: Our means of earning a livelihood, the globalization of society, and the relationship of economic resources to social justice tend to heighten mutual hostility. In short, we respond as we do based on both our individual and collective socioeconomic cultural encounters. For example, the fact that middle management workers are being hit hard in the corporate hierarchy because some of their jobs are being eliminated, and the fact that some workers see affirmative action practices pertaining to women and minorities as a central reason for loss of jobs, should have an effect on intercultural contact. By the same token, knowing that "for starving children in the Brazilian city of Recife, to have a Barbie doll seems more important than having food" (Hannerz, 1992, p. 223) tells us much about the complexity of human perception. Keep in mind that economic differences can serve as stumbling blocks to competent communication.

Political
By political we mean the extent to which the *state* (e.g., the United States government) accommodates the "disparate urges, goals and motivations of

people . . .to the need for public safety and order, and to the requirement that the work of life be done" (Murphy, 1986, p. 142). The way in which our political institutions serve our purposes for "primary goods" such as income, health care, education, the right to vote, and due process help to determine not only our orientations toward the state but also how we respond to others within it (Gutmann, 1992, p. 4). For example, much of the discussion concerning affirmative action centers on African Americans', women's, Latinos', and Native Americans' sense of how they should be regarded by other citizens, as well as how they should be treated politically (Taylor, 1992). Think of the complex interpersonal interactions that characterize answers to the following key political questions: What is the relationship of particular ethnic and social groups to other citizens? Should we ignore cultural particularities and focus on universal themes that transcend race and class? Should the public recognize specific ethnic groups?

These important questions focus on the relationship between culture and political practice. In communicating with others, you can expect the interplay between politics and culture to have a distinct effect on your everyday talk, the image you form of people, and the meanings you attach to what people say. Be prepared to reflect upon or modify your own cultural heritage in order to improve your intercultural knowledge and skills. Rarely will this orientation toward flexibility involve a radical change from what you value.

Stereotypes and Prejudices

LaRay Barna (1994) identified "preconceptions and stereotypes" as one of the six stumbling blocks in intercultural communication. We indicated earlier, when discussing stereotypes and prejudices, that these modes of thinking and behaving can blind us to the individuality of people. Barna indicates that stereotypes are stumbling blocks in intercultural communication for several reasons. First, they interfere with our ability to view the other objectively. Because prejudiced and stereotypical judgments are made in advance of our interaction with individuals, the person who is the object of hatred or aversion is not given a chance and is at a comparative disadvantage. The severity of this mode of thinking is evident in the innocent, yet disturbing question that a little girl put to her mother, "Mother, what is the name of the children I am supposed to hate?" Imagine a criminal court judge pronouncing sentence on a person before the lawyers and witnesses have presented all of the evidence!

Second, prejudiced and stereotypical attitudes "sabotage trust" (Carr-Ruffino, 1996). It is difficult to build trust-establishing relationships when comments such as, "You can't trust whites" or "Beware of the Jews," or "Italians are excitable" are part of our linguistic repertoire. Trust-establishing relationships move us toward individuals; nontrust-establishing relationships move us away from individuals.

Third, prejudiced and stereotypical attitudes increase our tendency to view the other selectively, that is, to take portions of information that sustain our worldview. For example, the Indian visitor who is accustomed to a life of asceticism and denial cannot fail to experience North American culture as materialistic and wasteful.

Your efforts to become a competent intercultural communicator will be greatly facilitated if you learn to become more open and understanding of others. Openness involves listening to others' points of view, weighing evidence objectively, and developing mutual respect. Reflect for a moment on any prejudices that you might have. A good, solid reflection should yield a search for the facts and your willingness to change when you have been exposed to new information that contradicts your prejudgment.

Religion

For most people, religion serves as a major source of rootedness. As we saw in Chapter 7, because religion gives us a comprehensive "picture of the way things in sheer actuality are," it is a source of much conflict and diversity in the world (Geertz, 1973, p. 89). Shweder (1991) gives us a fine feel for the diversity of religious practices. He notes that "if we look in the right places and with the right clearance," we can see human beings hunting for witches, propitiating dead ancestors, sacrificing animals to hungry gods, scapegoating their sins, waiting for messiahs, seeking salvation by meditating naked in a cave for several years, and wandering on pilgrimage from one dilapidated shrine to the next (p. 30).

If these practices challenge your beliefs, you have confronted the many religious differences that exist worldwide. Regardless of your worldview, however, you must remember that most people feel strongly about their religion, and that *differences between religious beliefs and practices do matter*. For example, among the Oriya Brahman of India, it is considered "shameless for a husband and wife to eat together" (Shweder, 1973, p. 30). Among some Christian faiths, however, "people who pray together, stay together." The Igbo of Nigeria distinguish between the physical aspects of the sun and its spiritual aspects (Uchendu, 1965).

Because various cultures differ radically, and because religions provide insights into actions and language, you should expect such values to manifest themselves in expression that you use everyday, as well as how you behave everyday. For example, if you have been taught that "cleanliness is next to godliness," this tenet will not only guide your behavior, but also incline you to judge others accordingly. Our religious norms are so internalized that they serve unconsciously as radar guiding, prompting, directing, moving, and urging on our thoughts and actions. As you communicate with others, be prepared to see manifestations of these throughout everyday talk. Expect norms to show up in discussions about notions of right and wrong, good and bad, in both form and content. Search for a way of framing your thoughts that will encourage you to "let go" of discussions over religious matters that lead to antagonism and hostility. Above all, try to develop sensitivity towards other religious practices and views.

Language and Context

In the chapter on language we noted that factors in the social environment influence how people respond to interpersonal interactions. As you become increasingly more interested in sharing yourself with others, you will observe that the social situation in which talk unfolds is an important consideration.

The human need to make sense of who speaks what language, to whom, and on what occasion, provides a framework for understanding what we mean by context. To behave appropriately and effectively in an intercultural exchange, you must make an accurate assessment about the social context in which communication occurs. For example, as Hymes (1973) notes, this can be facilitated by "a knowledge of what kinds of codes, channels and expressions to use, in what kinds of situations and to what kinds of people." For example, Mai-Li, a Chinese immigrant, arrived in the United States a decade ago and made a genuine effort to learn English, including metaphors, proverbs, humorous sayings, and slang. One of the slang expressions that she learned was, "to kick the bucket," which is term that cowboys use to indicate that an individual has died or passed away. Soon after Li had learned the expression, her history professor's wife died. While standing in line to express her condolences to her professor, Li said, "Professor Akbar, I am sorry that your wife has 'kicked the bucket!' " Despite Li's great intentions (and despite multiple variations of this story), her comments were inappropriate because the informal expression, "to kick the bucket," was unsuitable for the occasion.

As you might expect, there are some factors in the communication environment that limit and control what you say. One factor is a speaker's ability to make decisions from among a range of available language choices. For example, in the case of Mai-Li, she might have chosen expressions such as, "passed away," "departed," or "final resting place." Obviously, we cannot provide you with enough specifics to manage every intercultural encounter. To improve intercultural relationships, however, you must make a conscious effort to use the appropriate word in the appropriate interpersonal context (Lee, 1997).

Another factor that influences the context is "know(ing) when not to speak as well as when to speak and what to say" (Basso, 1972, p. 69). For example, Native Americans are more likely than white Americans to use silence. Basso (1972) studied how Western Apache use silence and found that they do not feel compelled to "introduce" persons who are unknown to each other; their rule is to wait for the stranger to speak first. Basso also notes that Western Apache remain silent after they have "been cussed out" because they believe that enraged persons are temporarily "crazy" (p. 76). In contrast, consider how often North Americans encourage others to speak because they are uncomfortable with silence.

Finally, communication and context are rule-governed. This means that there are patterns or rules that guide interpersonal interactions and that these rules reflect cultural beliefs and knowledge. Once a group has established communication rules, there is an expectation that they will be observed. For example, there are communication rules governing when to pause and for how long. In one culture, a 5-second pause is an invitation for an individual to speak while in another culture, it simply means that the person is organizing his or her thoughts. To be a successful communicator, you must know which rules apply, to whom, when, and how.

Local and Global Dimensions

Having looked at the notion of context, we shall now look at the interplay between local and global dimensions. A story relating to this follows in which Hannerz (1992) illustrates the power of these connections.

> *Each year in the spring, the countries of Europe meet in a televised song contest, a media event watched by hundreds of millions of people. There is first a national contest in each country to choose its own entry for the international competition. A few years ago, a controversy erupted in Sweden after this national contest. It was quite acceptable that the tune which was first runner-up had been performed by a lady from Finland, and the second runner-up by an Afro-American lady who was by now a naturalized Swede. Both were highly thought of and somehow represented that new heterogeneity of Swedish society which had evolved over the last couple of decades. What was controversial was the winning tune, the refrain of which was "Four Buggs and a Coca Cola;" Bugg, like the name of the soft drink, was a brand name (for a chewing gum). Many thought it improper that the national entry in the European contest should revolve around two brand names. But of the two, Coca Cola was much the more controversial, as it was widely understood as a central symbol of "cultural imperialism." Indeed a synonym for the latter is the cococolonization of the world. (p. 217)*

Hannerz 's story is important for what it tells us about the interrelatedness of cultures. First, today it is more difficult to see the world as a cultural mosaic, with separate and discrete parts. Coca Cola, reggae music, Pepsi, and other cultural products are part and parcel of cultures worldwide. And they influence how people view the presentation of and use of such products. Note, for instance, that in Hannerz's story, the Swedes were concerned about whether a local song contest should use lyrics expressing a global orientation. The Swedes demanded lyrics closer to their own culture and folkways. What the Swedes paid less attention to, however, was the fact that the winning number was a calypso, which also represented global culture. Because local products and their accompanying messages are extending beyond specific borders, you can expect these changes to challenge deeply held values and beliefs worldwide.

Second, although there is cultural flow between borders, we should not conclude that old customs and traditions will easily fade away. Knowing this, we should adjust our communication practices and attitudes to reflect an on-going, dynamic flow of ideas and meanings across borders. Again, the Swedish controversy over "Four Buggs and Coca Cola" struck at the heart of Swedish culture.

IMPROVING INTERCULTURAL COMMUNICATION COMPETENCE

As we have seen, the specter of factors haunts our ability to communicate competently. Knowledge of self, sociocultural roots, religion, stereotypes and prejudices, and local and global dimensions of culture encourage fidelity to communication practices, but they can also be "iron cages." We have noted some ways that we might free ourselves of these "iron cages," but we have as yet only hinted at the most important ways of doing so. Next, we discuss some concrete things that you can do in order to become an effective communicator. This is through a complex and challenging approach to intercultural competence.

Framing an Approach to Intercultural Competence

Our practical approach is based on Shweder's (1991) notion of what happens when individuals "confront diversity in belief, desire and practice" (p. 30). Before we outline our approaches to improving intercultural communication effectiveness, you should consider the following points.

Overcoming "either-or-ism"

Either-or-ism is a form of human thought that uses binary opposition as a way of classifying people, ideas, and things into categories such as good or bad, virtue or vice, fat or thin, black or white. This mode of categorical, pair-forming thinking forces people to deny that there is a middle ground. For example, the categorization of certain groups in the United States as either black or white means that children who are a mixture of black and white are forced to belong to one group or the other rather than to both.

The ability to overcome either-or-ism is a basic requirement of a competent communicator. The first step in overcoming either-or-ism is to accept that *human cultures are complex and various*. Because people and cultures differ in all sorts of ways, you should try to look beyond simplistic categories and search for significant or deeper ways of talking about your experiences and interacting with others. To take an example, suppose a white North American female is visiting the Zulu of South Africa because her company has sent her there. Then, suppose that the company president, who is a black male, takes the female to dinner and insists that he enter the restaurant first (McNeil, 1996). Imagine the reaction this would bring! Some individuals would possibly classify this as either good or bad before learning that in South Africa, it is customary for Zulu men to go first to clear the way of danger.

The second step in overcoming either-or-ism is to test whether an idea or concept can be explained beyond "either-or." For example, in the above Zulu incident, there is a vast middle ground of options to which we might appeal by using qualifiers such as "unless," "assuming," "if," and "until." Thus, rather than denouncing the behavior of the black, Zulu male as "bad," we could make a statement such as, assuming that this is a cultural rule of the Zulu, it is neither "good" or "bad," but "just is." Or we could make a statement such as, "Until I learn more about the cultural practices of the Zulu, I shall simply withhold judgment." Our point is until we know more about the specifics of situations, events, and ideas, the general rule is to be especially cautious regarding cultural interpretations. We don't want to give you the impression that no categorical thinking should occur. People do think categorically; however, the thought pattern should flow directly from the available evidence.

Distinguishing between "in spite of" and "because of" Thinking

As you consider your thoughts, actions, and feelings and how they relate to the thoughts, actions, and feelings of others, you can improve your overall intercultural competence by making distinctions between "in spite of" and "because of" thinking. We introduced you to these concepts in our discussion of economics and culture. Let us begin with definitions. *Because of thinking* is the assumption that A (one's race, sex, ethnicity, age, etc.) is responsible for B (whatever is happening as a result of human interaction). For example, you have probably heard people say things like, "Susie neglected to acknowledge Shinika's presence because Shinika is black," or "Koreans don't like Roberto because of his Spanish accent," "Don't hate me because I'm beautiful—" the line from a classic television commercial featuring a gorgeous female with silky hair. Statements of these kind clamor for additional information.

There is a mathematical and social equation inherent in "because of" thinking, because it assumes there is a one-to-one, direct causal relationship between A and B. In our way of thinking, "because of" thinking is asymmetrical because it works against harmonious relationships with others.

"In spite of" thinking is accountability reasoning. It assumes that A (whatever is happening) might or might not cause B. It is symmetrical thinking because it promotes congenial relationships. For instance, although "the store clerk, who is British and Protestant, serviced John Majors, a British Protestant before servicing McIntosh, who is Irish Catholic, it is impossible to determine whether it is based on assumptions about religion."

Perhaps a concrete example can make the point clearer. A group of students (all Puerto Rican) are having a wonderful time in the lobby of a Chicago hotel. There are three women and two men. As the conversation continues, Morales (male) sits down next to an elegantly scrubbed, middle-aged Jewish American female. As soon as he sits down, the Jewish woman leaves immediately, in about 10 seconds. The question is, why did the Jewish woman leave suddenly? How many reasons can you think of? If you are adjusting your thoughts along the lines of "in spite of" symmetrical thinking, rather than "because of" thinking, some reasons might include:

> *The Jewish woman suddenly remembered that she had to make a telephone call.*
> *She was scheduled to meet a friend at a restaurant and discovered she had left the street address in her car.*
> *She saw a person across the room whom she wished to avoid.*
> *Nature called.*

This exercise illustrates that we must have enough pieces of the intercultural puzzle to arrive at appropriate decisions about human attitudes and behavior.

Developing a both/and orientation

In building your interpersonal competence, you might process similar incidents in the following way:

> **Describe the situation.** *"We noticed that the Jewish woman left as soon as Morales sat down beside her." Include other factors in the communication context, such as nonverbal behaviors. For example, did Mrs. Stein shrug her shoulders or utter a "nasty" word about Puerto Ricans before leaving?*

Identify your feelings. "Mrs. Stein was rude, but in the scheme of things, it doesn't matter."

Try to infer others' feelings. "I believe Mrs. Stein felt awful about leaving suddenly and I have no reason to believe that she is a bad person."

Seeking Common Ground

Our discussion of how to improve intercultural competence is nearly complete. We have defined "either-or-ism," examined the difference between "because of" and "in spite" of thinking, and considered how to develop a "both/and orientation." Our discussion of improving intercultural communication, however, is still incomplete, because we have not emphasized common ground.

Although there are fascinating variations in human culture—from region to region and from society to society—and although we have stressed diversity, if we are to succeed in communicating interculturally, we must also search for significant or deeper points of similarity within cultures. Some scholars assume with George Peter Murdock (1945) that there are many things that unite us. Murdock reminds us that all people have a concept of beauty, follow rules of etiquette, tell jokes, dance, make music, feel anger, participate in sport, gather food, and use systems of economic exchange, ranging from cowrie beads to the French franc, to the Nigerian nira.

In all sorts of ways, though, we tend to emphasize the things that divide us rather than the things that unite us. We are astonished to learn, for instance, that in some cultures people believe that a neighbor's envy can make you sick or that snakeskin can ward off evil. In your efforts at being adaptable, keep the similarities that bind you to others in the foreground. When you greet someone from another culture, what is the first thing that you focus on? If your powers of perception are similar to those of others, you will probably notice details such as hair color, facial features, skin color, height, weight, and clothing. Focusing on similarities means that you should also move to the next level of perception, which is to consider those human traits, attitudes, customs, and behaviors that you share with others.

Think of this emphasis on similarities as observing what commonalities remain in your interactions with others long after the immediate "strangeness" has disappeared. As Desmond Morris (1994) nicely puts it, "We may wear different hats but we all show the same smile; we may speak different languages but they are all rooted in the same basic grammar; we may have different marriage customs but we all fall in love" (p. 6).

TEN BASIC RULES OF
INTERCULTURAL EFFECTIVENESS

To improve relations with others, observe the following rules:

1. **Give people the benefit of the perceptual doubt. Assume goodwill.**
   This rule assumes that most individuals seek psychological comfort and
   congeniality.
2. **Minimize confrontations** by asking questions such as, "How's that?"
   and "How so?" Or say, "Please help me to understand why you see A or
   B the way you do." Here the emphasis is on giving the "other" an opportunity to explain his or her point of view.
3. **Ask for clarification.** "Would you give me an example of A or B?" or
   "I'm not sure I understand what you mean, would you elaborate further?"
4. **Use "I" instead of "you" to deflect blame.** Say, "I'm having some difficulty understanding A or B" rather than "You are not explaining the origins of chopsticks very well."
5. **Try to look at people as individuals rather than as members of ethnic
   groups.** Some stereotyping will occur, of course, since we generally do
   not start each encounter with a clean slate of impressions.
6. **Seek common ground.** Learn about things that you share in common
   with others. For example, "My friend Yoshiko and I both love the musical group Hootie and the Blowfish."
7. **Be flexible in selecting words and actions.** Learn how to respond positively to conditions, people, and situations as they arise.
8. **Learn how to distinguish between** things that happen to you **because**
   you are white, Latino, Chinese, male, or female, and things that happen
   to you **in spite of** your sex or ethnicity.
9. **Recognize the fact that people communicate differently.** For example,
   some people smile a lot; others do not.
10. **Develop empathy.** Try to infer the feelings and actions of others.

These are general rules and will, of course, vary from situation to situation and from person to person. Also, remember that sometimes it is most
difficult to communicate with some individuals despite your good and no-
ble intentions. This can lead to a special kind of anguish when communicating.

CONCLUSION

Certain principles and practices are basic to the achievement of competent intercultural communication. Competent intercultural communication (1) makes full use of cognitive, affective, and behavioral dimensions, (2) has an appreciative orientation and a movement in the direction of empathy, (3) relies on knowledge of self and sociocultural roots such as ties to one's family as well as connections to political, religious, and economic attitudinal structures, (4) does not permit stereotypes and prejudices to "sabotage trust" with others, (5) is positive and other-directed, and (6) acknowledges both local and global dimensions of human relations.

Among the various ways of improving intercultural competence, learning to overcome "either-or-ism" and to distinguish between "because of" and "in spite of" events and situations is most necessary. A both/and orientation toward developing intercultural competence emphasizes the relatively rich complexity of human behavior. We have sought to offer you advice and counsel about human diversity. The ten basic rules of intercultural communication should serve as guides for you as you seek to minimize misunderstandings between yourself and others.

QUESTIONS

1. What are some crucial factors in developing intercultural competence?
2. How are cognitive, affective, and behavioral dimensions related to intercultural competence?
3. In what sense can one say that an individual is acting locally? Globally? What are some key differences between the two?

ACTIVITIES

Case Studies/Narratives

Case Study 1

Yoko is a Japanese student in an Eastern university. Her fiancee, also Japanese, lives in Japan. Although Yoko is delighted about her approaching marriage, she is troubled because she would like to retain her maiden name. In Japan, it is legally established that the wife must take the husband's last name. Yoko knows that parliament is scheduled to discuss changes in the law soon; however, the change will not occur before her wedding date.

Assume that Yoko is asking your advice as a friend. What would you say to her?

Case Study 2

Mary Jo and her roommate were walking home on Railroad Street in Bernice, Louisiana, and were stopped by a young East Indian man (around 18 years old) carrying incense sticks. He walked up to Mary Jo and her roommate and asked them to smell the incense sticks. In response, Mary Jo said, "I have a cold and cannot smell much of anything," and her roommate said, "No, thank you."

The young man, much to the surprise of Mary Jo and her friend, became very angry, and began to shout at them.

Later, Mary Jo felt devastated by the East Indian's response and wondered why he had felt they "owed him a conversation."

Discuss the interpersonal implications of "owing" others a conversation. Was Mary Jo obligated to respond to the young East Indian's request? What might have accounted for his anger?

Case Study 3

Soo Kim works in a gift shop in a southern town. One day a Middle Eastern male entered the shop to buy a small gift, which cost a little over two dollars. As he was writing a check for the purchase, Kim told him he should make it payable to the shop, and that she would also require a piece of identification. Kim's request to see identification, however, infuriated the Middle Eastern male.

What do you think accounted for the man's behavior?

REFERENCES

Appiah, K. (1992), *In my father's house*. New York: Oxford University Press.

Barna, L. (1994). Stumbling blocks in intercultural communication. In L. Samovar & R. Porter (Eds.), *Intercultural communication: A reader* (pp. 337–346). Belmont, CA: Wadsworth.

Basso, K. (1972). To give up on words: Silence in Western Apache culture. In P. P. Giglioli (Ed.), *Language and social context* (pp. 67–86). New York: Penguin.

Berlin, I. (1991). *The crooked timber of humanity: Chapters in the history of ideas*. New York: A. Knopf.

Carr-Ruffino, N. (1996). *Managing diversity, people skills for a multicultural workplace*. New York: Thomson Executive Press.

Condon, J., & Yousef, F. (1975). *An introduction to intercultural communication*. Indianapolis, IN: Bobbs-Merrill.

Geertz, C. (1973). *The interpretation of cultures*. New York: Basic Books.

Gudykunst, W., & Ting-Toomey, S. (1988). *Culture and interpersonal communication*. Newbury Park, CA: Sage.

Gutmann, A. (1992). Introduction. In C. Taylor, *Multiculturalism and the politics of recognition*. Princeton, NJ: Princeton University Press.

Hannerz, U. (1992). *Cultural complexity: Studies in the social organization of meaning*. New York: Columbia University Press.

Hudson, R. (1980). *Sociolinguistics*. New York: Cambridge University Press.

Hymes, D. (1973) Toward ethnographies of communication. In M. Prosser (Ed.), *Intercommunication among nations and peoples* (pp. 45–66). New York: Harper & Row.

James, W. (1890). *The principles of psychology* (p. 294). (reprint). Dover, 1950.

Kim, Y. (1991). Intercultural communication competence. In S. Ting-Toomey & F. Korzenny (Eds.), *Cross-cultural and interpersonal communication* (pp. 259–275). Newbury Park, CA: Sage.

Lee, W.-S. (1997). In L. Samavor & R. Porter, (Ed.), *Intercultural communication: A reader* (pp. 213–220). Belmont, CA: Wadsworth.

McNeil, D.G. Jr. (1996, July 21). In Johannesburg? *The New York Times*, p. B1.

Morris, D. (1994). *The human animal: A personal view of the human species*. New York: Crown Publishers.

Murdock, G. (1945). Common denominator of cultures. In R. Linton (Ed.), *Science of man in the world crises*. New York: Columbia.

Murphy, R. (1986). *Cultural and social anthropology: An overture*. Englewood Cliffs, NJ: Prentice-Hall.

Pollack, A. (1995, July 27). The pen is mightier than the germ? *The New York Times*, p. A4.

Samovar, L., & Porter, R. (1991). *Communication between cultures*. Belmont, CA: Wadsworth.

Selznick, P. (1992). *The moral commonwealth: Social theory and the promise of community*. Berkeley, CA: University of California Press.

Spitzberg, B.H. (1989). Issues in the development of a theory of interpersonal competence in the intercultural context. *International Journal of Intercultural Relations, 13*, 241–268.

Spitzberg, B.H., & Cupach, W.R. (1984b). *International communication competence*. Beverly Hills, CA: Sage.

Spitzberg, B.H., & Cupach, W.R. (1984a). *Handbook of interpersonal competence research*. New York: Springer-Verlag.

Shweder, R.A. (1991). *Thinking through cultures: Expeditions in cultural psychology*. Cambridge, MA: Harvard University Press.

Taylor, C. (1992). *Multiculturalism and the politics of recognition*. Princeton, NJ: Princeton University Press.

Tuan, Y-F. (1977). *Space and place: The perspective of experience*. Minneapolis: The University of Minnesota Press.

Uchendu, V. (1965). *The Igbo of southeast Nigeria*. New York: Holt, Rinehart and Winston.

14

FUTURE DIRECTIONS

Objectives

After reading this chapter, you should be able to:

1. Discuss the major trends that are shaping our move to the twenty-first century.
2. Identify and discuss some of the options and issues we have in handling the challenges of an increasingly diverse society.
3. Discuss the prospects for successful intercultural communication in the twenty-first century.

A major television network in the United Kingdom, ITN, ran two reports in October 1996 on the reactions of Canadians and New Zealanders respectively to the increasing flow of Chinese from Hong Kong into their countries. The white population in each report largely had problems with the increasing flow. In New Zealand, a political party that called for a practical halt to immigration was shown to be gathering momentum. The rise in anti-Chinese feelings in New Zealand was markedly more pronounced than in Canada. In both situations, the problem was not just the increase in numbers but the *quality* of the Chinese immigrants that were moving into the countries—they were wealthy Chinese. Because of their enormous wealth, they purchased huge homes in the most desirable neighborhoods and spent lavishly on luxury cars. Several of the whites interviewed for the report expressed resentment, and it was clear that the economic divide—between rich Chinese immigrants and the struggling white middle-class—was driving a wedge that would turn out to be catastrophic if not properly handled.

We start with the above because there is a global manifestation of a rapid movement of people from one region of the world to another, bringing about a complex set of reactions by host countries that are ill-prepared to deal with the magnitude of the trend. The trend is moving so fast that it is sweeping the world into a problematic sociocultural situation that will characterize the nature of intercultural contacts and communication in the early twenty-first century. It is important to note right from the start that this chapter does not involve "forecasting" within the context of futuristic studies by great futurists such as Alvin Toffler (1974).

We focus on some of the scenarios that will characterize the early twenty-first century, examining the implications of the increased movements of people from region to region, the potential for resistance by host countries, perceived threats to privileged positions by dominant groups, and the emerging learning needs on issues such as alternative lifestyles, gender and race, and the new communication and information technologies that require careful strategies in efforts to satisfy such needs. We expect to provide the basis for discussion stemming from a series of rhetorical questions aimed at the render. Because this chapter deals with "future directions," we see our role as catalyst—stimulating discussion by you on what the future holds for intercultural communication.

ROOTS OF THE IMMIGRATION FLOW

The Chinese example given above is symptomatic of the fears people have regarding transformation from one of way of life to another. Hong Kong is now part of the People's Republic of China. When it was a British territory, citizens of Hong Kong operated businesses in a capitalist economy and the entrepreneurial class amassed a lot of wealth. With the taking over by the People's Republic of China, a socialist state, there is fear among the wealthy Hong Kong Chinese that their wealth will be appropriated and that socialism will restrict their business operations. This fear of the unknown—the extent to which they will be allowed to keep their businesses—creates tensions and uncertainties that force the business people to flee to Western countries where capitalism is the deeply entrenched practice.

Besides the Chinese immigrants, there are other groups of people from various parts of the world that are also gravitating towards the West. The fall of the Berlin Wall—the most well-known symbol of the collapse of communism in Eastern Europe—is also a root cause for the flow of immigrants to the West. There is, however, a fundamental distinction: The immigrants from Eastern Europe moving into the West are white not Chinese. Furthermore, the overall economic status of the immigrants from Eastern Europe cannot be equated with the Chinese. Immigrants from former Communist regimes in Europe and Latin America (Cuba) are given preferential treatment compared with immigrants form the rest of the world because of the declared anticommunist stance by the West.

There are others besides the Eastern Europeans who are also gravitating to the Western countries: Medical professionals from South Asia, Africa, and the Caribbean are moving to the West for various reasons ranging from economic to political. The trend is constant and all indications are that it will continue to manifest itself into the twenty-first century. The future direction and result are written on the wall: a more diverse population with varying levels of wealth and skills. With the rapid rate at which the population is becoming diverse, the problems involved in developing intercultural communication skills and competency are going to be exacerbated.

It is precisely because of this realization of a trend that is taking us to the twenty-first century that we stress throughout this book the need to understand roots and routes as a critical concept. The millions of Africans, Asians, Europeans, Latin Americans, and others moving West are deeply rooted in their cultures. Even though they are en route to becoming residents or citizens in the West, we cannot expect them to automatically shed their beliefs, values, and attitudes. As Barrett (1991) observes, "most individuals, most of the time, are deeply committed to their own customs" (p. 99). The immigrants moving across continental and cultural boundaries cannot be Americans, Britons, or French or New Zealanders overnight. Their routes are complex and acculturation is a process that is painful at times and time-consuming.

Resistance to immigration flows can be seen also within a wider context of what See (1986) refers to as *ethnic nationalism*. Our understanding of the concept of roots and routes prepares us to be more cautious in handling intercultural communication situations and less prone to stumbling over the blocks discussed by Barna (1997). Given the complex nature of the cultural transformation taking place at the level of the mass international flow of immigrants, what are some of the options available to handle the emerging complex and diverse societies in the West and elsewhere? Let us examine briefly three options and three critical factors.

SCENARIOS AND OPTIONS

Creolization of Culture

We may understand and be sensitive to the impact of roots and routes. What, however, will be the resultant society with such a rapid transformation from a largely Anglo-Saxon culture in the United States for example, to a *creolized* culture? A *creole* is someone of a mixed racial and/or ethnic origin. The important characteristic feature of a creole is the merging of a diverse cultural heritage in a person or a language. In Haiti, for example, the lingua franca is creole, which is a mix of French and African languages. Many countries in West Africa speak *pidgin*, which is a creolized version of English and several African languages. In Louisiana, there is group of people referred to as Creole who are of mixed Spanish, French, and African descent.

A creolized culture can be the resultant culture of a country such as the United States given the emerging numbers of Asians, Hispanics, and other immigrants from non-Western cultures who are "merging" their indigenous cultures with that of their new host culture in the United States. In such a resultant culture, each of the major ethnic, racial, religious, and co-cultural groups will contribute significantly to the creolization process. The new culture will have to manifest several elements of each of the major co-cultural blocks in society, incorporating, for example, values and belief systems and attitudes (Hannerz, 1992). However, the merging cultural systems may clash. For instance, rituals in some Asian and African cultures involving controversial practices such as female circumcision and the use of herbal medicines brought in from Asian and African countries can create serious areas of dispute and confrontation as the creolization process evolves.

In addition to such potential clashes, cultural changes and adjustments do not occur in revolutionary ways. Cultural changes *evolve*. Geertz (1973) observes that moving from imagining change to actually living under conditions that have changed are radically different things (see Chapter 10 especially). So even though we can imagine creolization as an option, living in a creolized culture will be an entirely different matter. The evolutionary process may prove to be difficult to a point of provoking violent resistance by certain groups in the host country.

Some critical issues that can be considered for discussion on the evolution of a creolized culture are the following: What will form the foundations of values in a creolized culture? How will the Christian, Jewish, Muslim, Buddhist, and other faiths create common ground in bringing about creolized cultural norms that will address the concerns and needs of a complex and diverse society? What will be the language of this creolized culture? What will be the implication for the judicial and legislative systems? How will the educational system function in a creolized cultural context? Is creolization a viable option? What are the advantages and disadvantages? These questions are rhetorical, requiring discussion and analysis.

Domestic Cultural Domination

In Chapter 12, dealing with the media, we discussed the concept of "cultural domination" within the context of the exportation of American/Western values to various nations in the world through television programming, film, and video. In this chapter, we focus on *domestic* cultural domination in an effort to examine the domestic reaction to an increasing tension between co-cultural groups over the rapid flow of immigrants to America. In Chapter 1, we referred to two ways people react to diversity: locally (particuliarism) and globally (universalism). Domestic cultural domination is treated in this chapter against the background of particuliarism.

A host country keen to preserve the fundamental elements of its cultural base can resist attempts to alter its fundamental cultural makeup. There are signs of such resistance already visible in the United States and other Western societies. Resistance to immigration is a major political issue in the United States. Politicians on the right argue forcefully for restriction on the flow of immigrants to the country on the grounds of cultural integrity and potential economic burdens on the state and federal governments.

The resistance trend cuts across political party lines and is a national phenomenon. If creolization is not an option, is the future option domestic cultural domination in which one co-culture can *impose* its values, belief systems, attitudes, and rituals on all other co-cultural group instead of negotiating among co-cultural group beliefs, attitudes, and value systems?

Power relations are at the heart of the domestic cultural domination option. If cultural domination is the chosen option, one dominant group will decide on the future of all co-cultural groups affecting their economic, social, and political well-being. The standards against which all are to be judged are those that the dominant group will determine as the norm. Opportunities for social mobilization by the nondominant co-cultural groups will be solely based on the standards and merit structure of the dominant group. The presence of highly qualified immigrant social scientists with different or alternative perspectives on social standards and organization, cultural practices that enhance intercultural communication, peace and harmony, based on experiences from their cultural roots will not matter. What will matter is the status quo—the dominant value-orientations and standards as the norm and bases for power and control.

Power relations as articulated above are not new. Prior to the reforms that followed the Civil Rights movement of the 1960s, one dominant group, represented by caucasians, controlled the whole nation. Folb (1997) claims that it is the same group that continues to manifest domination. She argues that "society [current] is maintained through instruction and indoctrination in the ways of the culture. But the question that pricks and puzzles the mind is, Whose culture is passed on? Whose beliefs and values are deemed appropriate? Whose norms, mores, and folkways are invoked?" (p. 140). Folb's rhetorical questions add to highlight the complexities involved in understanding the dynamics of power relations and, subsequently, domestic cultural domination.

With the increased level of diversity and the imbalance in economic opportunities for some of the co-cultural groups in society, the viability of the domestic cultural domination option has to be closely scrutinized. It is an option that by its nature points to the continued tensions among co-cultural groups. The scrutiny of this option will encompass an examination and analysis on potential for violent resistance from co-cultural groups that will result in outbreaks of civil disorder, civil wars, and major population dislocations. Is domestic cultural domination a viable option? Again, it is a scenario that provokes discussion.

Regionalization

The focus thus far has been on the existing reality: the flow of immigrants from various countries in the world to the major leading Western countries—the United States, Britain, France, Italy, Germany, Australia, and New Zealand. We need to look beyond the immigration issues prompted by political and economic reasons that accelerate the flow of immigrants to the West from *all* parts of the world, to other diversity moves going on in other parts of the world and their possible impact.

Regionalism is a visible trend that is becoming a viable option in Europe, Africa, Asia, and the various Pacific countries with varying degrees of success. Regionalism is a mechanism by which countries of a given geographic region in the world form a coalition that uses an integrative approach to economic, social, and political collaboration. We focus only on the European example here because it is at the most advanced stage of its formulation. In Europe, the main outgrowth of regionalism is the formation of the European Union (EU). The European continent is moving rapidly towards economic and political union.

The European Community is now a reality, in many respects. Many Europeans travel from country to country in Europe without visas. A borderless continent is emerging in which all Europeans regardless of color, creed, economic status, or political orientation can move without undue harassment. If agreed to by *all* European nations, borderless Europe will look like the United States where Americans travel freely within the fifty states of the Union. A United Europe with economic opportunities for all under a democratic system of government may prove to be successful to the extent that people may feel less inclined to leave for perceived greener pastures in the United States or elsewhere. This may be good for America. There will be less immigrants. But there are some thorny issues that require mentioning.

Europe lacks some of the favorable factors that make the United States a successful borderless country. In the United States, there is one major language, one economic system, one currency, and a long history of a federal government that links the fifty states. There is also the presence of institutional structures that have served the functions of governing a borderless state. The European situation is the opposite—many languages, different currencies, even though the various countries in Europe are working hard on the common currency issue, different institutions of governance, and different national cultures, just to mention a few.

Regionalism has sparked some ugly confrontations already among Europeans. People from Southern Europe—Turkey, for example—suffer from physical attacks by extremist groups in Germany, who are opposed to the presence of Turks and non-whites in Germany. Besides the racial dimension of the problem, Europeans from economically weaker and poorer countries move in huge numbers into the stronger economies such as Germany, provoking challenges and attacks by Germans who feel threatened by the flow of "immigrants" (Europeans) into their country, creating problems of unemployment and conflicts over different cultural values and habits. While regional grouping as an option to deal with an emerging diverse future may be promising, it brings along with it potential for explosive co-cultural conflicts over resources and opportunities.

The three options mentioned above are directly linked to the massive cultural and linguistic transformation taking place as we move to the twenty-first century. As you discuss the options, and probably more of them that you can come up with, consider all implications for intercultural communication and the demands on everyone to become more culturally sensitive. Regardless of what option seems to be feasible, a transformation is taking place that requires serious attention. It may be the case that we have to consider a combination of options to ensure a smooth transition from a largely unicultural power base to a more balanced approach to power sharing and the provision of mechanisms that will ensure equal access for all and equal opportunity for every individual regardless of race, creed, or religion.

While pondering over the options, let us take a brief look at other factors that we need to address in terms of future directions. Three critical factors are readily discernible: alternative lifestyles, gender and race issues, and the impact of the new information and communication technologies, which we will discuss briefly.

Alternative Lifestyles

The options we discussed earlier focused on co-cultural groups as entities. When we discuss alternative lifestyle, we begin at the individual level: the right to be what one feels is right for him or her. At the heart of the alternative lifestyle factor is the issue of family values as articulated by organizations such the Christian Coalition. The Supreme Court of Hawaii is presently reviewing an appeal case regarding two men who argue that a lower court is wrong in denying them the right to marry. The issue goes beyond the gay/lesbian debate because of the level at which it is being adjudicated. The 104th Congress, for example, and the United States Senate voted against a bill that called for reciprocal recognition of same sex marriages by states. Heterosexual marriages are recognized by all states regardless of the state that issues the license.

Increasingly, gay and lesbian groups throughout the United States are gaining grounds on issues of right to alternative lifestyle patterns. Many professional organizations have gay and lesbian caucuses. Decisions by courts in favor of gays and lesbians throughout the country are strengthening the arguments of the right of individuals to alternative lifestyles. The United States Congress has openly gay members who advocate on the floor of the house for gay rights. This is in stark contrast to the manner in which gay and lesbian issues were treated as late as the 1980s (see Gross, 1991, for an excellent analysis of the negative manner in which issues on gays and lesbians were handled). As the momentum accelerates, what are the prospects for a resultant society in which the issue of alternative lifestyle will not be a an issue but rather a fact of life, with like-minded people constituting a co-cultural group?

During the debate on same sex marriages in the United States Senate, Senator Carol Mosley Brown of Illinois argued in favor of the bill, saying that the issue was similar to those articulated during the Civil Rights movement, namely, prohibition of interracial marriages. Fifty years ago, interracial marriages were not popular and in some states were prohibited. The issue at hand with regard to alternative lifestyle is, what do we anticipate fifty years from now and what will be the implications for intercultural communication? Will gay and lesbian "culture" be a viable co-culture in the United States and perhaps elsewhere? We wish to stress again that we are raising questions on future directions for discussion by the class, not providing answers. How do you see the debate shaping as we move to the twenty-first century?

Gender and Race Concerns

A quotation by Audre Lorde serves as a transition from the alternative lifestyle issue to gender and race concerns. She writes: "As a forty-nine-year-old black lesbian feminist socialist mother of two, including one boy, and a member of an interracial couple, I usually find myself a part of some group defined as other, deviant, inferior, or just plain wrong" (in Rothenberg, 1995, p. 445). Lorde is everything that is perceived as questionable, debatable, or wrong in a society deeply rooted in a Judeo-Christian tradition that censures several aspects of her being. She raises the question of gender, sex, race, and ideology in one sentence and points towards the direction the twenty-first century is shaping up to be: Issues on culture, race, gender, sex and politics are intertwined. To talk about one is to talk about the others. In this regard, even though we have separate headings for each factor identified, we do this for convenience.

The larger issue raised by Lorde is the responsibility to society, of people who are seen as out of the mainstream. Lorde sees herself as "oppressed." She claims that "it is the responsibility of the oppressed to teach the oppressors their mistake" (p. 445). She continues, "I am responsible for educating teachers who dismiss my children's culture in school" (p. 445). Lorde made these statements in 1980, when it was not in vogue to reveal a person's sexual orientation. Nineteen years later, groups that consider themselves "oppressed," among whom are women, are actively engaged in teaching about womanhood through writing and other forms of communication. Articles are written by women about how men communicate differently from women and identifying the characteristic feature of male speech and female speech (Wood, 1997).

It is a foregone conclusion that action on issues of women's rights is more discernible than it has been since Lorde made her statement. It is this action dimension that seems to be the future direction on this issue. In short, the problem—women's rights—has been carefully and vigorously defined and articulated over the past several decades. Society is in the action phase of ensuring that the rights are upheld and that it is better educated about the concerns women have and why. Does this fall within the purview of intercultural communication? The answer is yes. Women's literature on several aspects of womanhood (Angelou, 1995; Hubbard, 1995) is providing insights that help facilitate our understanding of gender concerns across racial, ethnic, and cultural boundaries.

On the issue of race, it remains an ever constant factor in multiracial societal settings. The O.J. Simpson criminal trial touted by the press as "the trial of the century" brought in an expression that points towards what may be a difficult future: the so-called *race card*. In Chapter 12, we looked at how the media reported on the O.J. Simpson trial, focusing on the racial divide.

The gender issue is increasingly moving towards the institutionalization of the action phase, but the future of race relations does not seem to hold well for increasing positive action. Vigilante and racist attacks are on the rise—the church burnings of 1996 and attacks on African Americans by white extremists are vivid replays of Jim Crowism in America as are the antics of the Ku Klux Klan.

The race factor is not just an issue of tension between African Americans and whites. Tensions have been on the rise between African Americans and Asians. An African child recently informed one of the authors about an experience she had on a school bus that points towards a troubled future for race and ethnic relations in the United States. During the ride to school, a recent immigrant child from the former Yugoslavia annoyingly questioned her newly found white girl friend why she sat beside a "black" person.

The incident is instructive. Immigrants from the former Eastern block countries are moving to the United States in significant numbers. There is a clear need for effective intercultural communication training programs that will facilitate their cultural adjustment so as to prevent potentially explosive scenes involving such immigrants and other racial and ethnic groups in the country. What future direction for race relations? Perhaps the answer is similar to that provided by Lorde: Teach people about the existing realities in society and provide mechanisms by which people can learn to function well in diverse contexts. Teaching and learning are essential future undertakings that will help facilitate a smooth transition to the twenty-first century. Peccei (1981), president of The Club of Rome, an international body that is active in future-related concerns, calls for the:

> *creation of a movement of innovative learning on the broadest possible bases; promotion of the development of alternative projects for the future by mobilizing the creativity of the young; and stimulation of a fundamental renewal in our current way of thinking.*

The above appeal points towards the importance of our commitment to learning as society becomes more and more complex. Peccei also stresses the centrality of learning and argues that we should learn "to live in consonance with the new, fantastic, half-artificial world of our own creation" (p. 168).

THE NEW INFORMATION AND COMMUNICATION TECHNOLOGIES

We preface this section by citing a passage from Berry's (1974) *The Next Ten Thousand Years*. He observes that "The one cardinal error. . . is to assume that man is free to choose his own long-term future. He is indeed free to choose it within narrow limits. Like a snake compelled to move through a tunnel, he may move from side to side, experimenting with this way of life or that. But there is only one forward path, the path to unending technological expansion" (p. 194).

Taking the cue from Berry, let us briefly examine the new technology that is rapidly sweeping the global scene—the internet. The global presence of the internet has serious future implications for intercultural communication. For instance, it was practically impossible for social groups opposed to oppressive domestic policies of certain countries in the Southern hemisphere to communicate their concerns to groups outside of their countries. Through the internet, like-minded groups residing in different continents exchange views on democracy and human rights that are shaping political behavior in countries that were once isolated from world public opinion.

With such power to access national and cultural groups in different parts of the world, the potential for collaboration is heightened. So, however, is the potential for the destruction of cultural norms revered by certain societies. A major dispute on the telecommunications law recently passed by the United States government is a case in point. The dispute surrounds the transmission of child pornography through the world wide web. Such content is offensive to some cultures. Even in the United States where freedom of expression is guaranteed, several groups fight consistently against the practice of using the world wide web for the sale of content featuring child pornography.

Besides issues of child pornography and other controversial content, the internet represents one of the most effective ways people can learn quickly about other cultures by visiting websites that specialize in providing such information. The potential for the new information and communication technologies for promoting intercultural understanding through rapid information sharing places them at the cutting edge of information packaging that could help quell international tensions. For example, email exchanges between the governments of various countries can facilitate the clarification of issues that otherwise could lead to misunderstandings resulting in conflict.

Information sharing holds the best prospect for the future in terms of the positive impact of the new technologies on the promotion of intercultural communication and understanding. By the same token, caution is required in determining the nature of the information that is transmitted so as not to cause unnecessary cultural damage domestically or internationally.

CONCLUSION

A lot of questions remain unanswered about the future directions of intercultural communication. Throughout the text, we have focused on the need to understand the significance of roots and routes as they impact upon our cultural attributes. From the discussion above, we can discern that the routes that are taken by people moving from one cultural context to another are becoming more and more complex. Furthermore, as the level of complexity rises, it is becoming apparent that the future of intercultural communication rests on our willingness to learn from each other regardless of our origin, creed, race, gender, class, or orientation. It is a challenging task. But who says intercultural communication is easy? The challenge is with us. Let us work towards its successful resolution.

REFERENCES

Angelou, M. (1995). Still I rise. In P. Rothenberg (ed.), *Race, class, and gender in the United States*. New York: St. Martin's Press

Barna, L. (1997). Stumbling blocks in intercultural communication. In L. Samovar & R. Porter (Eds.), *Intercultural communication: A reader* (8th ed). Belmont, CA: Wadsworth.

Barrett, R. (1991). *Culture and conduct*. Belmont, MA: Wadsworth.

Berry, A. (1974). *The next ten thousand years*. New York: Saturday Review Press/E.P. Dutton.

Folb, E.A. (1997). Who's got the room at the top? Issues of dominance and non-dominance. In L. Samovar & R. Porter (Eds.), *Intercultural communication: A reader* (8th ed.). Belmont, CA: Wadsworth.

Geertz, C. (1973). *The interpretation of cultures*. New York: Basic Books.

Gross, L. (1991) Gays, lesbians and popular culture. In M. Wolf & A. Kielwasser (Eds.), *Gay people, sex, and the media*. New York: Harrington Park Press.

Hannerz, U. (1992). *Cultural complexity: Studies in the social organization of meaning*. New York: Columbia Press.

Hubbard, R. (1995). Rethinking women's biology. In P. Rothenberg (Ed.), *Race, class, and gender in the United States*. New York: St. Martin's Press.

Lorde, A. (1995). Race, class and sex: Women redefining difference. In P. Rothenberg (Ed.), *Race, class and gender in the United States*. New York: St. Martin's Press.

Peccei, A. (1981). *One hundred pages for the future*. New York: Pergamon.

Rothenberg, P. (1995). *Race, class, and gender in the United States*. New York: St. Martin's Press.

See, K.O. (1986). First world nationalisms: *Class and ethnic politics in Northern Ireland and Quebec*. Chicago: University of Chicago Press.

Toffler, A. (1974). *Learning for tomorrow*. New York: Random House.

Wood, J.T. (1997). Gender, communication and culture. In L. Samovar & R. Porter, (Eds.), *Intercultural communication: A reader* (8th ed.). Belmont, CA: Wadsworth.

INDEX